USNA.

The United States
of North America

USNA: The United States of North America is based on an original screenplay by David Longworth and Allan Stanleigh. The graphic novel, USNA: The United States of North America, written by Harry Kalensky, Davy Longworth and Allan Stanleigh. Artwork, book design and visual concepts by Dave Casey www.dave-casey.com

© 2012 USNA Publications Incorporated, Vancouver, B.C. Canada. Canadian Copyright Number: 1093496

USNA Publications Inc.
Vancouver, B.C. Canada
www.usna.ca

This book is dedicated to the following people whose wit, energy, creativity and heart helped in the creation of this graphic novel:

Kathy Chan, Cordell Wynne, Craig Laven and Linden Banks. With a special thank-you to Dr. Larry Stanleigh, Calgary's foremost and wittiest dentist, whose sense of humour, keen business sense, intellect, love and support literally saved this project.

For Jill Ann Moreton, who provided the pen and paper to Davy so that he could record the original thoughts exploding in his awareness, the seeds of the story, USNA.

For John 'Man Bear' Curtis, whose support and inspiration helped in the creation of this project and who is the model for the character, Solo.

For Blu Mankuma, Vancouver B.C. actor, for his inspiration for the character, Conrad.

Dave Casey wishes to thank his family and friends for their support.
You know who you are.

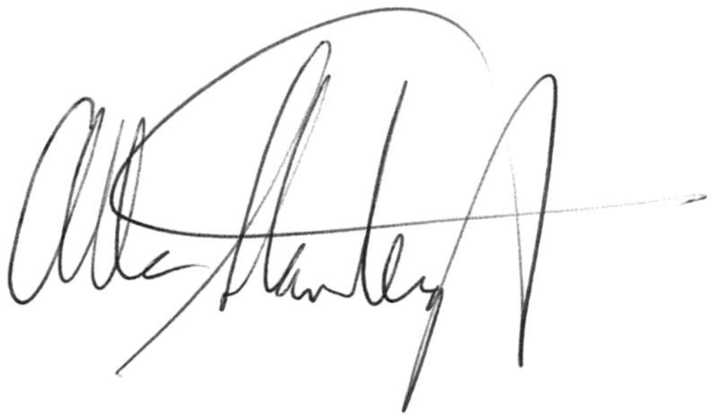

USNA: the United States of North America

Words by David Longworth, Harry Kalensky, and Allan Stanleigh
Pictures and Design by Dave Casey

with foreword by Will Ferguson

ALASKAN
NORTH
CENTRAL
PACIFIC
ATLANTIC
SOUTH
CENTRAL

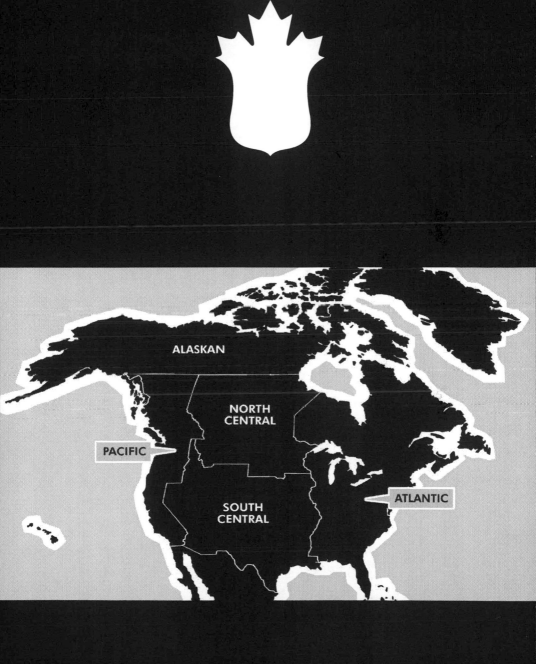

FOREWORD

"Living next door to the United States," Pierre Trudeau famously observed, "is like sleeping next to an elephant. No matter how friendly and even-tempered is the beast, one is affected by every twitch and grunt."

Canadians have long learned to sleep with one eye open. Indeed, it is one of the great myths of history that Canada's divergent destiny in North America was one charted peaceably. Far from it. Canada was founded on conquest. From the exile of the Acadians, scattered as far afield as Louisiana (where they are known now as 'Cajuns), to the Fall of New France and the Native uprisings led by Pontiac, it is a story soaked in bloodshed.

It is also worth remembering that the American Revolution was, above all, a civil war, one that split the continent down the middle along lines of loyalty. One of the first acts of the newly minted United States of America was to invade the northern colonies. "To the inhabitants of Canada," George Washington's army proclaimed, "Come, unite with us in an indissoluble Union!" The Americans were rebuffed, and the invasion of Canada was turned back in a howling snow storm at the very gates of Quebec City.

The Americans would try again in 1812, with yet another bombastic proclamation, this one issued by an invading general who warned Canadians "The United States offers you Peace, Liberty, and Security. Your choice lies between these and War, Slavery, and Destruction. Choose then, but choose wisely . . ."

But once again, the Canadian colonies stood firm. The American invasion was thwarted by ragtag Canadian militias and disciplined British troops, who counterattacked with a raid on Washington D.C that set both the capital—and the White House—ablaze.

From Canada's failed republican rebellions in 1837 to the Fenian raids launched by Irish radicals thirty years later—covertly supported by American interests—to the Aroostook Cold War in northern New Brunswick and the "Pig War" on San Juan Island south of Victoria, B.C. (wherein the two sides almost went to war over a single slain swine), the Canada-U.S. border has long been an arena of competing claims and looming threats.

These conflicts were fuelled by an American belief in "Manifest Destiny," a doctrine that claimed the entire continent for the United States. It was the threat of an imminent American invasion that was one of the driving forces behind Confederation, after all. There was safety in numbers, as the union of British North America demonstrated.

Canada's central defense plans were predicated on an assumed invasion from the United States well into the 1920s. And in USNA, David Longworth, Harry Kalensky and Allan Stanleigh envision a different outcome to this history. Dave Casey's gritty illustrations, in turn, provide a vivid reimagining of manifest destiny, one in which the American Empire has solidified its grasp on the continent. It is a story in the tradition of Richard Rohmer's novels Ultimatum and Exxoneration writ large on the canvas of a graphic novel. It is a story our forebears would find eerily familiar.

Will Ferguson
Co-author of 'How to be a Canadian' and Winner of the Pierre Berton Award for History from Canada's National History Society

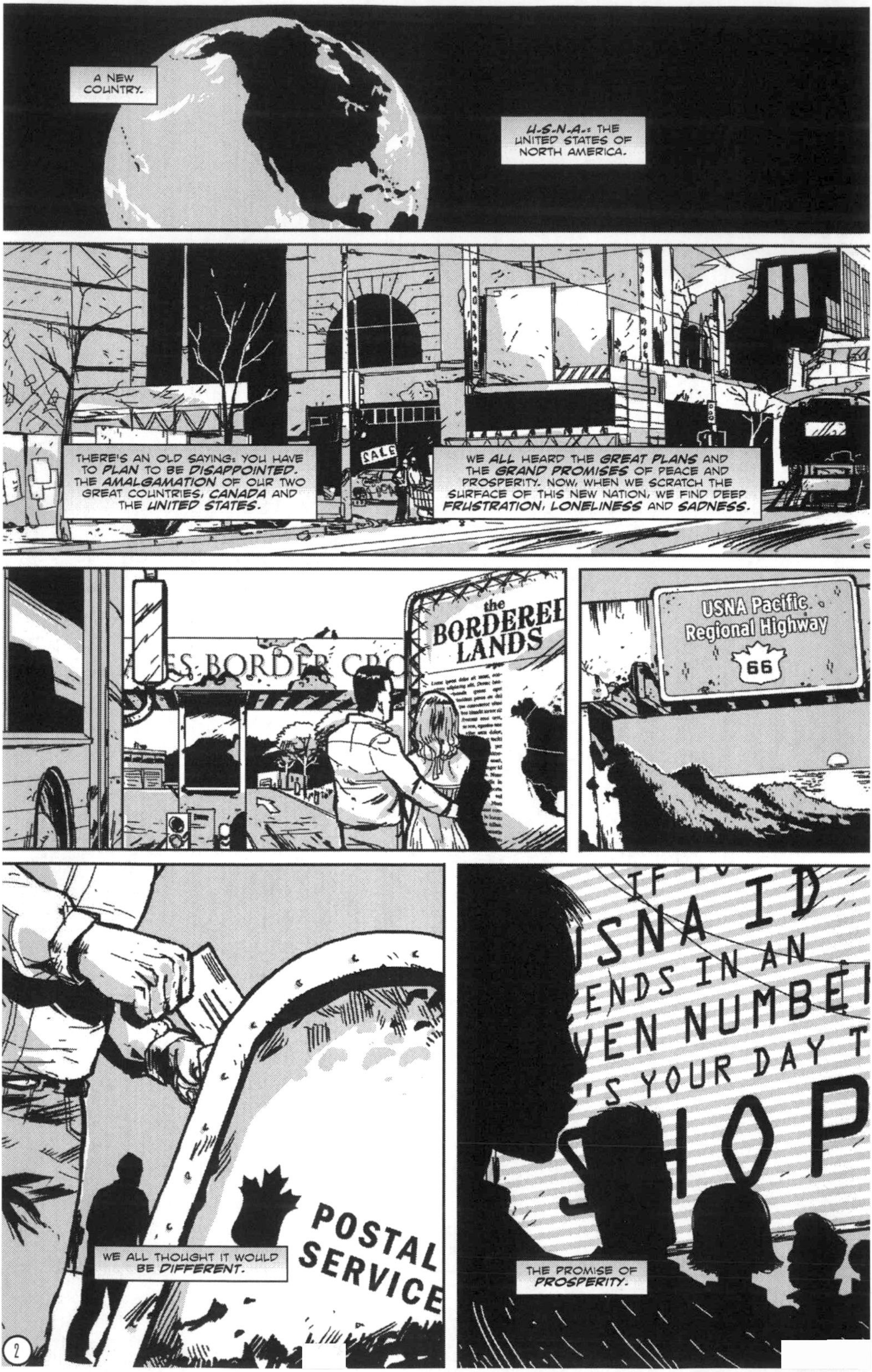
A NEW COUNTRY.
U.S.N.A.: THE UNITED STATES OF NORTH AMERICA.
THERE'S AN OLD SAYING: YOU HAVE TO PLAN TO BE DISAPPOINTED. THE AMALGAMATION OF OUR TWO GREAT COUNTRIES, CANADA AND THE UNITED STATES.
SALE
WE ALL HEARD THE GREAT PLANS AND THE GRAND PROMISES OF PEACE AND PROSPERITY. NOW, WHEN WE SCRATCH THE SURFACE OF THIS NEW NATION, WE FIND DEEP FRUSTRATION, LONELINESS AND SADNESS.
the BORDERED LANDS
USNA Pacific Regional Highway
66
POSTAL SERVICE
WE ALL THOUGHT IT WOULD BE DIFFERENT.
USNA ID
ENDS IN AN
VEN NUMBE
'S YOUR DAY T
HOP
THE PROMISE OF PROSPERITY.

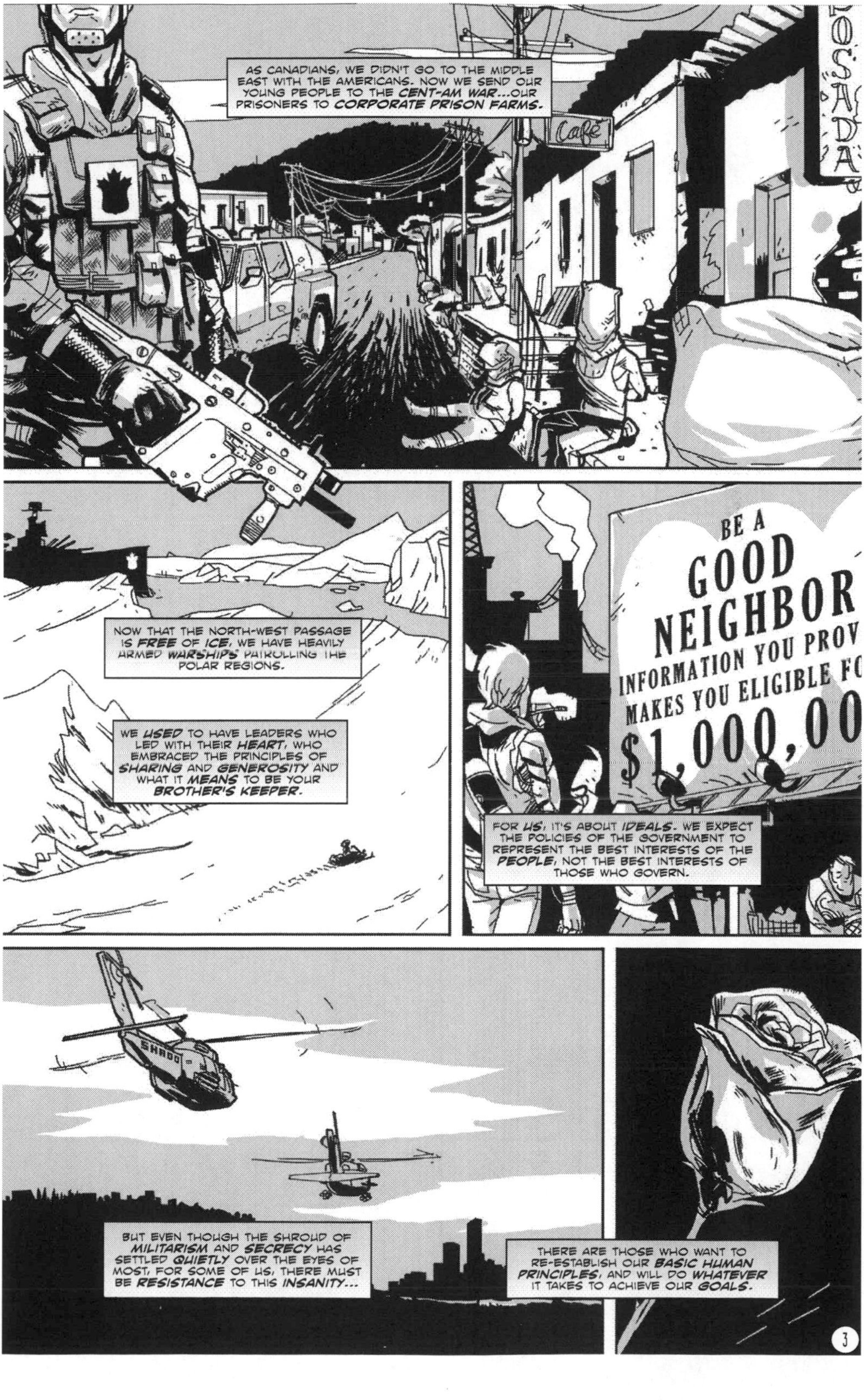
AS CANADIANS, WE DIDN'T GO TO THE MIDDLE EAST WITH THE AMERICANS. NOW WE SEND OUR YOUNG PEOPLE TO THE CENT-AM WAR...OUR PRISONERS TO CORPORATE PRISON FARMS.
Café
NOW THAT THE NORTH-WEST PASSAGE IS FREE OF ICE, WE HAVE HEAVILY ARMED WARSHIPS PATROLLING THE POLAR REGIONS.
WE USED TO HAVE LEADERS WHO LED WITH THEIR HEART, WHO EMBRACED THE PRINCIPLES OF SHARING AND GENEROSITY AND WHAT IT MEANS TO BE YOUR BROTHER'S KEEPER.
BE A GOOD NEIGHBOR
INFORMATION YOU PROV
MAKES YOU ELIGIBLE FO
$1,000,00
FOR US, IT'S ABOUT IDEALS. WE EXPECT THE POLICIES OF THE GOVERNMENT TO REPRESENT THE BEST INTERESTS OF THE PEOPLE, NOT THE BEST INTERESTS OF THOSE WHO GOVERN.
BUT EVEN THOUGH THE SHROUD OF MILITARISM AND SECRECY HAS SETTLED QUIETLY OVER THE EYES OF MOST, FOR SOME OF US, THERE MUST BE RESISTANCE TO THIS INSANITY...
THERE ARE THOSE WHO WANT TO RE-ESTABLISH OUR BASIC HUMAN PRINCIPLES, AND WILL DO WHATEVER IT TAKES TO ACHIEVE OUR GOALS.

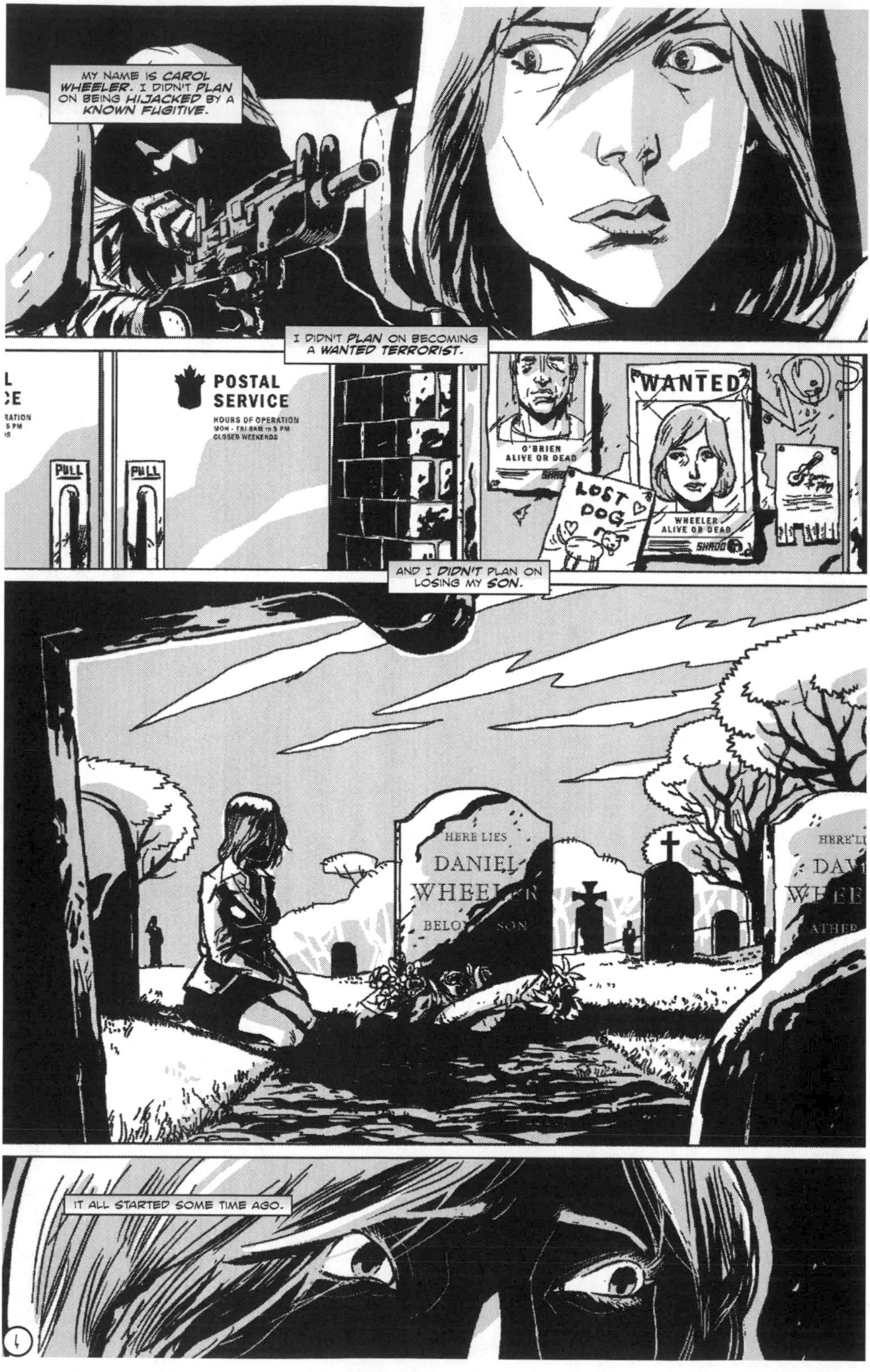
MY NAME IS CAROL WHEELER. I DIDN'T PLAN ON BEING HIJACKED BY A KNOWN FUGITIVE.
I DIDN'T PLAN ON BECOMING A WANTED TERRORIST.
POSTAL SERVICE
HOURS OF OPERATION
MON - FRI 8AM TO 5 PM
CLOSED WEEKENDS
PULL
PULL
O'BRIEN
ALIVE OR DEAD
WANTED
WHEELER
ALIVE OR DEAD
LOST DOG
AND I DIDN'T PLAN ON LOSING MY SON.
HERE LIES
DANIEL
IT ALL STARTED SOME TIME AGO.

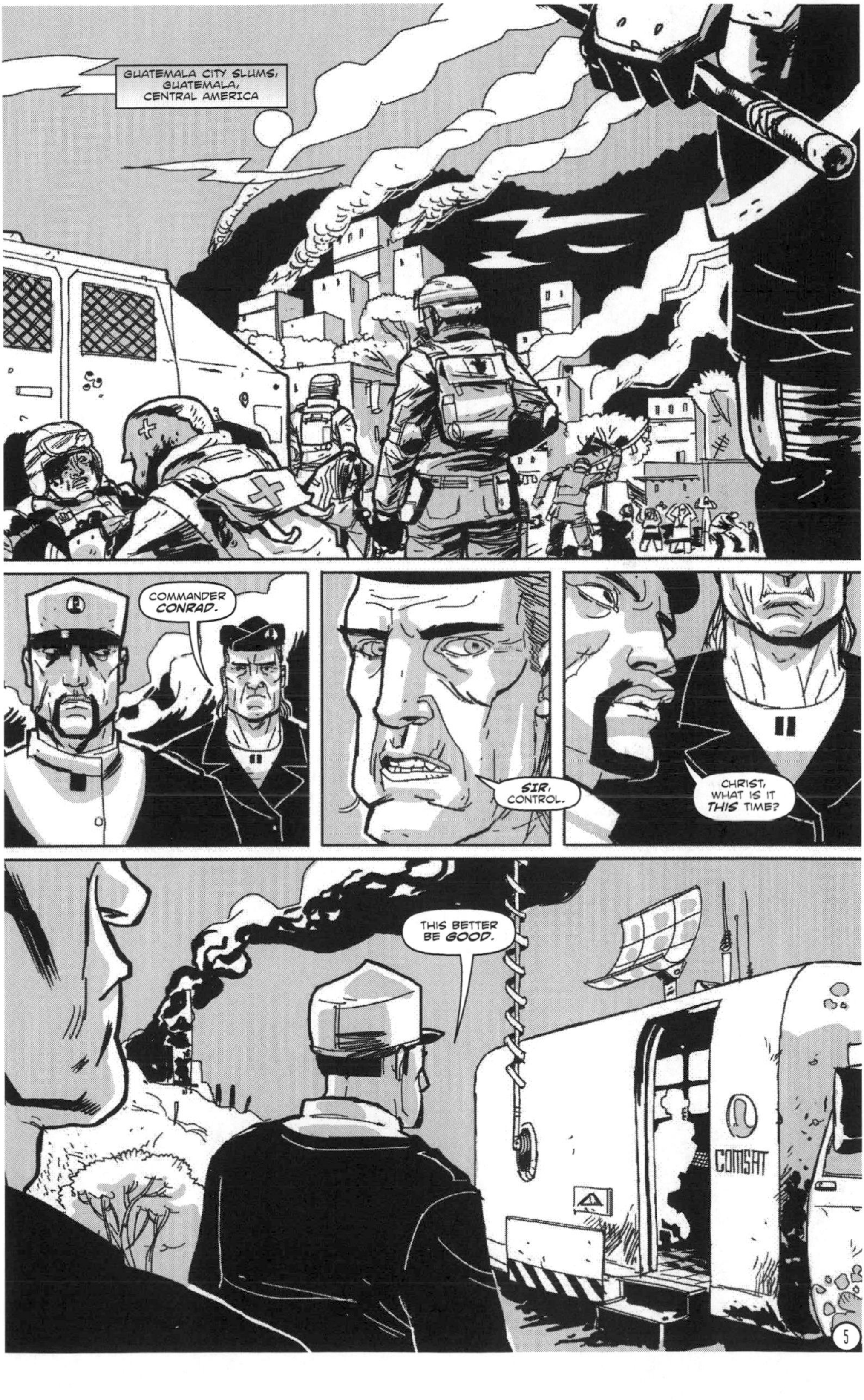
GUATEMALA CITY SLUMS, GUATEMALA, CENTRAL AMERICA
COMMANDER CONRAD.
SIR, CONTROL.
CHRIST, WHAT IS IT THIS TIME?
THIS BETTER BE GOOD.
COMSAT

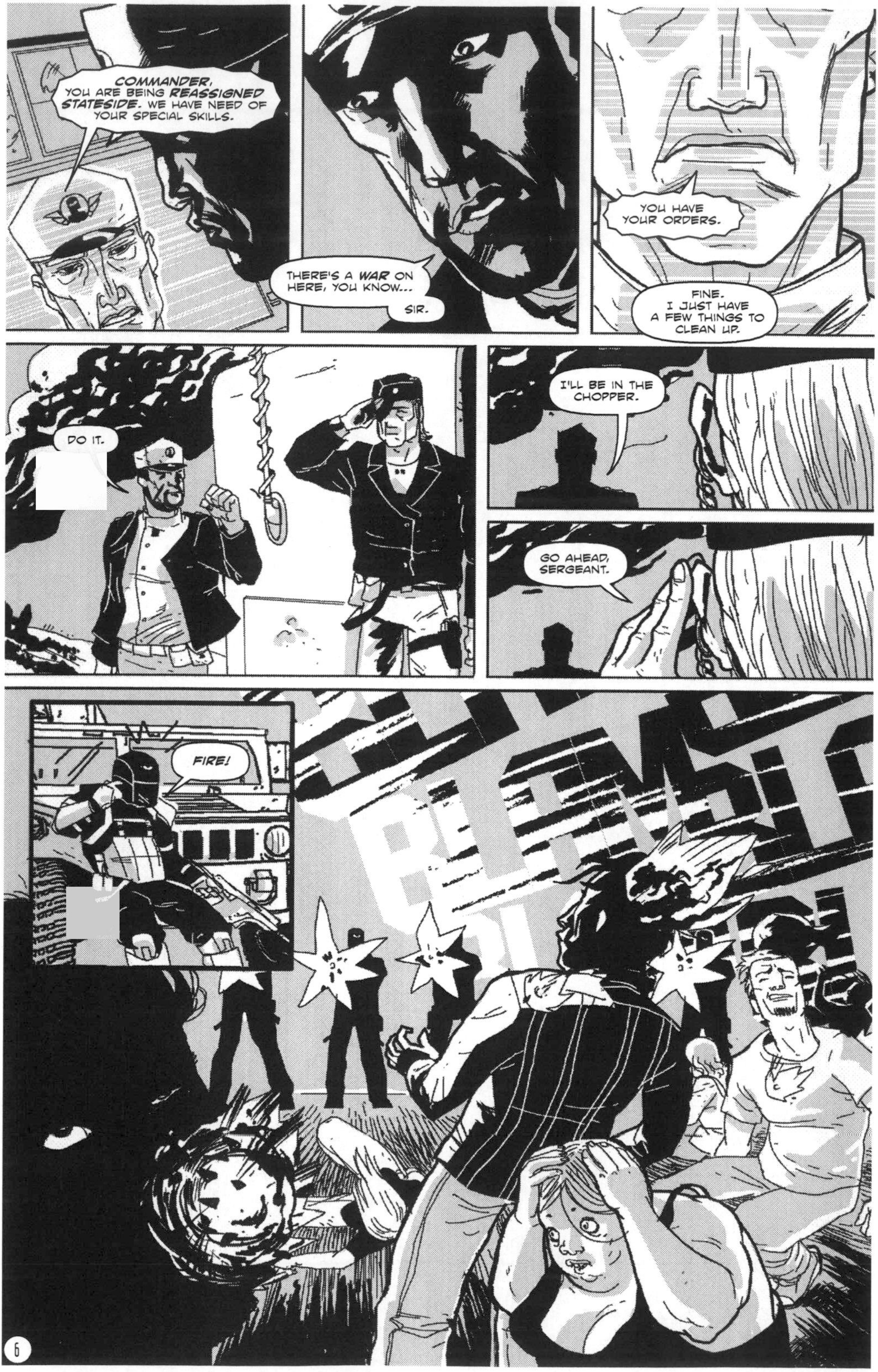
COMMANDER, YOU ARE BEING REASSIGNED STATESIDE. WE HAVE NEED OF YOUR SPECIAL SKILLS.
THERE'S A WAR ON HERE, YOU KNOW...
SIR.
YOU HAVE YOUR ORDERS.
FINE. I JUST HAVE A FEW THINGS TO CLEAN UP.
DO IT.
I'LL BE IN THE CHOPPER.
GO AHEAD, SERGEANT.
FIRE!

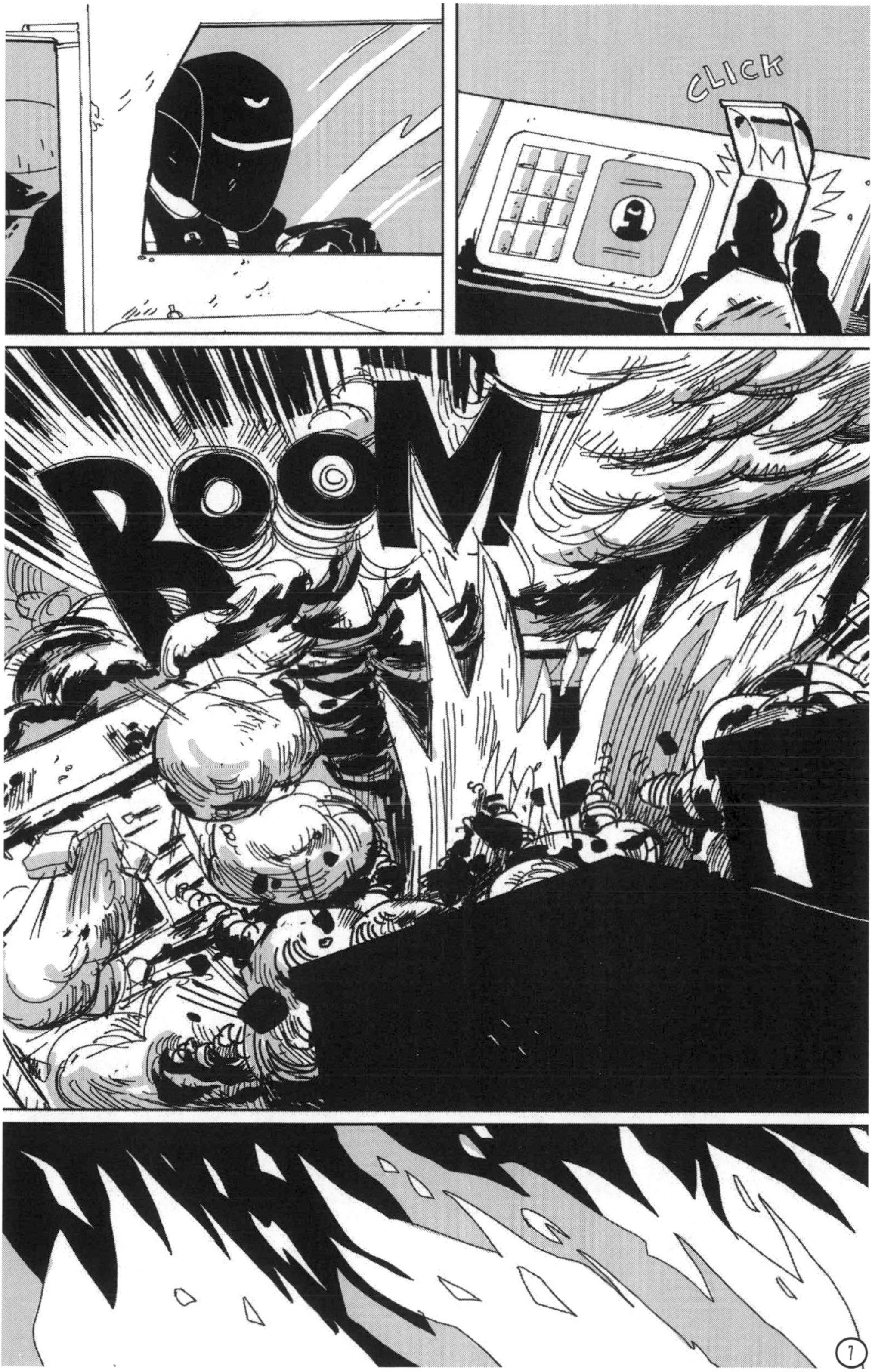
CLICK
BOOM

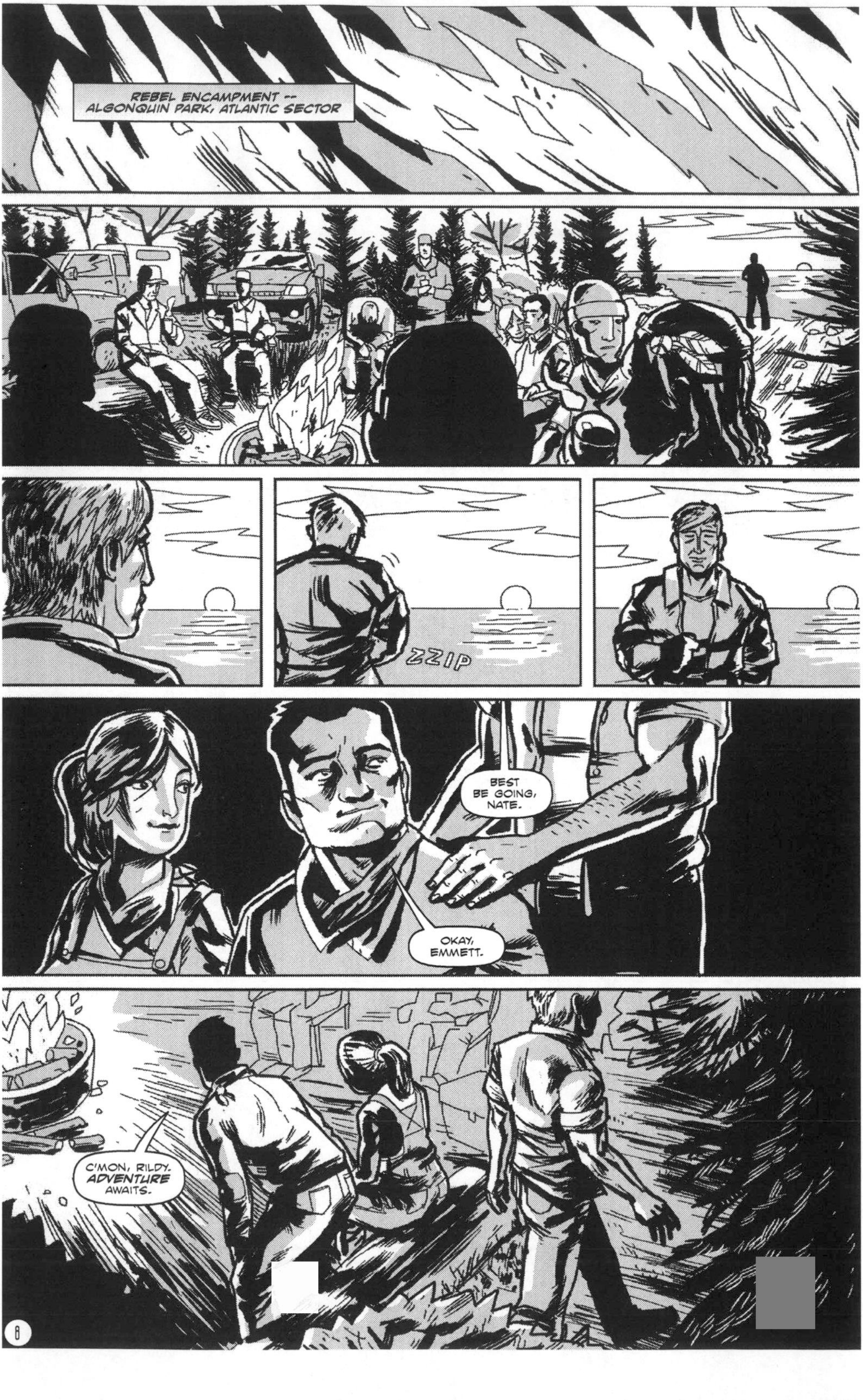
REBEL ENCAMPMENT --
ALGONQUIN PARK, ATLANTIC SECTOR
ZZIP
BEST BE GOING, NATE.
OKAY, EMMETT.
C'MON, RILDY. ***ADVENTURE*** AWAITS.

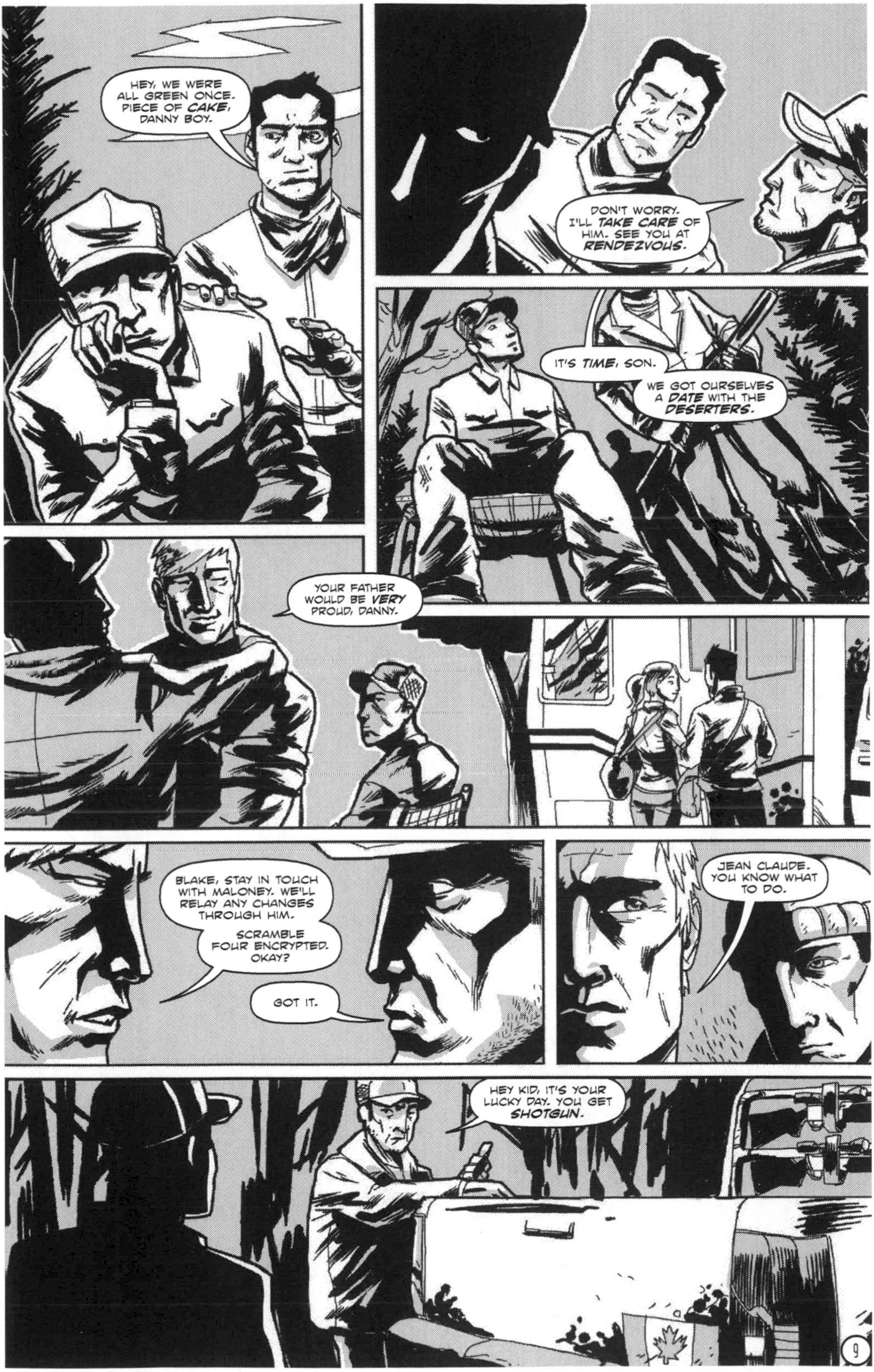
HEY, WE WERE ALL GREEN ONCE. PIECE OF CAKE, DANNY BOY.
DON'T WORRY. I'LL TAKE CARE OF HIM. SEE YOU AT RENDEZVOUS.
IT'S TIME, SON.
WE GOT OURSELVES A DATE WITH THE DESERTERS.
YOUR FATHER WOULD BE VERY PROUD, DANNY.
BLAKE, STAY IN TOUCH WITH MALONEY. WE'LL RELAY ANY CHANGES THROUGH HIM.
SCRAMBLE FOUR ENCRYPTED. OKAY?
GOT IT.
JEAN CLAUDE. YOU KNOW WHAT TO DO.
HEY KID, IT'S YOUR LUCKY DAY. YOU GET SHOTGUN.

```
-----------------------------------
From:  Mr.Carter2U@usna.net
Subject: Me First, bro                CLASSIFIED
Date:  April 8 10:06:18 PM EDT
To: Dwheeler <dwheeler@usna.net>
```

Hey Danny,

    I know you said to wait until you got back from your camping trip but I couldn't wait to write. I want to hear all about your adventures. Yea, I know you couldn't take me along this time and you promised to sometime....sometime? When is sometime going to happen anyhow? You know I've never gone camping or been out in the country. Now that they have all those roadblocks and check points, no-one seems to want to venture too far out of the city. What's the problem? Is it really so dangerous? Or have the lions gone rogue? Or is it wolves? lol :)

    So anyhow, you have to email me as soon as you get back. Okay! I want to hear all about it. Where were you going again?

    Mom was a little concerned, like she always is, about the people you have been hanging with recently. You know how she gets those 'feelings' about things. Women's intuition, or some such stuff. What do I know? I ain't no woman. Anyhow, that Blake guy who picked you up. I know you said he was some friend's dad, but where was the friend? And she said she'd never met that friend before. I know she hasn't met any of your new friends at graduate school but still, it did seem a little weird that his dad picked you up. Maybe your friend is a 'she?' That would explain everything. Like you don't want mom to know you're hanging with some girl in the woods. So, just to clear up any confusion, you can tell me. With dad gone, I don't have anyone to explain to me all this dating stuff. I mean, you know how shy I can be around girls, especially the nice looking ones. You seem to have a kind of easy way about you. You're a smooth operator, man.

    So call me as soon as you're back. Okay bro?

    Carter

```
-----------------------------------
```

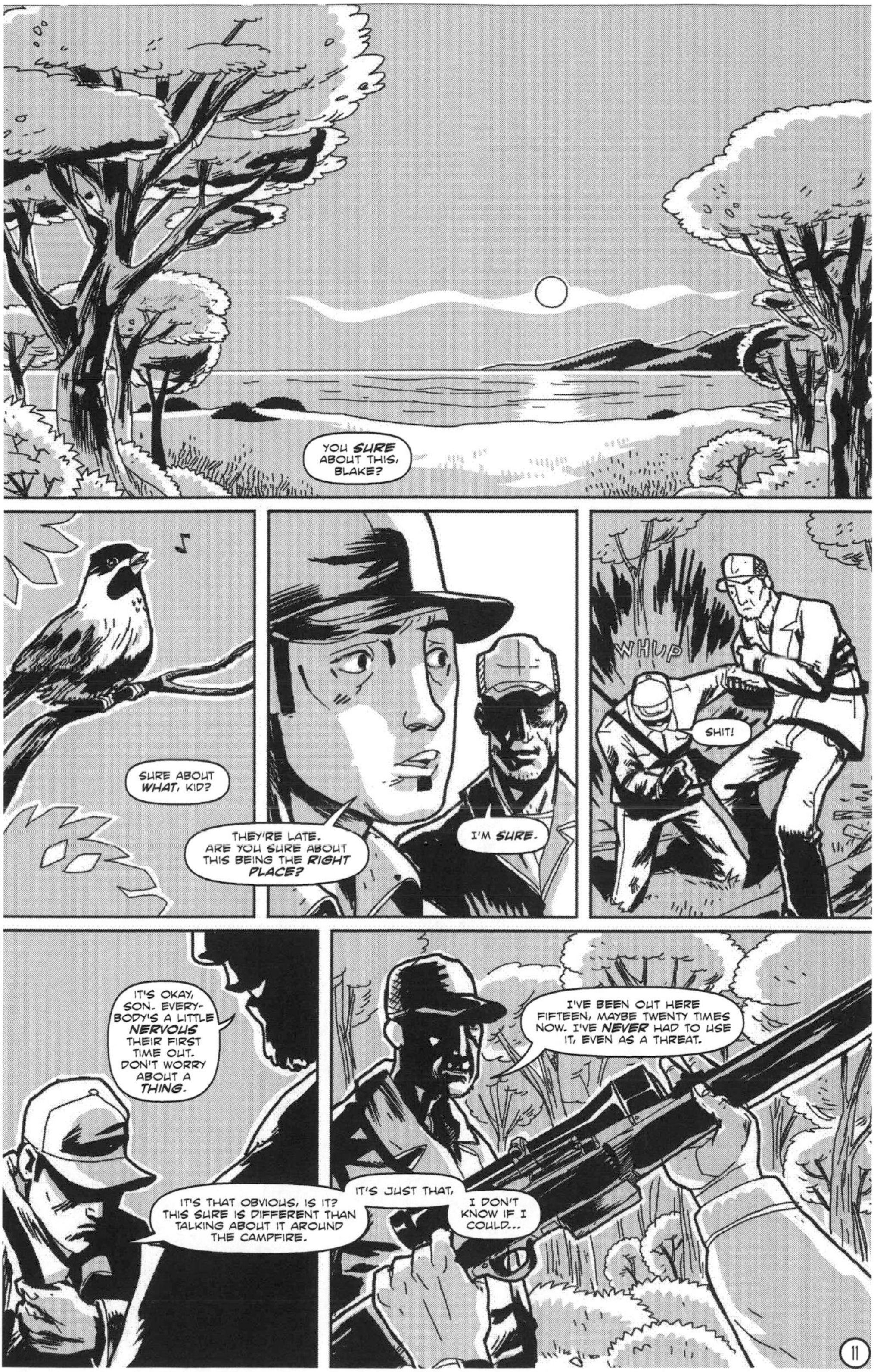
YOU SURE ABOUT THIS, BLAKE?
SURE ABOUT WHAT, KID?
THEY'RE LATE. ARE YOU SURE ABOUT THIS BEING THE RIGHT PLACE?
I'M SURE.
WHUP
SHIT!
IT'S OKAY, SON. EVERYBODY'S A LITTLE NERVOUS THEIR FIRST TIME OUT. DON'T WORRY ABOUT A THING.
IT'S THAT OBVIOUS, IS IT? THIS SURE IS DIFFERENT THAN TALKING ABOUT IT AROUND THE CAMPFIRE.
I'VE BEEN OUT HERE FIFTEEN, MAYBE TWENTY TIMES NOW. I'VE NEVER HAD TO USE IT, EVEN AS A THREAT.
IT'S JUST THAT,
I DON'T KNOW IF I COULD...

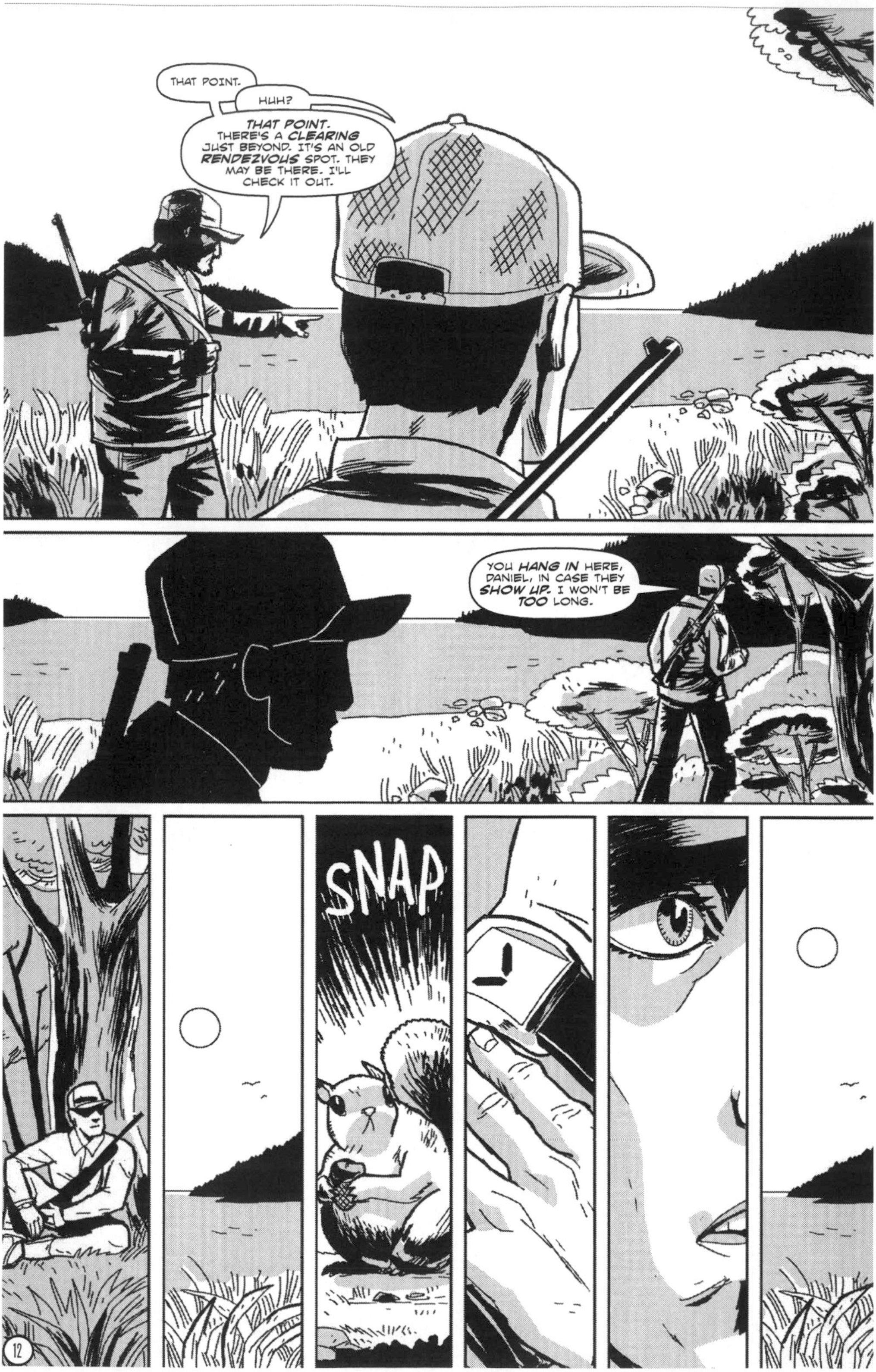
THAT POINT.
HUH?
THAT POINT. THERE'S A CLEARING JUST BEYOND. IT'S AN OLD RENDEZVOUS SPOT. THEY MAY BE THERE. I'LL CHECK IT OUT.
YOU HANG IN HERE, DANIEL, IN CASE THEY SHOW UP. I WON'T BE TOO LONG.
SNAP

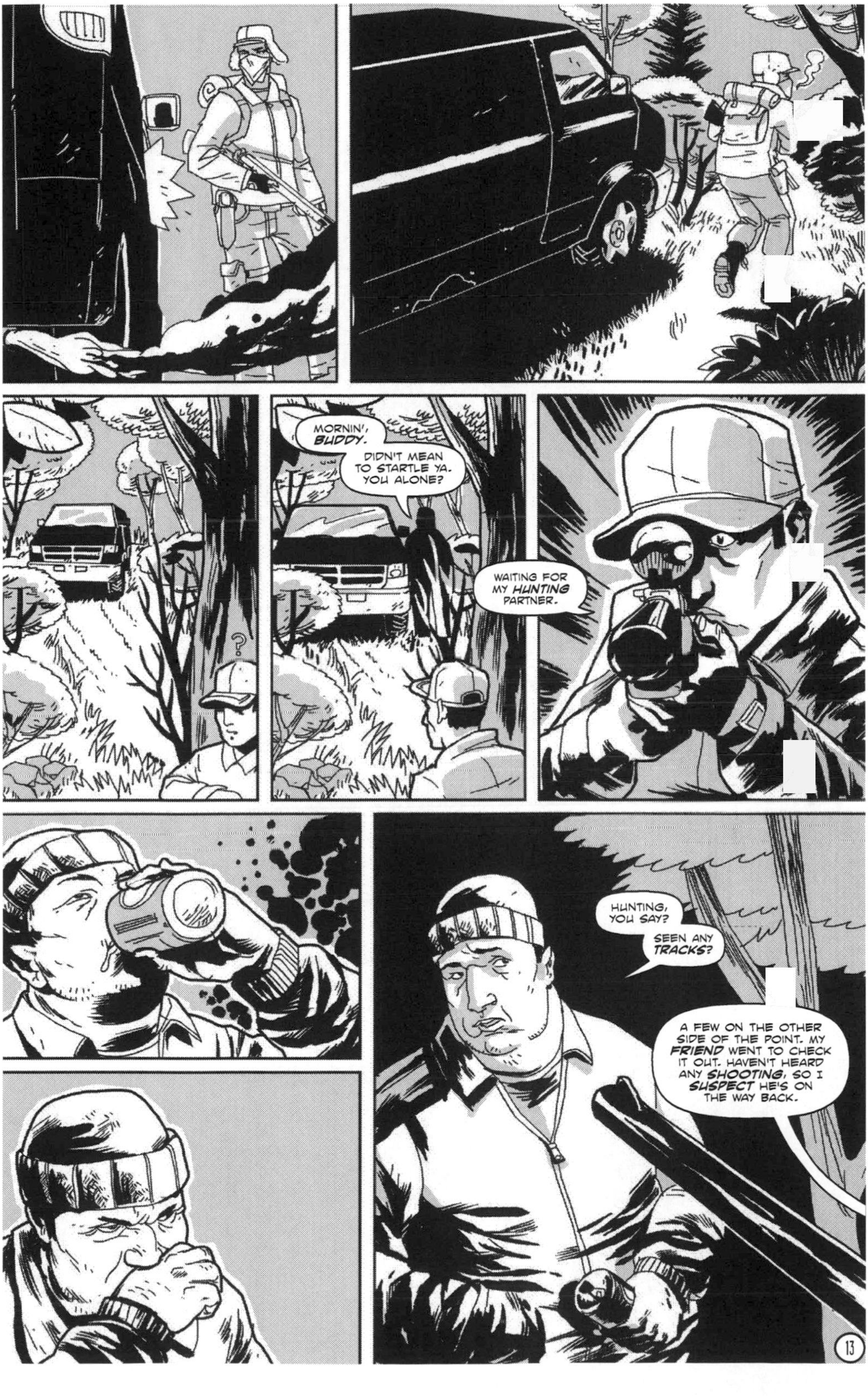
MORNIN', BUDDY.
DIDN'T MEAN TO STARTLE YA. YOU ALONE?
WAITING FOR MY HUNTING PARTNER.
HUNTING, YOU SAY?
SEEN ANY TRACKS?
A FEW ON THE OTHER SIDE OF THE POINT. MY FRIEND WENT TO CHECK IT OUT. HAVEN'T HEARD ANY SHOOTING, SO I SUSPECT HE'S ON THE WAY BACK.

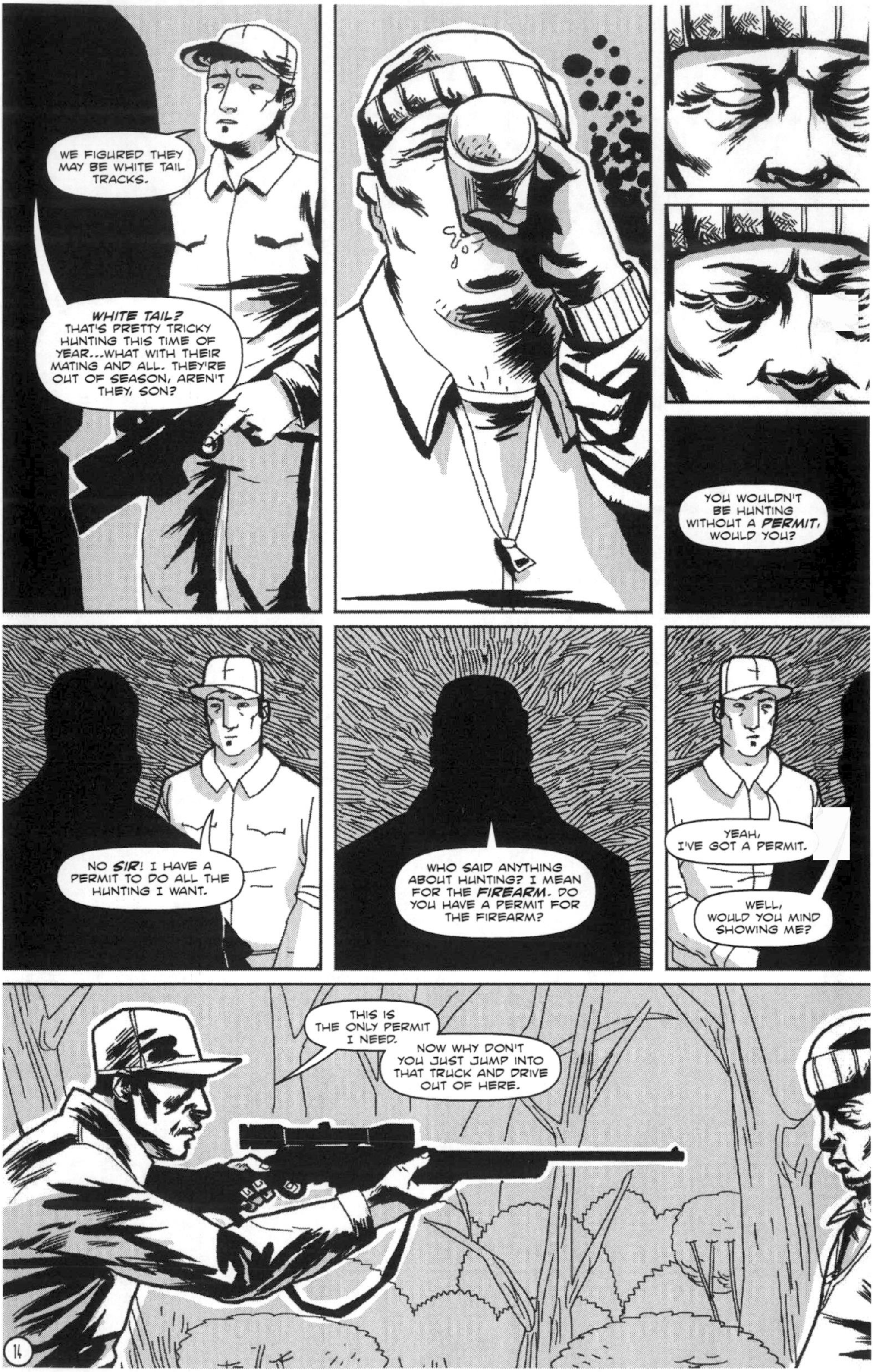
WE FIGURED THEY MAY BE WHITE TAIL TRACKS.
WHITE TAIL? THAT'S PRETTY TRICKY HUNTING THIS TIME OF YEAR...WHAT WITH THEIR MATING AND ALL. THEY'RE OUT OF SEASON, AREN'T THEY, SON?
YOU WOULDN'T BE HUNTING WITHOUT A PERMIT, WOULD YOU?
NO SIR! I HAVE A PERMIT TO DO ALL THE HUNTING I WANT.
WHO SAID ANYTHING ABOUT HUNTING? I MEAN FOR THE FIREARM. DO YOU HAVE A PERMIT FOR THE FIREARM?
YEAH, I'VE GOT A PERMIT.
WELL, WOULD YOU MIND SHOWING ME?
THIS IS THE ONLY PERMIT I NEED.
NOW WHY DON'T YOU JUST JUMP INTO THAT TRUCK AND DRIVE OUT OF HERE.

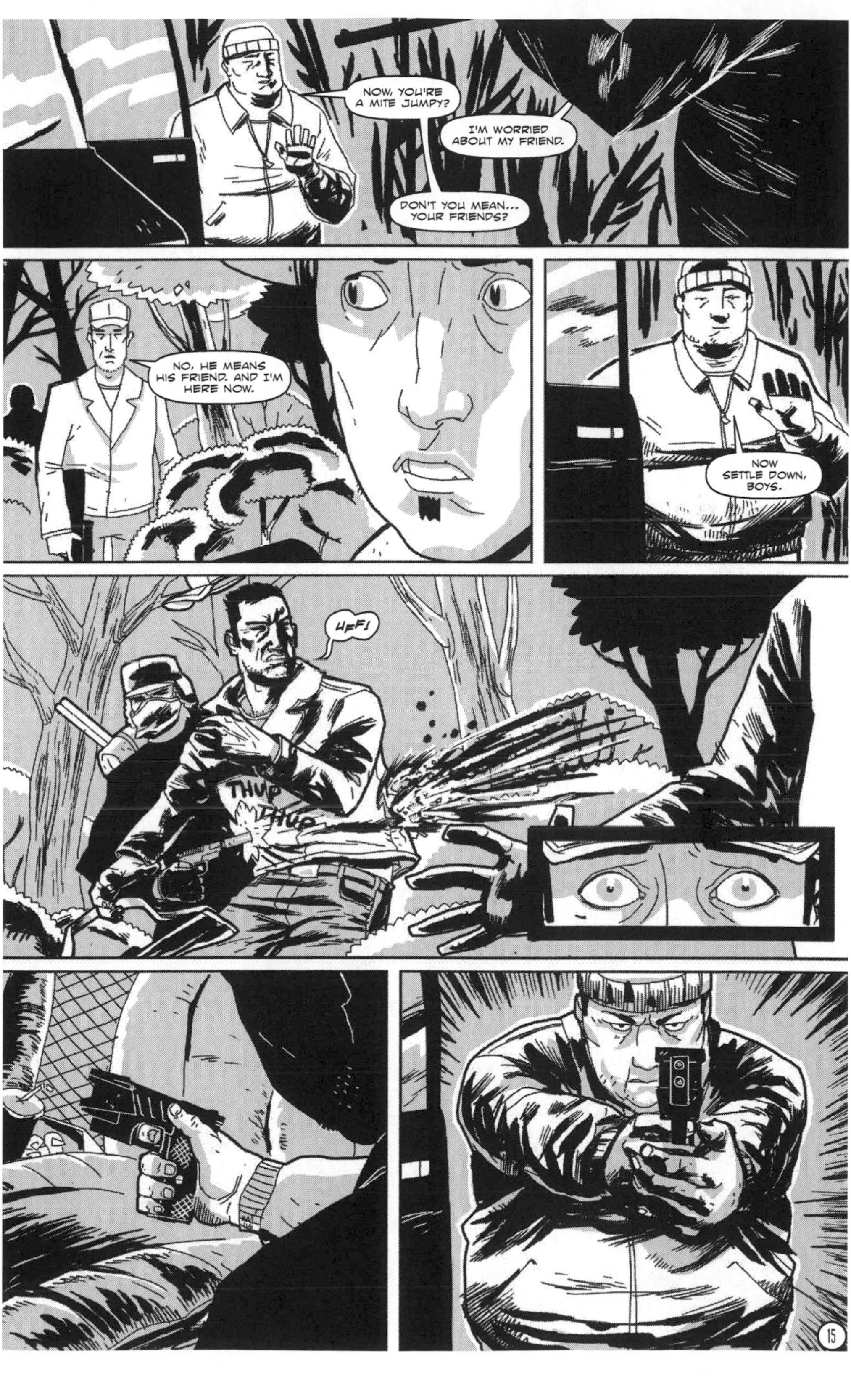
NOW, YOU'RE A MITE JUMPY?
I'M WORRIED ABOUT MY FRIEND.
DON'T YOU MEAN... YOUR FRIENDS?
NO, HE MEANS HIS FRIEND. AND I'M HERE NOW.
NOW SETTLE DOWN, BOYS.
UFF!
THUP
THUP

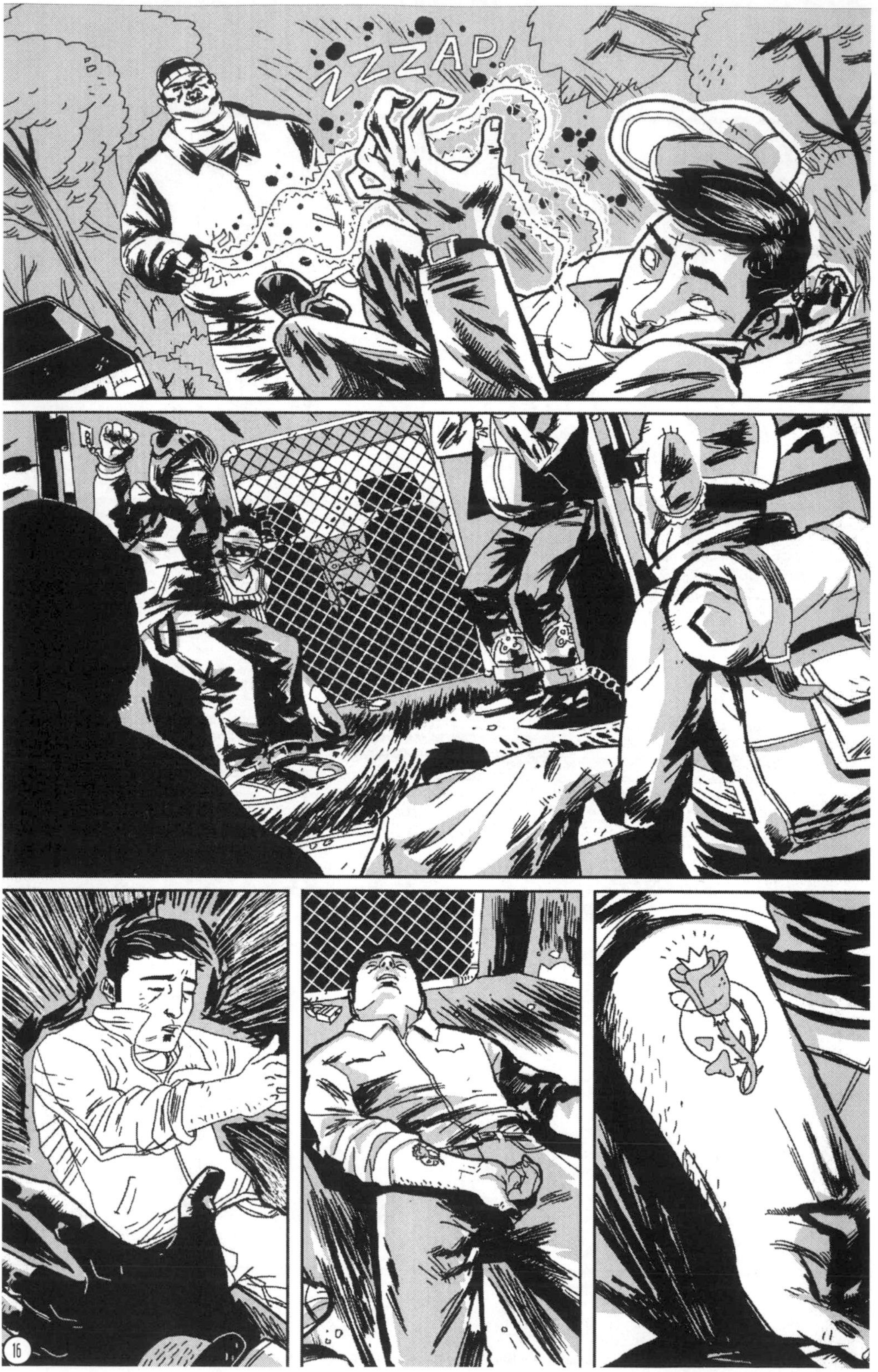
ZZZAP!

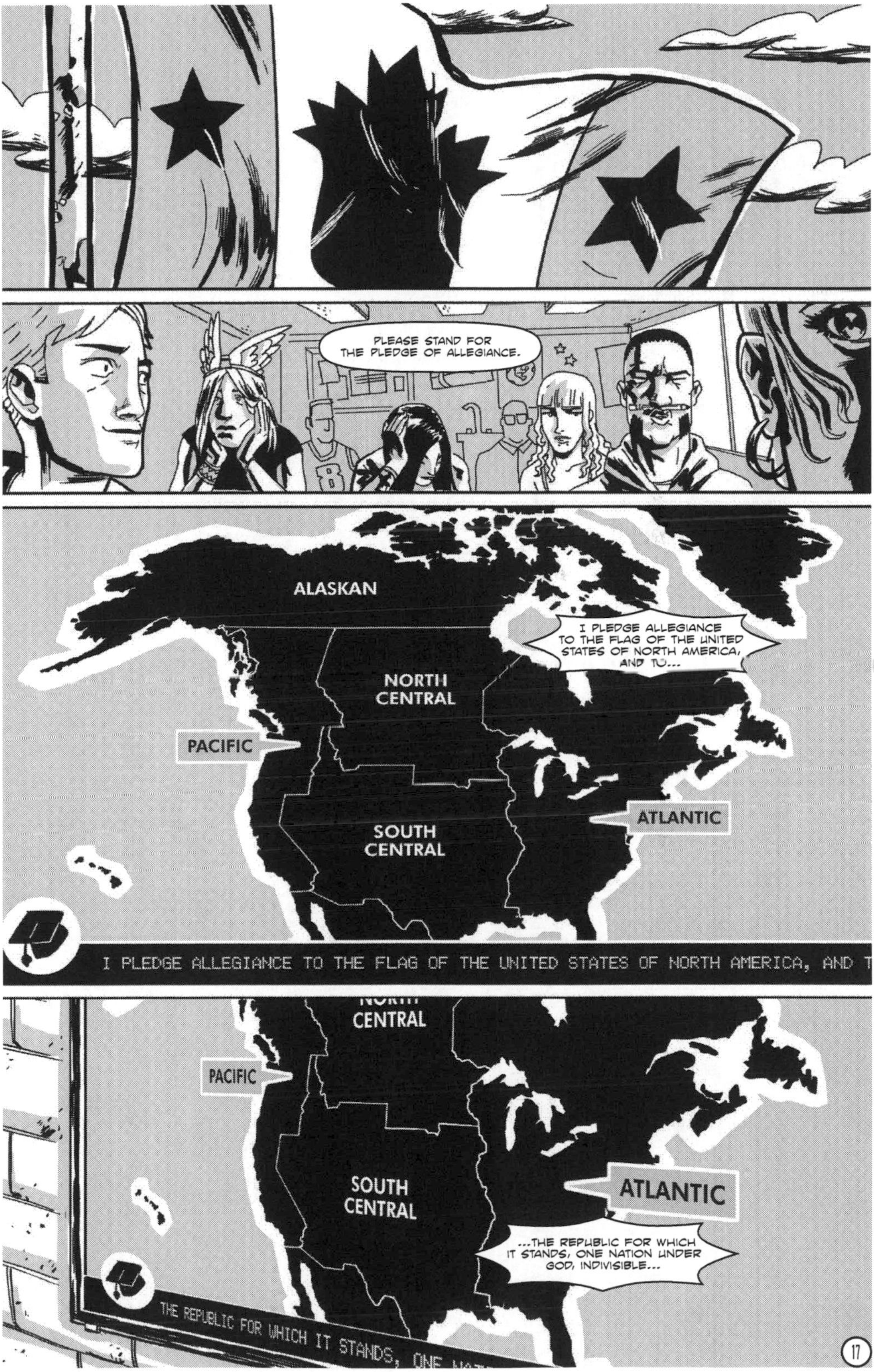
PLEASE STAND FOR THE PLEDGE OF ALLEGIANCE.
ALASKAN
I PLEDGE ALLEGIANCE TO THE FLAG OF THE UNITED STATES OF NORTH AMERICA, AND TO...
NORTH CENTRAL
PACIFIC
ATLANTIC
SOUTH CENTRAL
I PLEDGE ALLEGIANCE TO THE FLAG OF THE UNITED STATES OF NORTH AMERICA, AND T
CENTRAL
PACIFIC
SOUTH CENTRAL
ATLANTIC
...THE REPUBLIC FOR WHICH IT STANDS, ONE NATION UNDER GOD, INDIVISIBLE...
THE REPUBLIC FOR WHICH IT STANDS, ONE

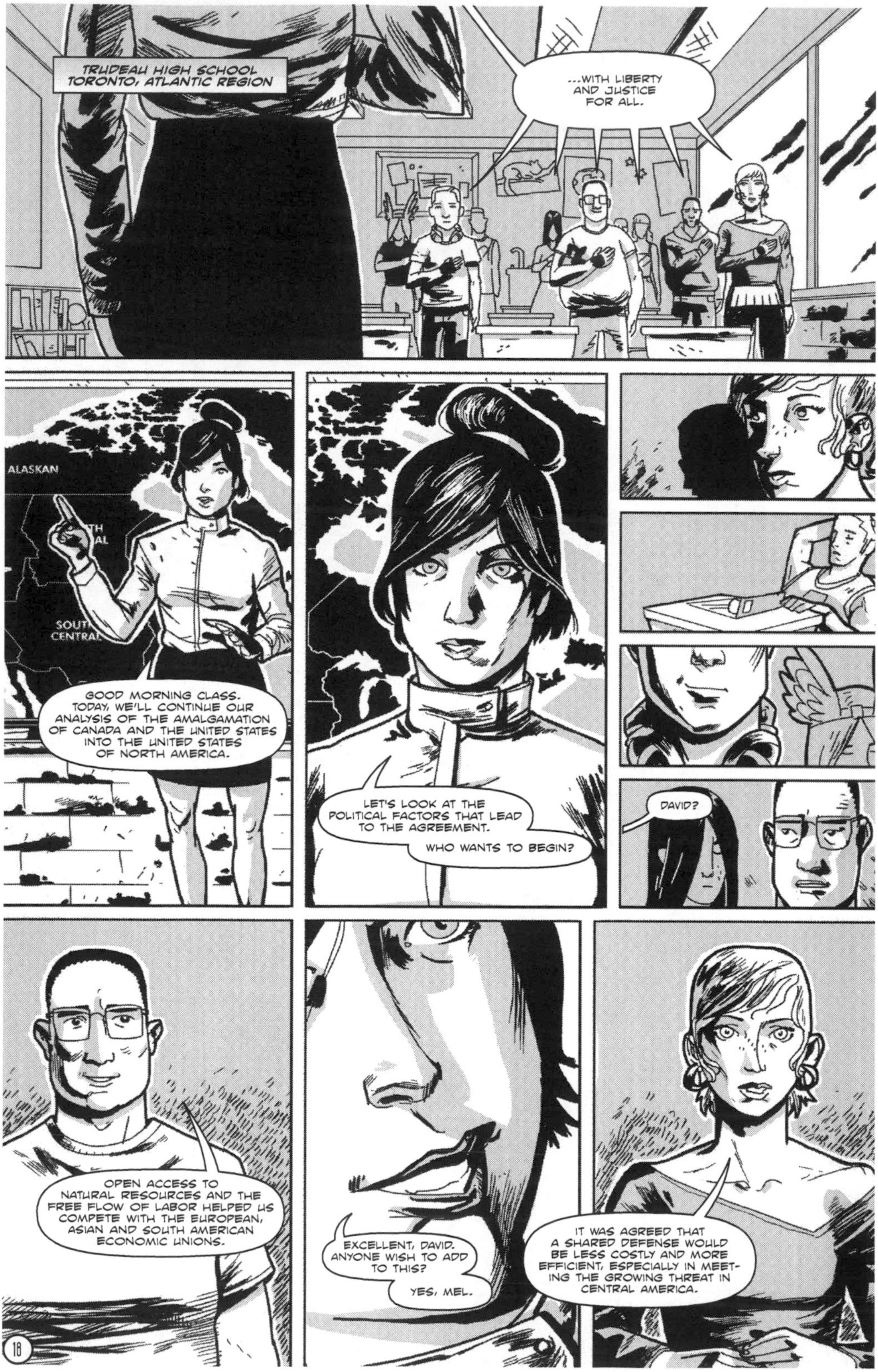
TRUDEAU HIGH SCHOOL
TORONTO, ATLANTIC REGION
...WITH LIBERTY AND JUSTICE FOR ALL.
ALASKAN
SOUTH CENTRAL
GOOD MORNING CLASS. TODAY, WE'LL CONTINUE OUR ANALYSIS OF THE AMALGAMATION OF CANADA AND THE UNITED STATES INTO THE UNITED STATES OF NORTH AMERICA.
LET'S LOOK AT THE POLITICAL FACTORS THAT LEAD TO THE AGREEMENT.
WHO WANTS TO BEGIN?
DAVID?
OPEN ACCESS TO NATURAL RESOURCES AND THE FREE FLOW OF LABOR HELPED US COMPETE WITH THE EUROPEAN, ASIAN AND SOUTH AMERICAN ECONOMIC UNIONS.
EXCELLENT, DAVID. ANYONE WISH TO ADD TO THIS?
YES, MEL.
IT WAS AGREED THAT A SHARED DEFENSE WOULD BE LESS COSTLY AND MORE EFFICIENT, ESPECIALLY IN MEETING THE GROWING THREAT IN CENTRAL AMERICA.

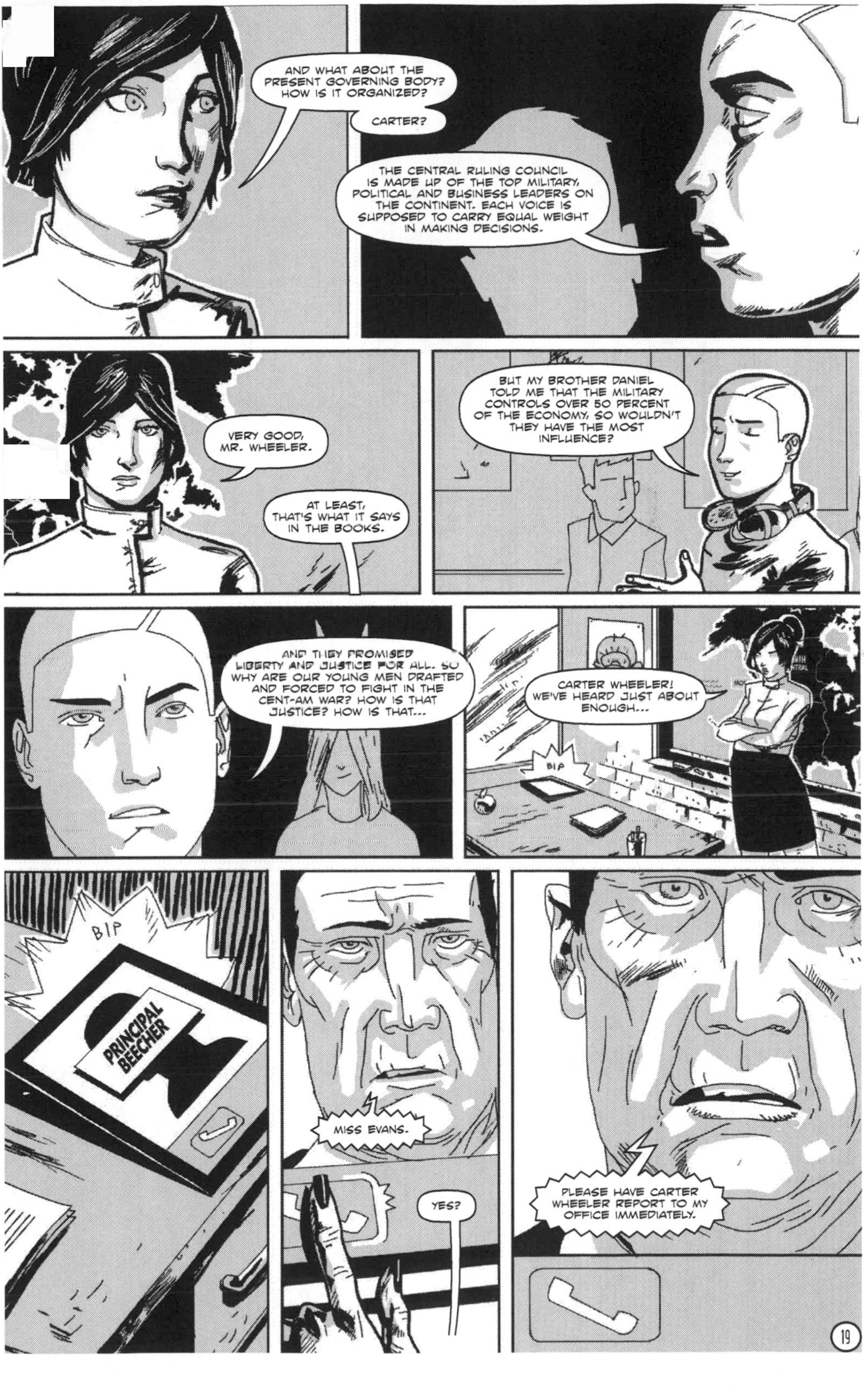
AND WHAT ABOUT THE PRESENT GOVERNING BODY? HOW IS IT ORGANIZED?
CARTER?
THE CENTRAL RULING COUNCIL IS MADE UP OF THE TOP MILITARY, POLITICAL AND BUSINESS LEADERS ON THE CONTINENT. EACH VOICE IS SUPPOSED TO CARRY EQUAL WEIGHT IN MAKING DECISIONS.
VERY GOOD, MR. WHEELER.
AT LEAST, THAT'S WHAT IT SAYS IN THE BOOKS.
BUT MY BROTHER DANIEL TOLD ME THAT THE MILITARY CONTROLS OVER 50 PERCENT OF THE ECONOMY, SO WOULDN'T THEY HAVE THE MOST INFLUENCE?
AND THEY PROMISED LIBERTY AND JUSTICE FOR ALL. SO WHY ARE OUR YOUNG MEN DRAFTED AND FORCED TO FIGHT IN THE CENT-AM WAR? HOW IS THAT JUSTICE? HOW IS THAT...
CARTER WHEELER! WE'VE HEARD JUST ABOUT ENOUGH...
BIP
BIP
PRINCIPAL BEECHER
MISS EVANS.
YES?
PLEASE HAVE CARTER WHEELER REPORT TO MY OFFICE IMMEDIATELY.

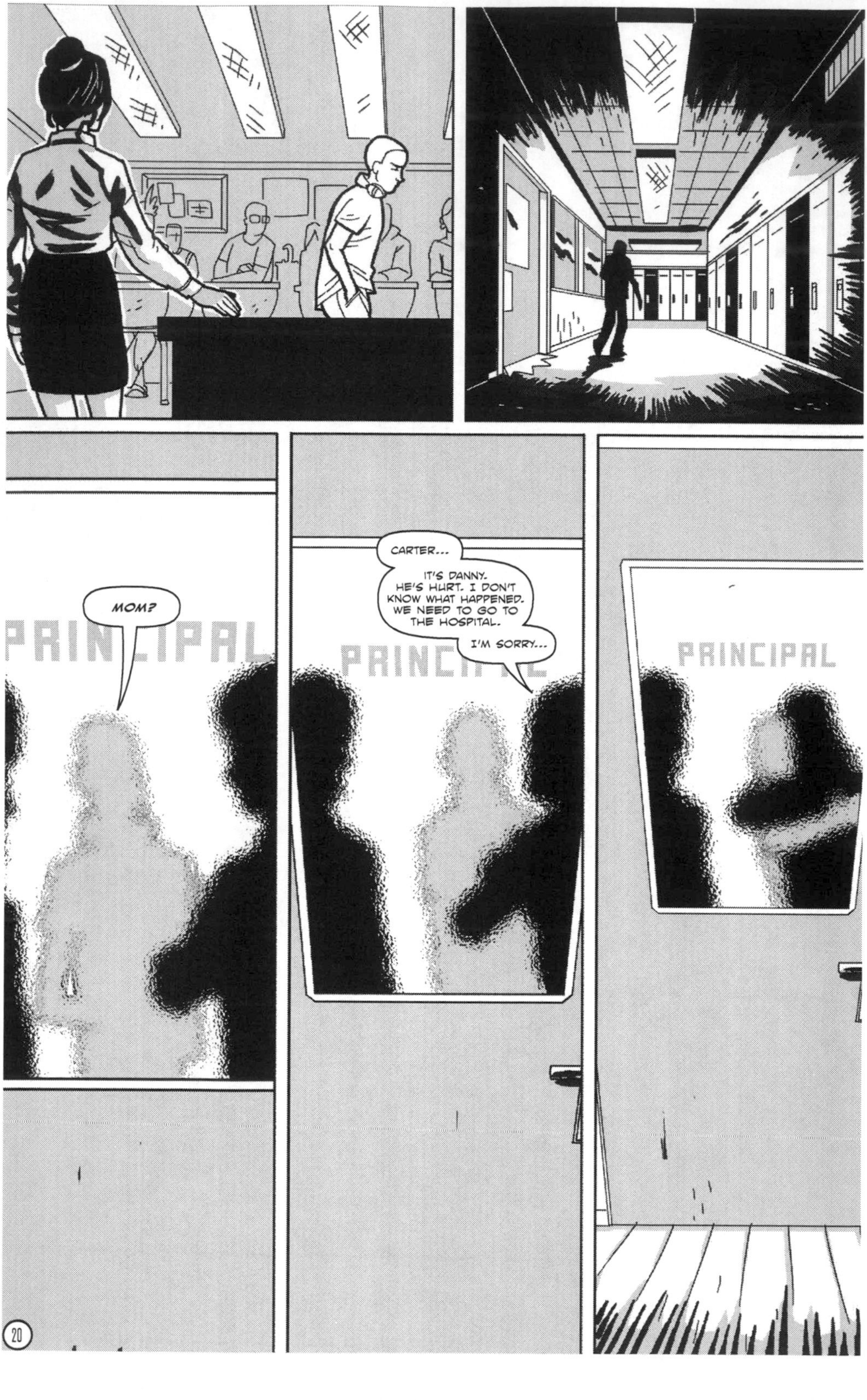
MOM?
PRINCIPAL
CARTER...
IT'S DANNY. HE'S HURT. I DON'T KNOW WHAT HAPPENED. WE NEED TO GO TO THE HOSPITAL.
I'M SORRY...
PRINCIPAL
PRINCIPAL

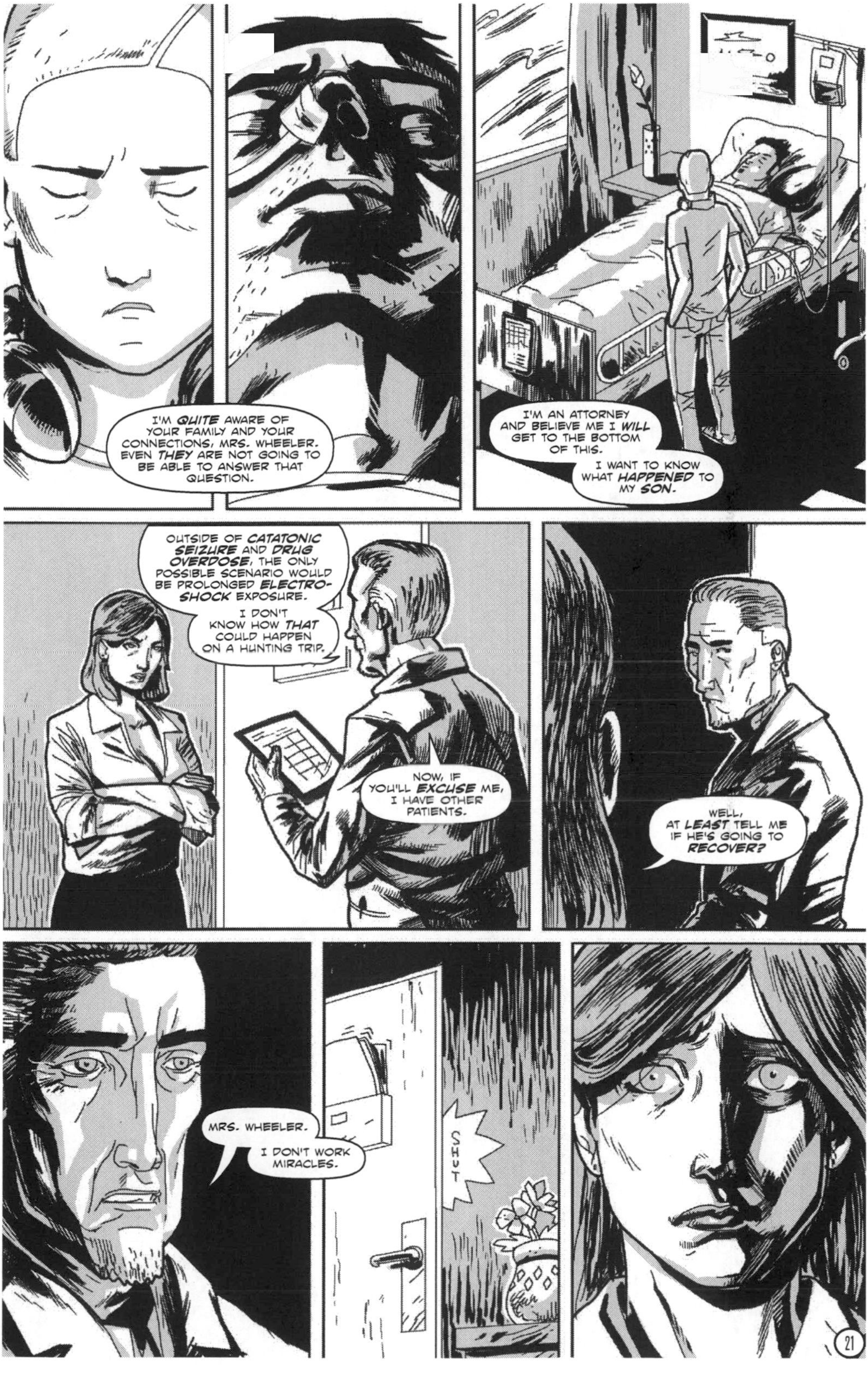
I'M QUITE AWARE OF YOUR FAMILY AND YOUR CONNECTIONS, MRS. WHEELER. EVEN THEY ARE NOT GOING TO BE ABLE TO ANSWER THAT QUESTION.
I'M AN ATTORNEY AND BELIEVE ME I WILL GET TO THE BOTTOM OF THIS.
I WANT TO KNOW WHAT HAPPENED TO MY SON.
OUTSIDE OF CATATONIC SEIZURE AND DRUG OVERDOSE, THE ONLY POSSIBLE SCENARIO WOULD BE PROLONGED ELECTRO-SHOCK EXPOSURE.
I DON'T KNOW HOW THAT COULD HAPPEN ON A HUNTING TRIP.
NOW, IF YOU'LL EXCUSE ME, I HAVE OTHER PATIENTS.
WELL, AT LEAST TELL ME IF HE'S GOING TO RECOVER?
MRS. WHEELER.
I DON'T WORK MIRACLES.
SHUT

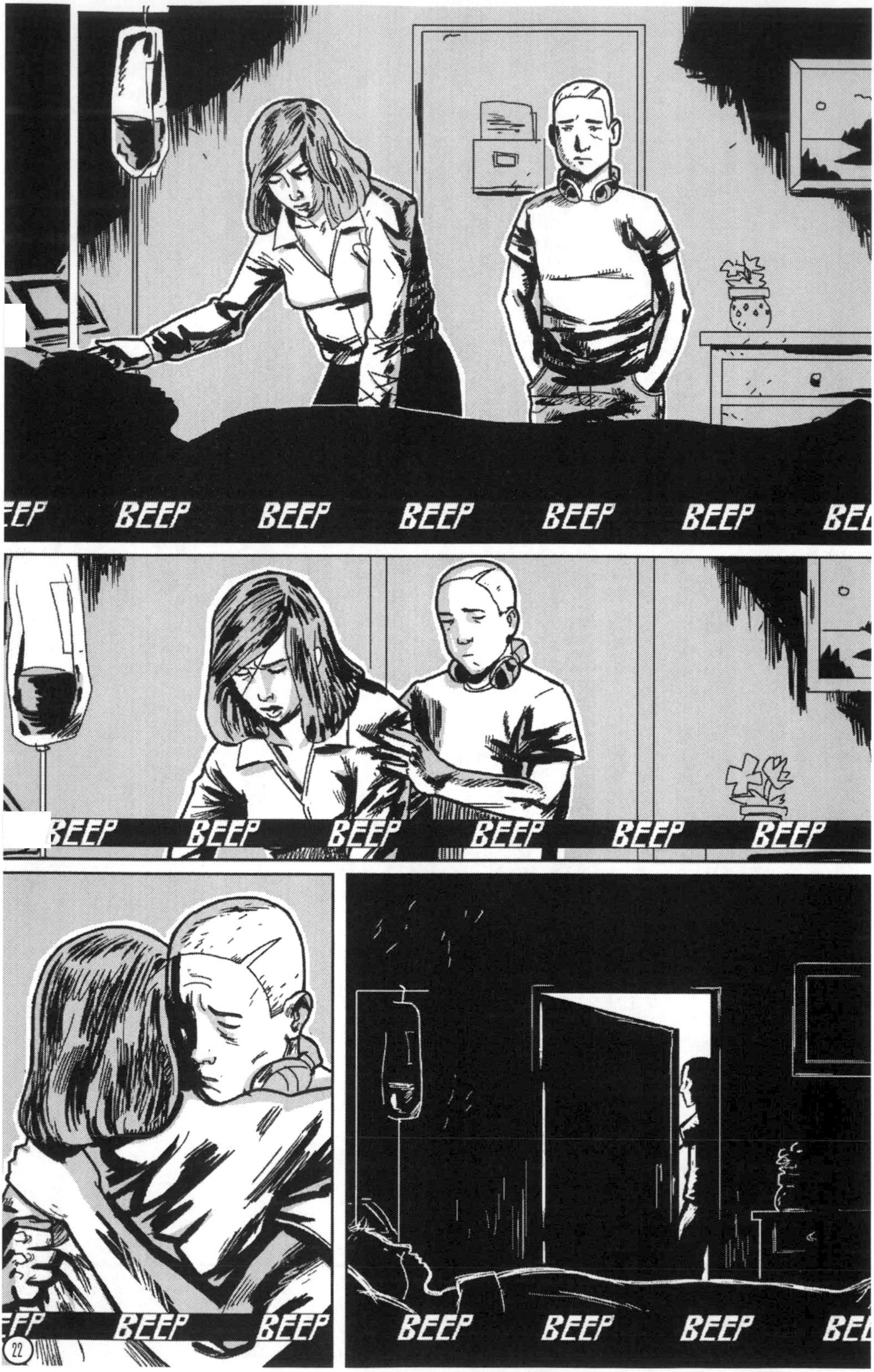
BEEP
BEEP
BEEP
BEEP
BEEP
BEEP
BEEP
BEEP
BEEP
BEEP
BEEP
BEEP
BEEP
BEEP
BEEP
BEEP

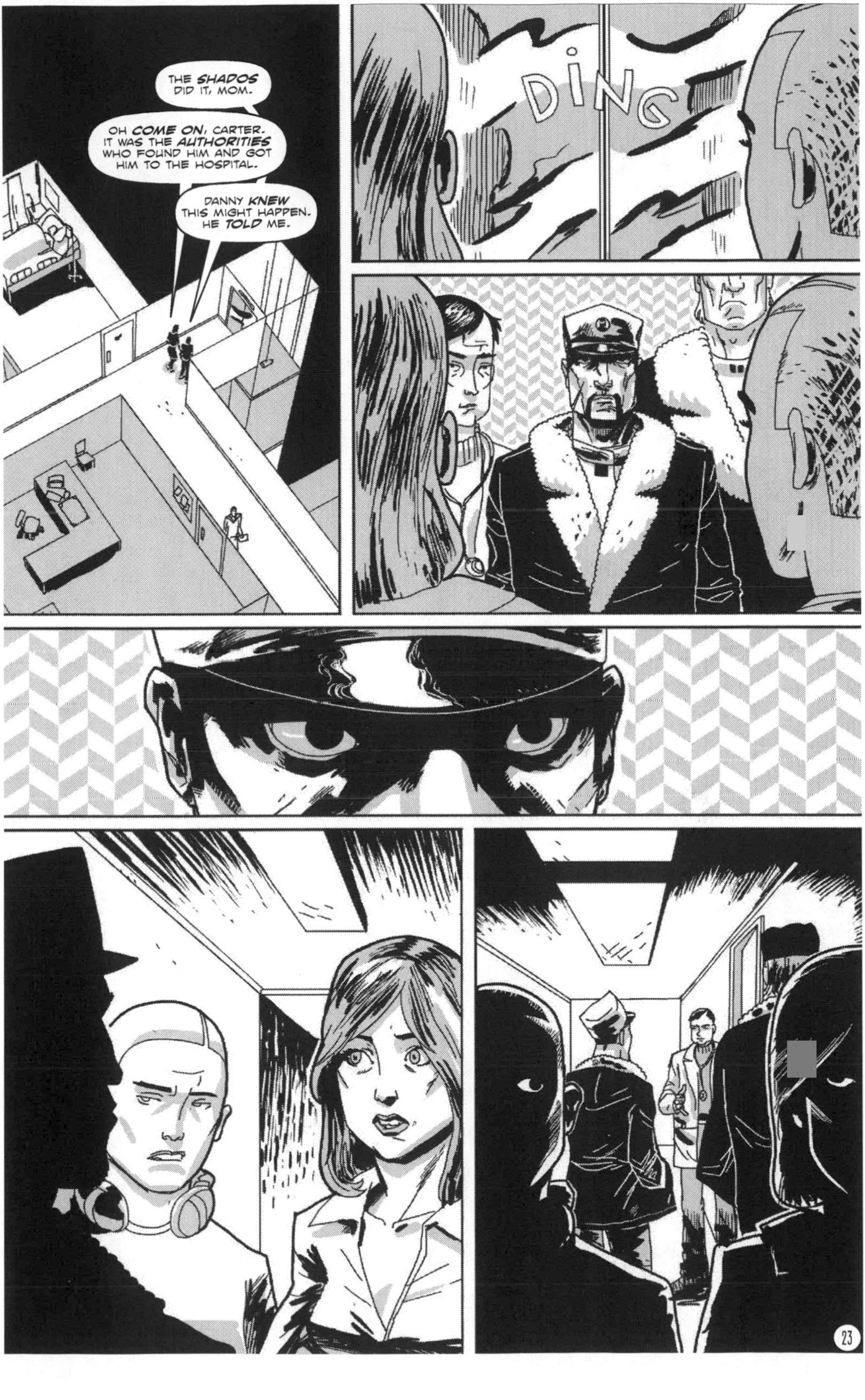
THE SHADOS DID IT, MOM.
OH COME ON, CARTER. IT WAS THE AUTHORITIES WHO FOUND HIM AND GOT HIM TO THE HOSPITAL.
DANNY KNEW THIS MIGHT HAPPEN. HE TOLD ME.
DING

BEEP   BEEP   BEEEEEEEEEEEEEEEEEEEEEEEEEEEEEEEEEEEEE

24

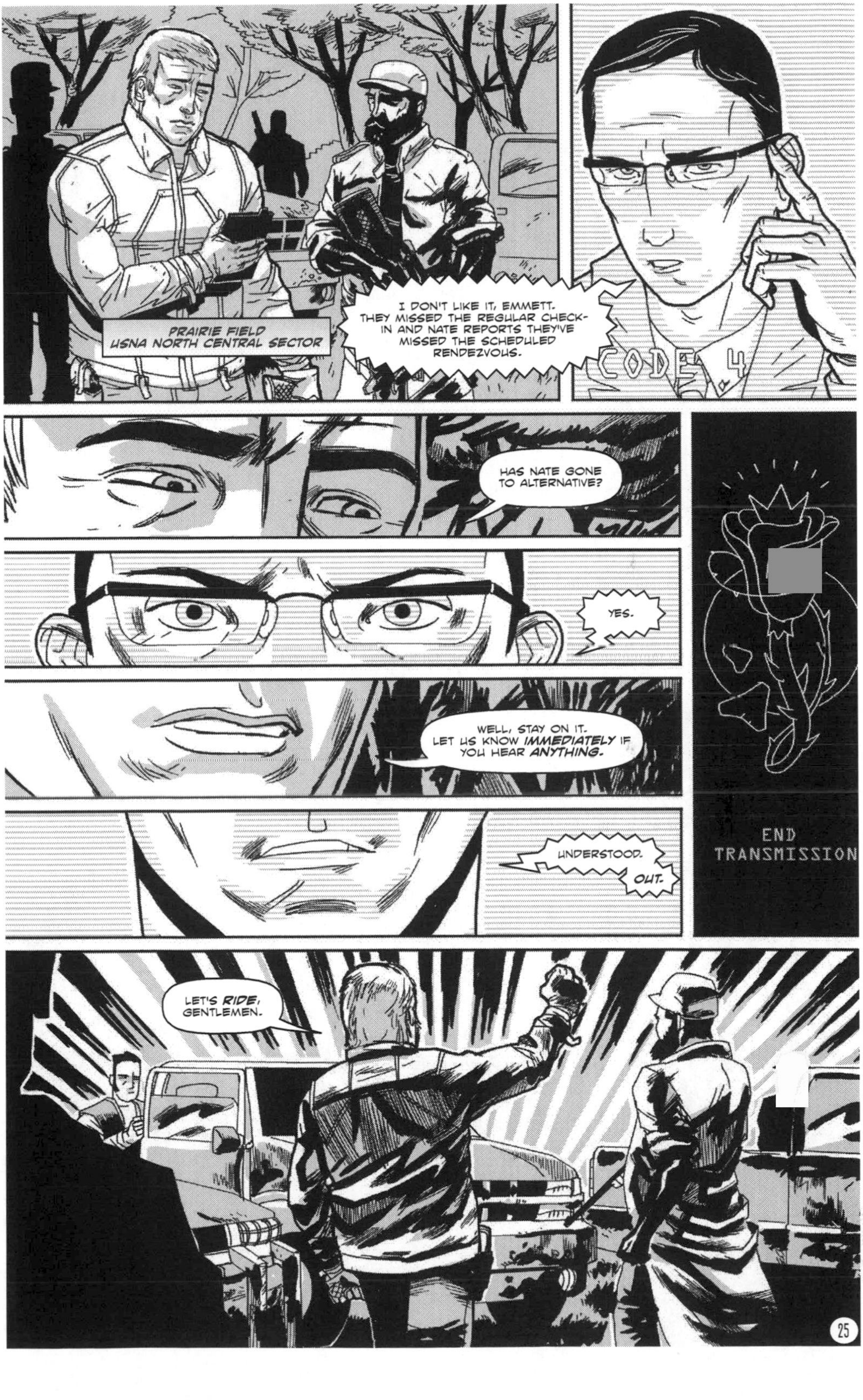
PRAIRIE FIELD
USNA NORTH CENTRAL SECTOR
I DON'T LIKE IT, EMMETT. THEY MISSED THE REGULAR CHECK-IN AND NATE REPORTS THEY'VE MISSED THE SCHEDULED RENDEZVOUS.
CODE 4
HAS NATE GONE TO ALTERNATIVE?
YES.
WELL, STAY ON IT. LET US KNOW *IMMEDIATELY* IF YOU HEAR *ANYTHING.*
UNDERSTOOD.
OUT.
END TRANSMISSION
LET'S *RIDE,* GENTLEMEN.

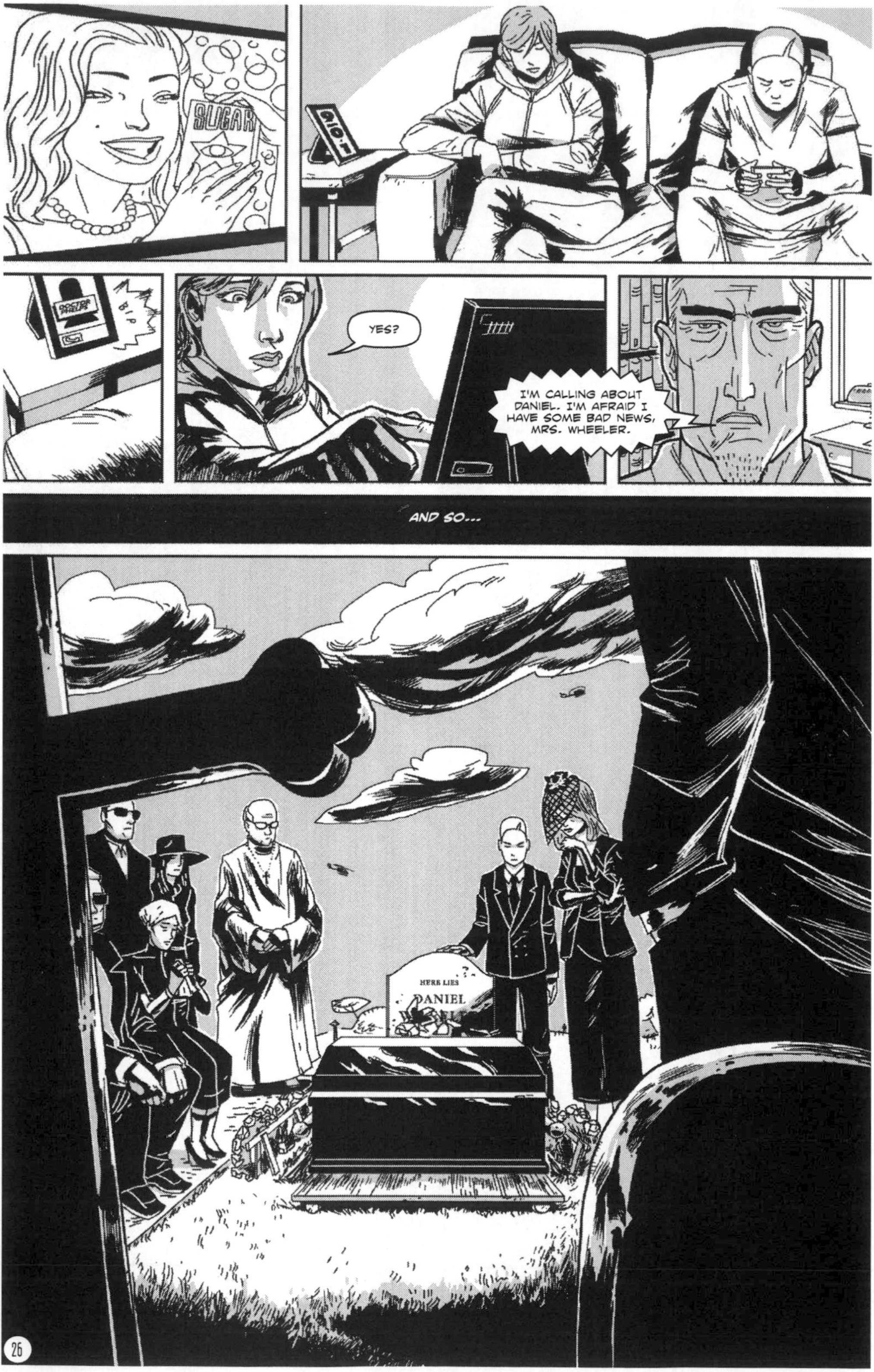
SUGAR
YES?
I'M CALLING ABOUT DANIEL. I'M AFRAID I HAVE SOME BAD NEWS, MRS. WHEELER.
AND SO...
HERE LIES
DANIEL

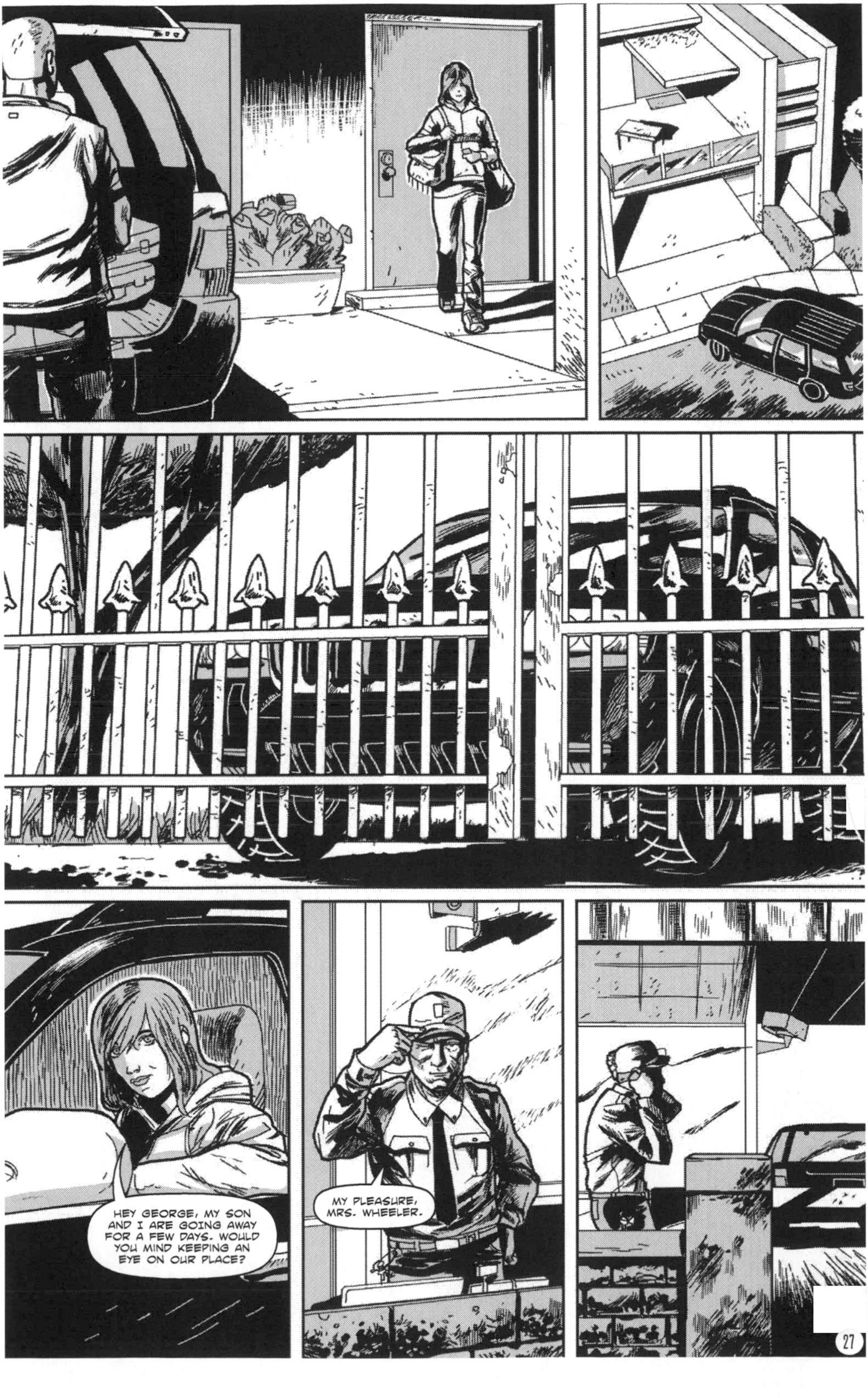
HEY GEORGE, MY SON AND I ARE GOING AWAY FOR A FEW DAYS. WOULD YOU MIND KEEPING AN EYE ON OUR PLACE?
MY PLEASURE, MRS. WHEELER.

Five Faces of the USNA

by Melissa Branigan - Staff Reporter

Every month, New Chronicle reporter Melissa Branigan presents her continuing series about the people of our new country.

Dr. Cameron Swanson drives his new all electric Cadillac Special Edition along the recently completed CS505 freeway which connects Chicago to the Eastern Seaboard. He punches his destination into his onboard computer, sets the autodrive parameters and lets go of the wheel. Electronic sensors embedded in the highway guide his vehicle safely to the outskirts of Philadelphia where he will disconnect from the grid and manually guide himself into the heart of the city. Dr. Swanson is the director of the combined Penn State and University of the Prairies team that designed the system. "By combining the talents of these universities with the financial clout of UADE (Universal Advanced Design Engineering), we were able to bring this project in under budget and months before the contracted completion date. We're very proud of what can by done without the hindrance of government controls and protections," states Dr. Swanson. This project is just one example of the advanced technology now being implemented throughout the USNA, a direct result of the amalgamation agreement.

Ben Fernie lifts a crate of apples onto the back of his aging pickup and heads from the inner city of Detroit to the Ambassador Bridge where he crosses over the Detroit River to Windsor. In the past, he would have had to undergo a thorough inspection of his vehicle and the agricultural products. Today, it's a quick trip to the growing metropolis of Windsor. A resident of Detroit, Fernie is now a farmer working his land on the site of USNA's largest urban farming community. First begun in 2010, after the recession of 2008 devastated the city's automobile industry, the shift from industrial to agriculture was accelerated with the amalgamation, as the vast markets of Southern Ontario became easily accessible without elaborate border and security protocols.

Ann Fellows is 46 years old, suffering from tuberculosis and living on the arid downtown streets of Los Angeles. Devastated by the crumbling California economy and the earthquakes that rocked the region, the downtown core has been deserted as people fled inland and north to safer locales. Many people, like Ann Fellows, were left behind. One of the most controversial elements of the amalgamation was the adoption of the old United States social model which emphasized individual responsibility for life's basics. This ran counter to the more socialist model of the former Dominion of Canada which preached the necessity of the social safety net. With the increasing population of urban homeless, there is a rising call for more government response to the growing crisis.

William Sanovich is a reluctant farmer. It's hot, backbreaking work for little pay and he's one of thousands working the industrial prison farms of the mid-west sector. The prison farm is a concept embraced by the ruling council of the USNA and reviled by those opposed to what they deem exploitation of labour. Deputy Secretary Hans Vellman oversees the prison farm network and believes the work is both healthy and necessary in rehabilitating the prisoners. "What would you have us do?" he asks. "Have them break rocks with sledge hammers and chisels? This system benefits the prisoner by teaching them useful skills and reconnecting them with the land. The consumer benefits by literally gaining the fruits of their labour. This system helps keep costs down." Sanovich disagrees. He sees little benefit in learning to pick, wash and pack lettuce, spinach and tomatoes. "Twelve hour days of kneeling in the dirt under the hot sun is about as far away from agricultural education and rehabilitation as you can get," he says. "We're slave labour for AAS (Advanced Agricultural Systems Inc.). They are the ones who benefit. Seen their stock prices lately? They ain't hurting."

Janet Michaels used to live in Denver. She now lives in Yellowknife, a city that has grown fourfold since the amalgamation. The melting ice cap and increased activity in the north has created job opportunities that didn't exist a decade ago. After a bitter divorce, Janet wanted to get as far away from her ex-husband as possible and a job in Yellowknife has proven the correct tonic to heal her emotional wounds. Trained in systems analysis and control, she heads a group coordinating the movement of goods and people north to the new mines that have opened in the past five years. "Sure, it gets cold during the winter but it lasts half as long as it did 10 years ago and the summers are warmer than ever before." Janet is thankful she could move from Colorado to the Alaskan sector without the old travel and immigration restrictions. "It's really a free country,' she enthusiastically proclaims. "Without the amalgamation, none of this would have been possible for me."

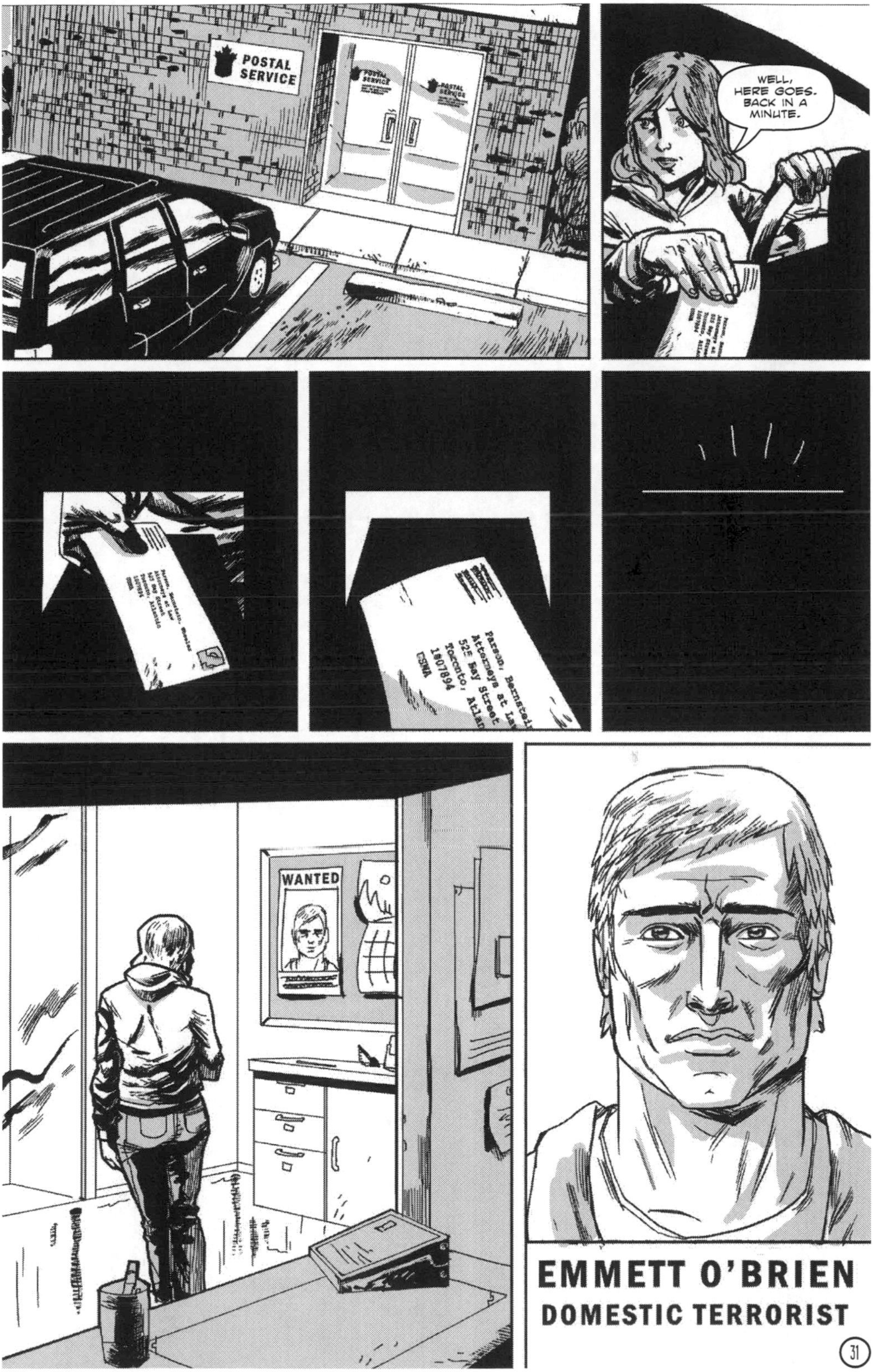
POSTAL SERVICE
WELL, HERE GOES. BACK IN A MINUTE.
525 Bay Street
1807894
USNA
WANTED
EMMETT O'BRIEN
DOMESTIC TERRORIST

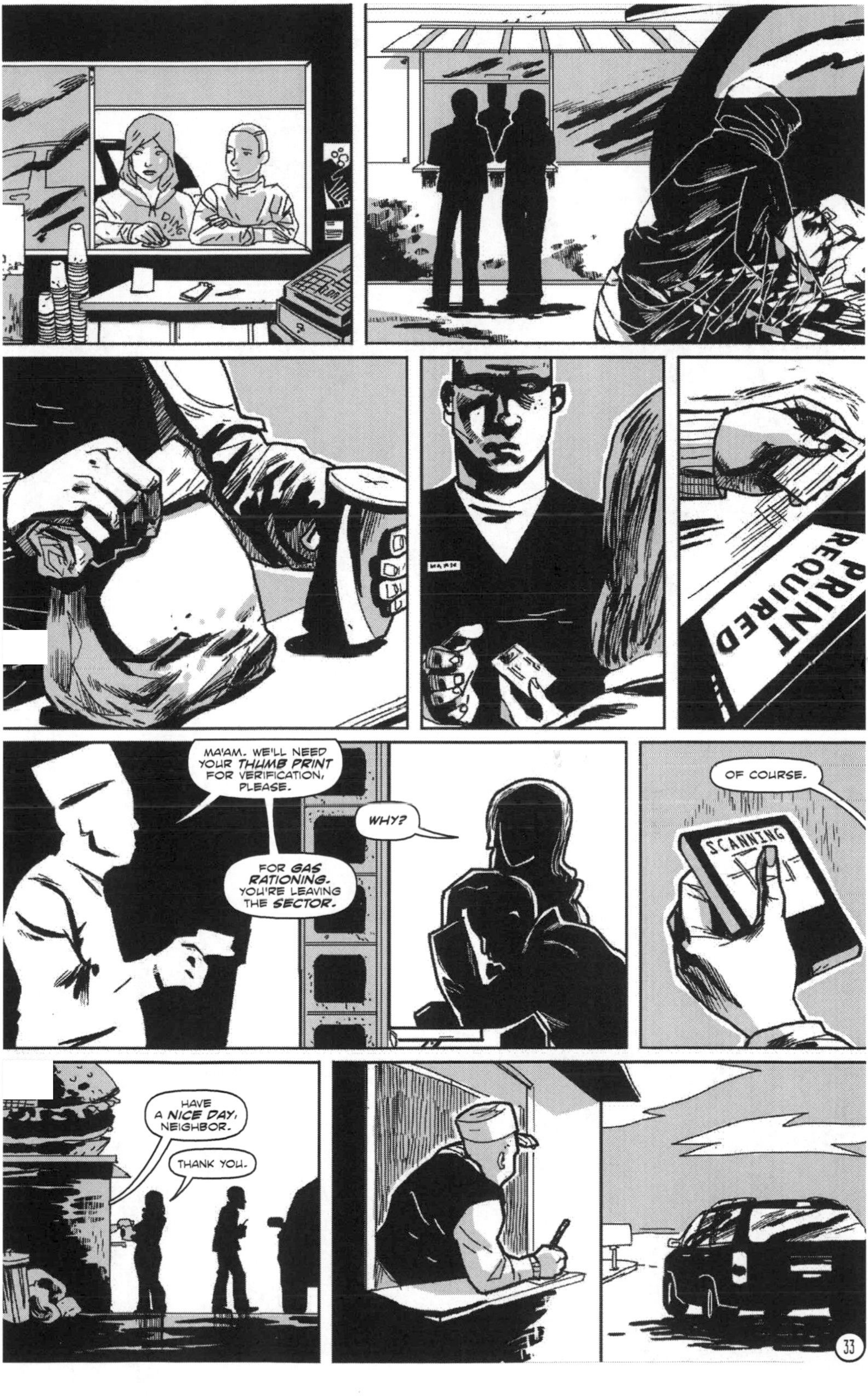
DING
PRINT REQUIRED
MA'AM. WE'LL NEED YOUR THUMB PRINT FOR VERIFICATION, PLEASE.
WHY?
FOR GAS RATIONING. YOU'RE LEAVING THE SECTOR.
OF COURSE.
SCANNING
HAVE A NICE DAY, NEIGHBOR.
THANK YOU.

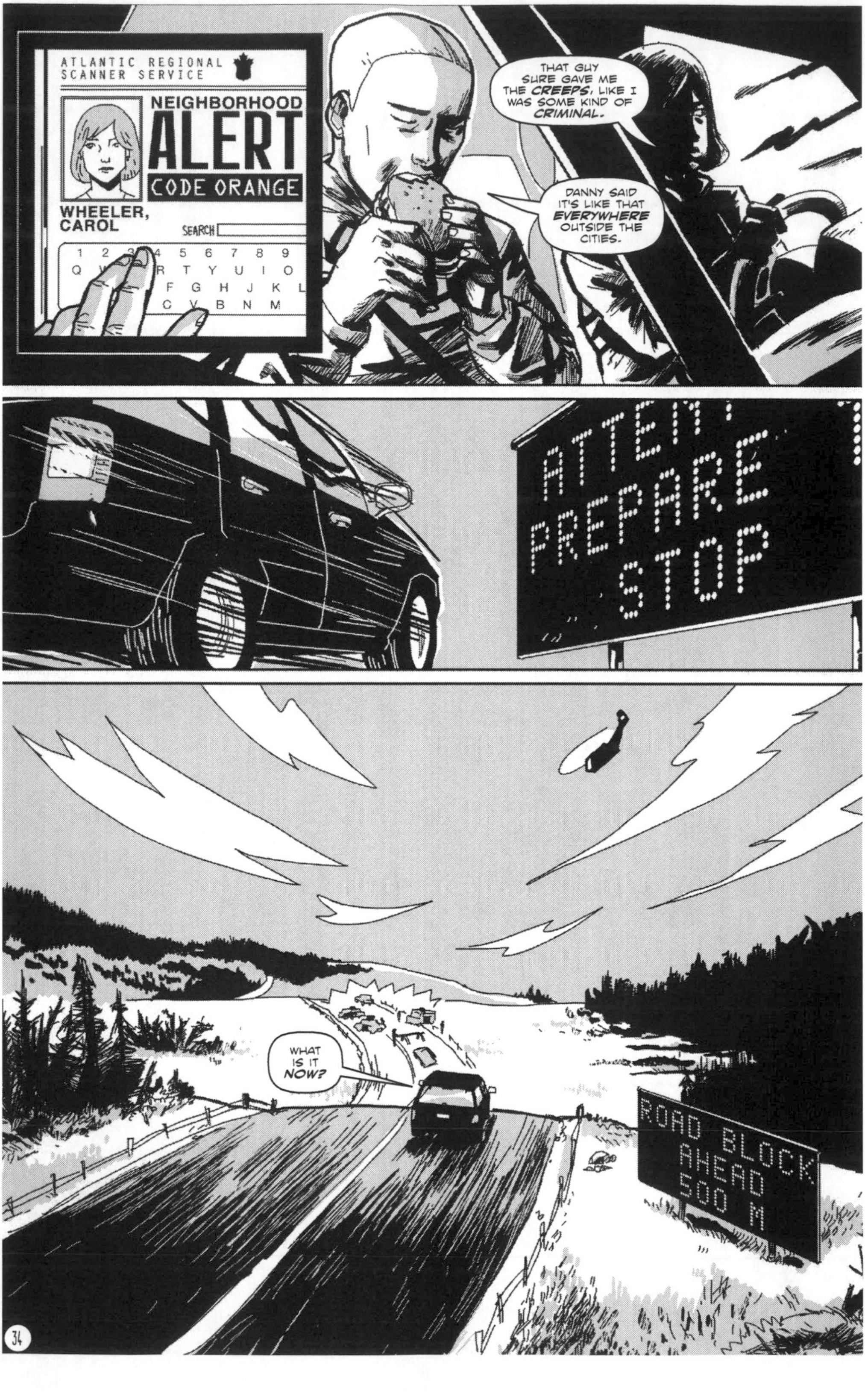
ATLANTIC REGIONAL
SCANNER SERVICE
NEIGHBORHOOD
ALERT
CODE ORANGE
WHEELER, CAROL
SEARCH
THAT GUY SURE GAVE ME THE CREEPS, LIKE I WAS SOME KIND OF CRIMINAL.
DANNY SAID IT'S LIKE THAT EVERYWHERE OUTSIDE THE CITIES.
ATTEN
PREPARE
STOP
WHAT IS IT NOW?
ROAD BLOCK
AHEAD
500 M

```
From:     Captain John Stanton-Mills
          Strategic Home Alliance Defense Organization
          Pentagon - Correspondence Analysis Division

To:       Commander M. Conrad
          Shado Counter Insurgency Team
          Central Regional Headquarters - Calgary

Re:       Analysis of Recently Intercepted eMail Between Carol Wheeler
          and Susan Parks (sister) of Calgary North Central Sector - USNA
```

Commander Conrad: Please find below a recently intercepted eMail from subject Carol Wheeler sent to her sister Susan Parks of Calgary, NCS. My analysis follows.

```
From:        Carol Wheeler <carolwheeler@usnaserve.com>
Subject:     Re: We're on the Way
Date:        May 12, 2025 5:26:28 PM EST
To:          Susan Parks <susanpk@usnaserve.com>
```

Hi Susan,

　　Just wanted you to know that we're finally on our way. We're planning to take our time. Heck, what's the hurry. We should be rolling into Calgary in about 10 days. Carter hasn't been anywhere outside of Toronto for over 10 years now so he's pretty excited. I must say, it is hard to travel, having just buried Daniel. I'm taking an extended leave of absence from the firm so we'll hang around the ranch as long as you can stand us. :)

　　I gotta tell you, this country sure has changed. I never realized how little they actually told us about life outside of Toronto. The highways are deserted. It's as if everyone is scared to travel. They keep warning us to keep vigilante, to not pick up strangers (like I would?). But all the checkpoints, the burnt out cars on the side of the road make you wonder. What other conclusion can you make but to proclaim that things have really gone downhill? Oh well, I guess you have to hit bottom before it improves.

　　I'm sorry I haven't told you much about Danny. I guess you never know how difficult dealing with these kind of situations are until sometime after, when you have a chance to just sit quietly and think. It's been very, very hard for me. And so very strange. The last time I saw him, he was in a coma. All I know is that they found Danny naked, in a park, in North York township. The doctor said he'd been electrocuted, subjected to electric shock. The doctor was either completely ignorant or hiding something. When I finally got to see Danny in the hospital, he was in a bed, under covers. I didn't have a chance to look for any wounds or marks on his body and, quite frankly, it was the last thing on my mind. I guess, in retrospect, it would have been a good idea, if just for peace of mind. But when you think about it, the only way someone could get an electrical jolt would be to be tasered. But it makes no sense? He was camping with his buds. He's a good kid, never in trouble and never looking for trouble. It just breaks my heart.

　　I contacted some of my political connections, government insiders, friends of David's. And I asked my law partner, Allan Goodman, to try to find out anything about the incident, the circumstances behind his injuries. All I got was denials and apologies. You'd think my husband's best friends would be a little more helpful. Danny was his son, after all. These days, you never know who to trust or what to believe.

　　What's happened to this country, the people, my family? It just makes you want to try to change things, get your hands dirty.

　　I look forward to seeing you and Jack and the kids. Carter and I really need the break. I know that mountain air will help clear our heads, maybe find a way to get centered. Are you still doing yoga? I'm thinking of getting back into yoga and meditation. It might be helpful.

　　See you soon, sis.
　　Love, Carol

Analysis:

      Subject is presently traveling via car to visit her sister in Calgary. This has been confirmed by checkpoints outside the Toronto region. Subject is traveling west towards the Central Sector. She is accompanied by her son, Carter, aged 16. She is presently vulnerable to detention for taking her son out of school during term, however she is a high profile citizen, and the publicity of such an act would be counter-productive to our goals.

      Her questions about her son Daniel Wheeler's activities and the nature of his death are disturbing. Suffice to say her inquiries drew the inevitable blanks but she is known to be persistent. Once she's had a chance to grieve the loss of her son, she may become more diligent in her pursuit of the truth. She is apparently still ignorant of his involvement in the rebel movement. Have the records on Daniel Wheeler's death been properly sealed?

      As subject has questioned the cause of death and queried the story of the electro-shock, we must also insure that all hospital records have been properly sealed. Carol Wheeler's statements about the state of the highway system, the lack of travelers and the checkpoints all point to a level of discontent that could flourish. Coupled with the recent loss of her son and her history of powerful political association vis a vis her husband's association with Samuel Stern's cabinet, she becomes a person of interest to us. Her emotional state makes her vulnerable to political sway and her statement about wanting to make change, getting her hands dirty bears scrutiny. I recommend that SHADO Command place her on the priority watch list with copies of all communications diverted to your office.

                    Captain John Stanton-Mills
                    Strategic Home Alliance Defense Organization
                    Pentagon - Correspondence Analysis Division

----

CLASSIFIED

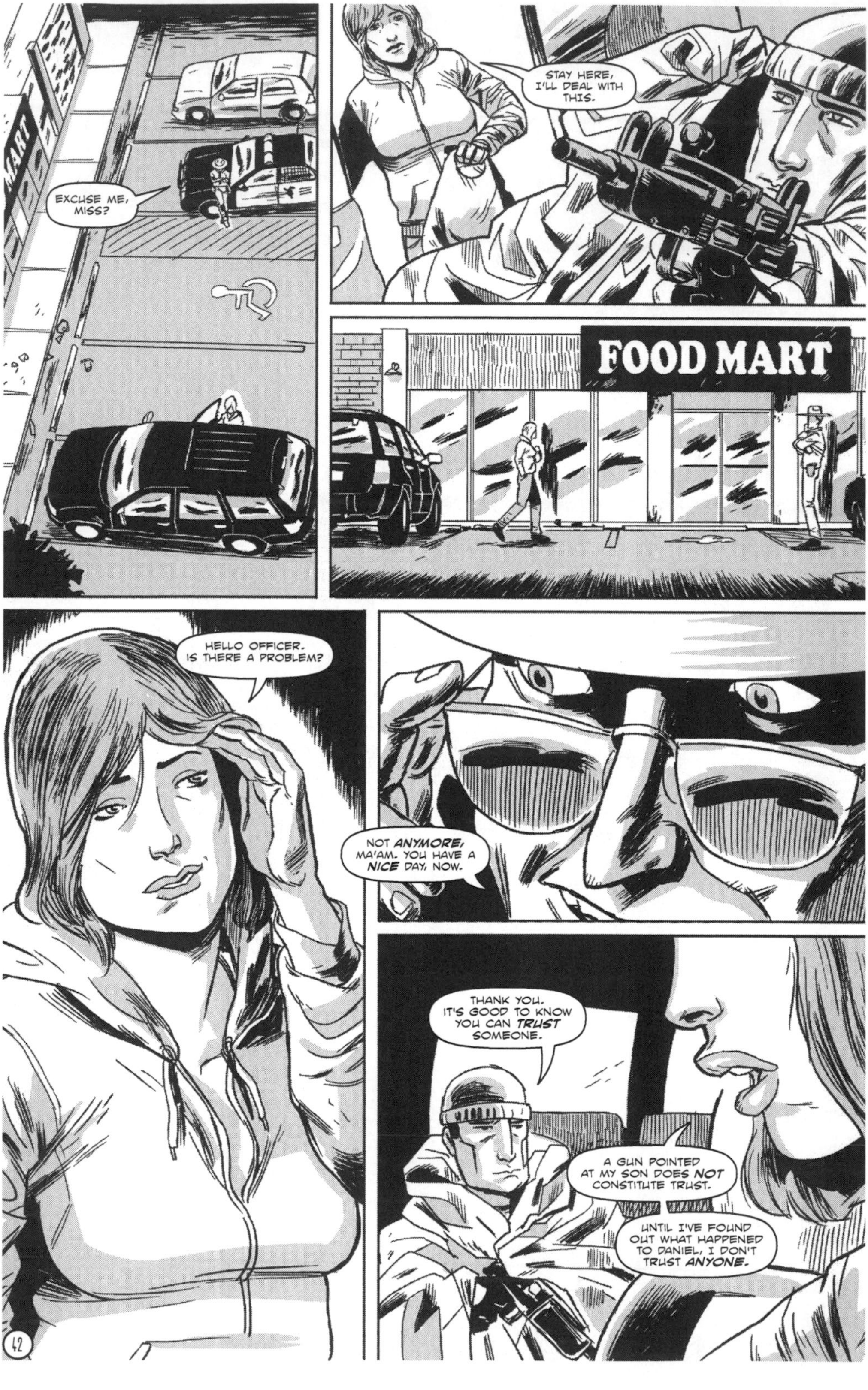
EXCUSE ME, MISS?
STAY HERE, I'LL DEAL WITH THIS.
FOOD MART
HELLO OFFICER. IS THERE A PROBLEM?
NOT ANYMORE, MA'AM. YOU HAVE A NICE DAY, NOW.
THANK YOU. IT'S GOOD TO KNOW YOU CAN TRUST SOMEONE.
A GUN POINTED AT MY SON DOES NOT CONSTITUTE TRUST.
UNTIL I'VE FOUND OUT WHAT HAPPENED TO DANIEL, I DON'T TRUST ANYONE.

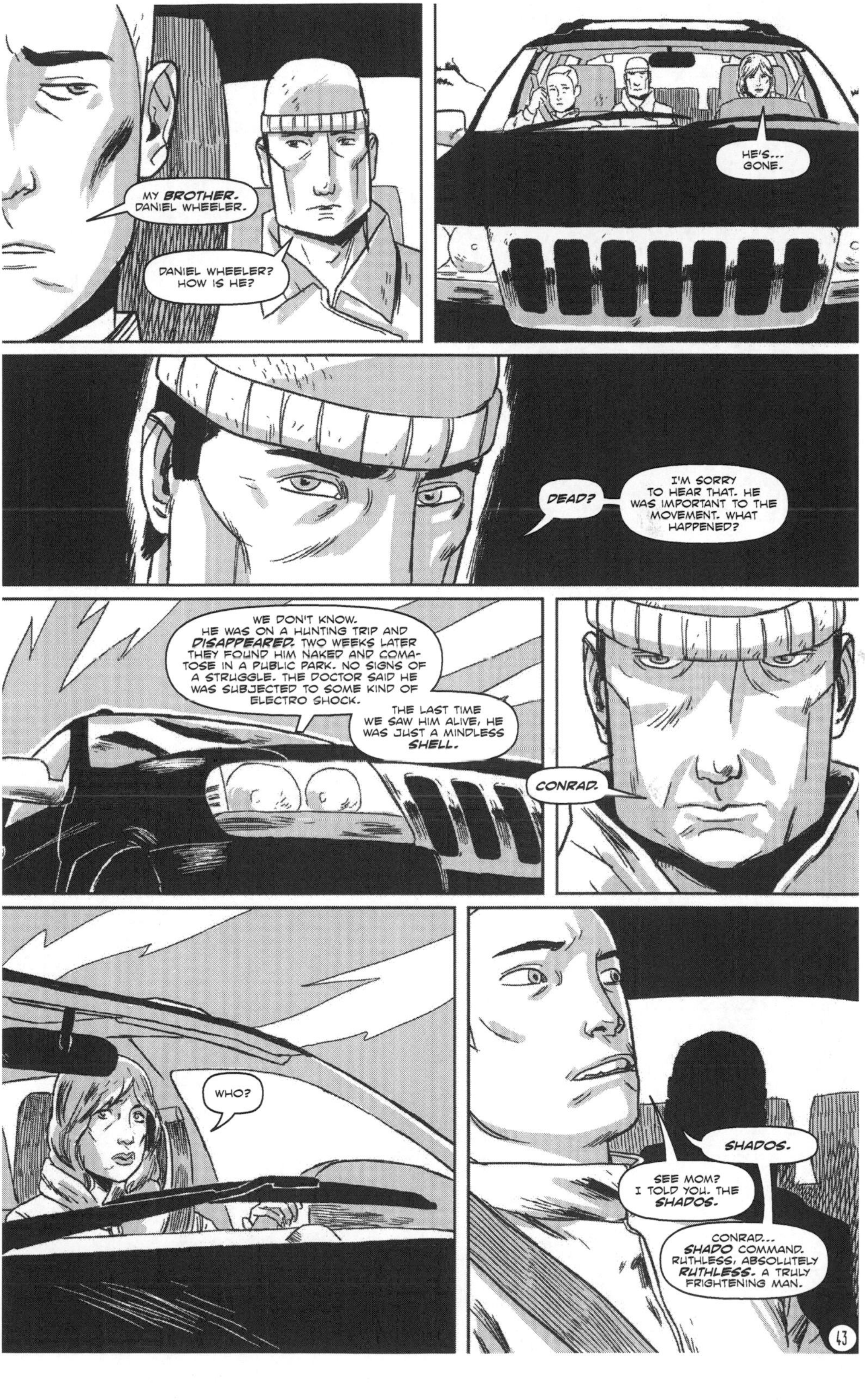
MY BROTHER. DANIEL WHEELER.
DANIEL WHEELER? HOW IS HE?
HE'S... GONE.
DEAD?
I'M SORRY TO HEAR THAT. HE WAS IMPORTANT TO THE MOVEMENT. WHAT HAPPENED?
WE DON'T KNOW. HE WAS ON A HUNTING TRIP AND DISAPPEARED. TWO WEEKS LATER THEY FOUND HIM NAKED AND COMATOSE IN A PUBLIC PARK. NO SIGNS OF A STRUGGLE. THE DOCTOR SAID HE WAS SUBJECTED TO SOME KIND OF ELECTRO SHOCK.
THE LAST TIME WE SAW HIM ALIVE, HE WAS JUST A MINDLESS SHELL.
CONRAD.
WHO?
SHADOS.
SEE MOM? I TOLD YOU. THE SHADOS.
CONRAD... SHADO COMMAND. RUTHLESS, ABSOLUTELY RUTHLESS. A TRULY FRIGHTENING MAN.
43

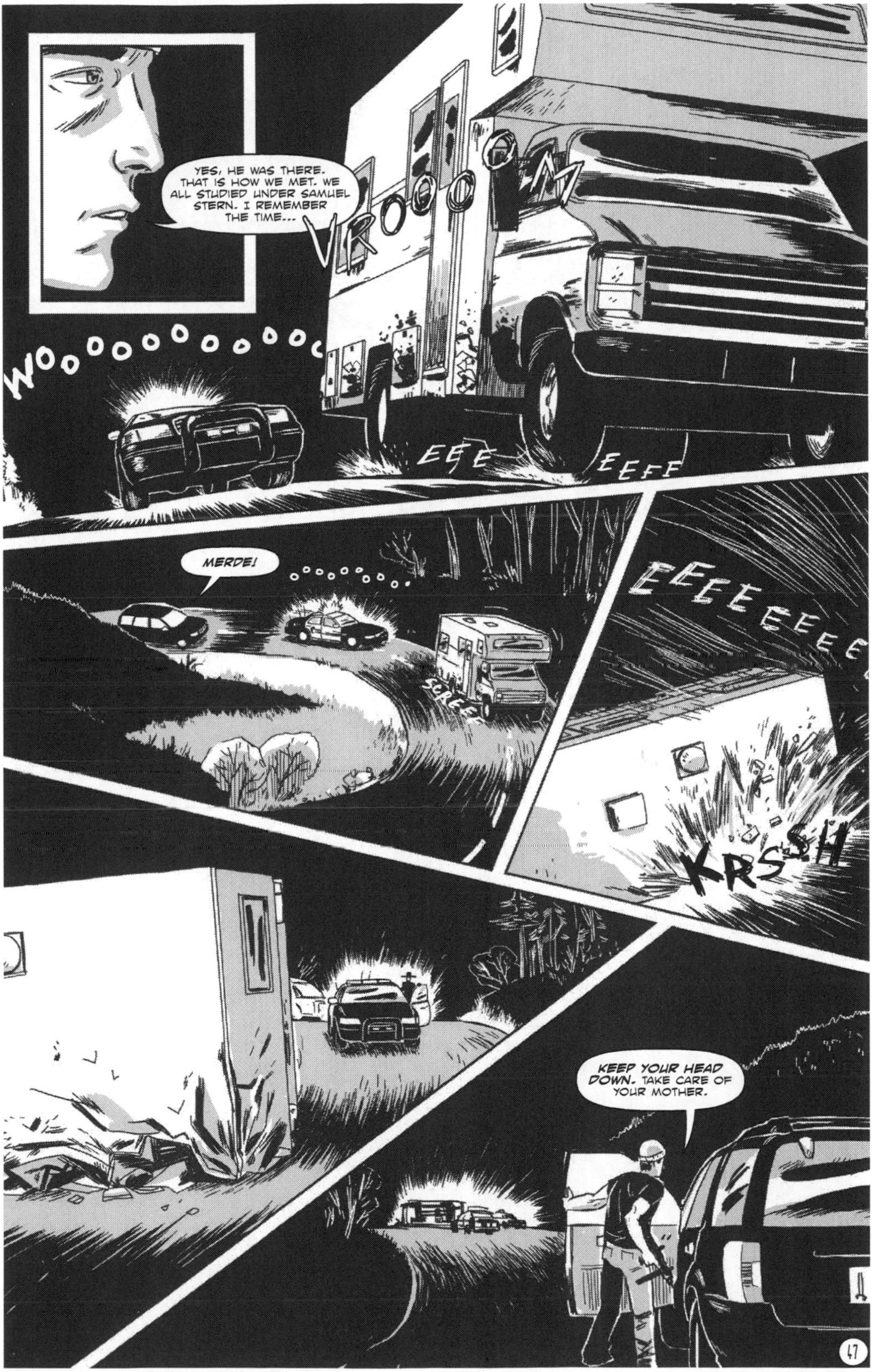

YES, HE WAS THERE. THAT IS HOW WE MET. WE ALL STUDIED UNDER SAMUEL STERN. I REMEMBER THE TIME...
VROOOOM
WOOOOOOOOOOO
EEE
EEFF
MERDE!
OOOOOOOOO
SCREE
EEEEEEEE
KRSSH
KEEP YOUR HEAD DOWN. TAKE CARE OF YOUR MOTHER.

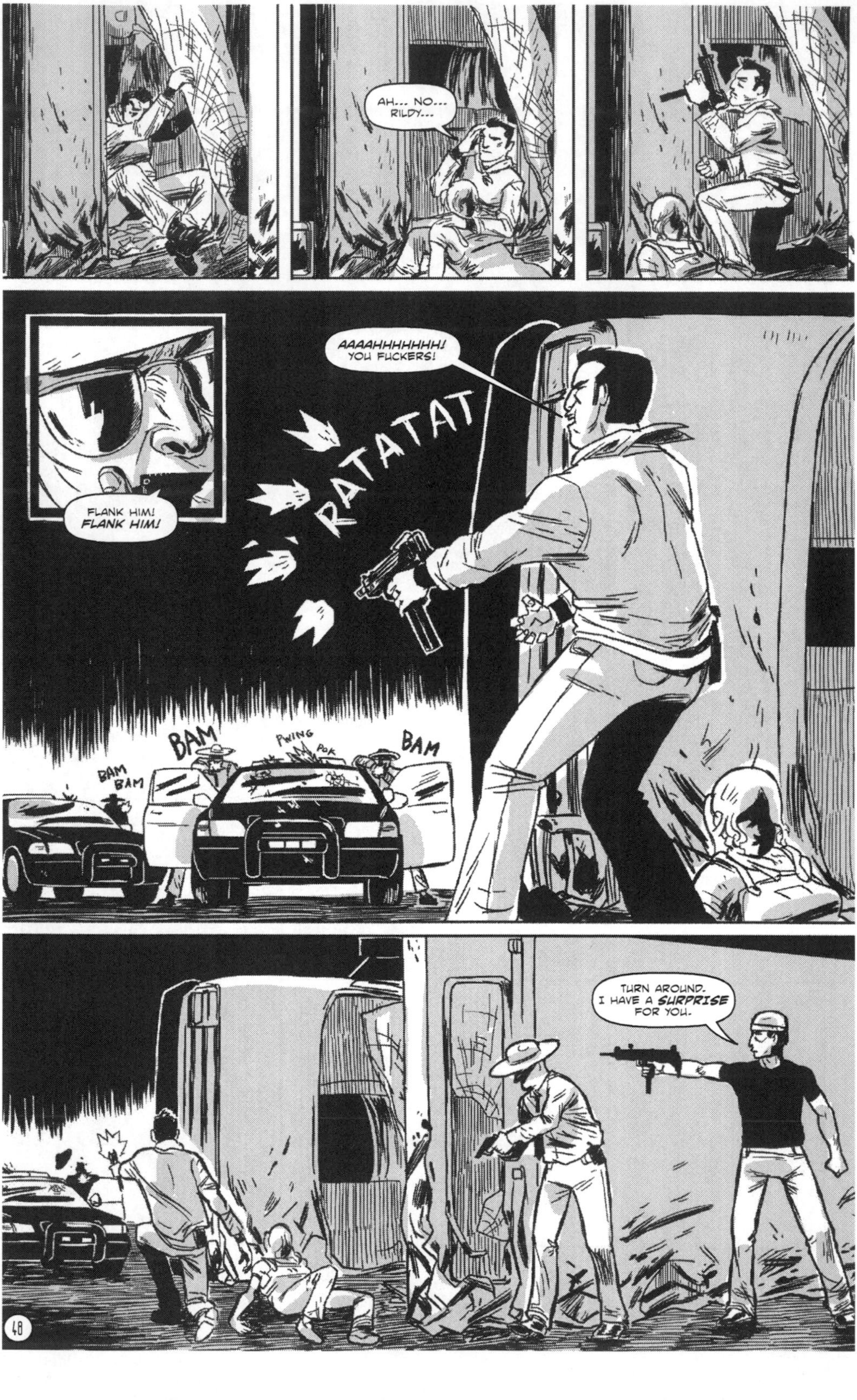
AH... NO... RILDY...
AAAAHHHHHHH! YOU FUCKERS!
FLANK HIM! FLANK HIM!
RATATAT
BAM
BAM BAM
PWING
POK
BAM
TURN AROUND. I HAVE A SURPRISE FOR YOU.

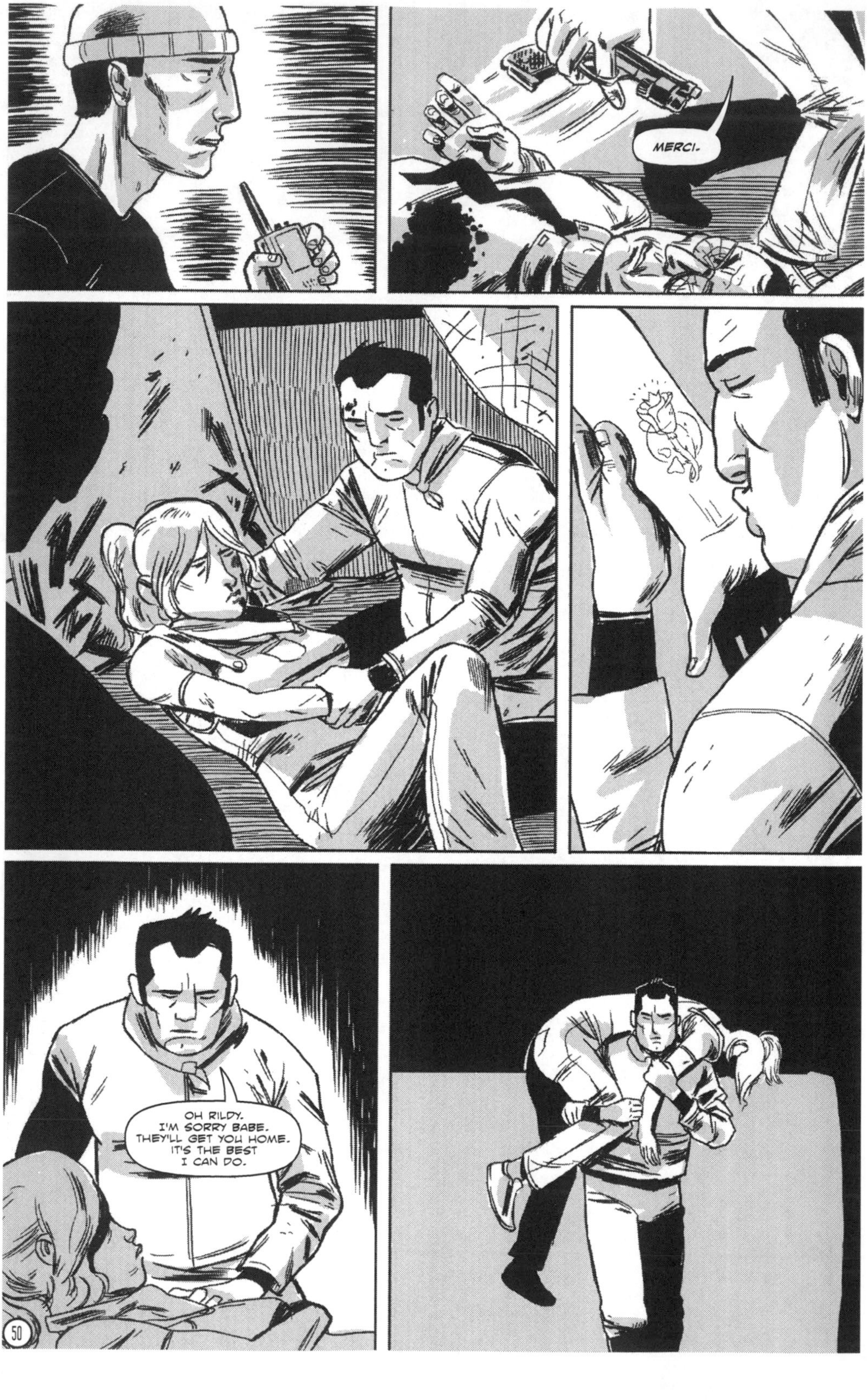
MERCI.
OH RILDY. I'M SORRY BABE. THEY'LL GET YOU HOME. IT'S THE BEST I CAN DO.

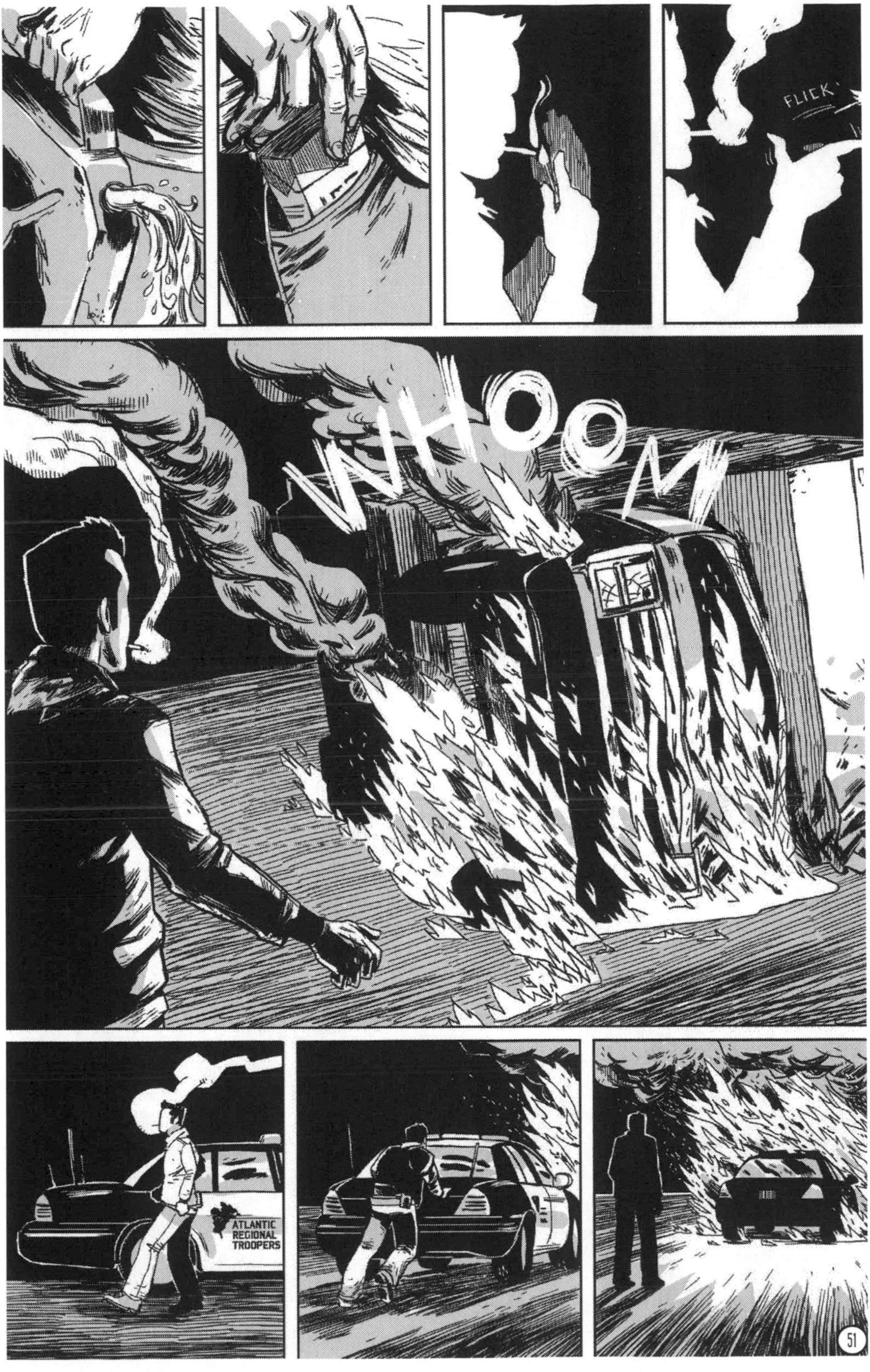
FLICK
WHOOM
ATLANTIC REGIONAL TROOPERS

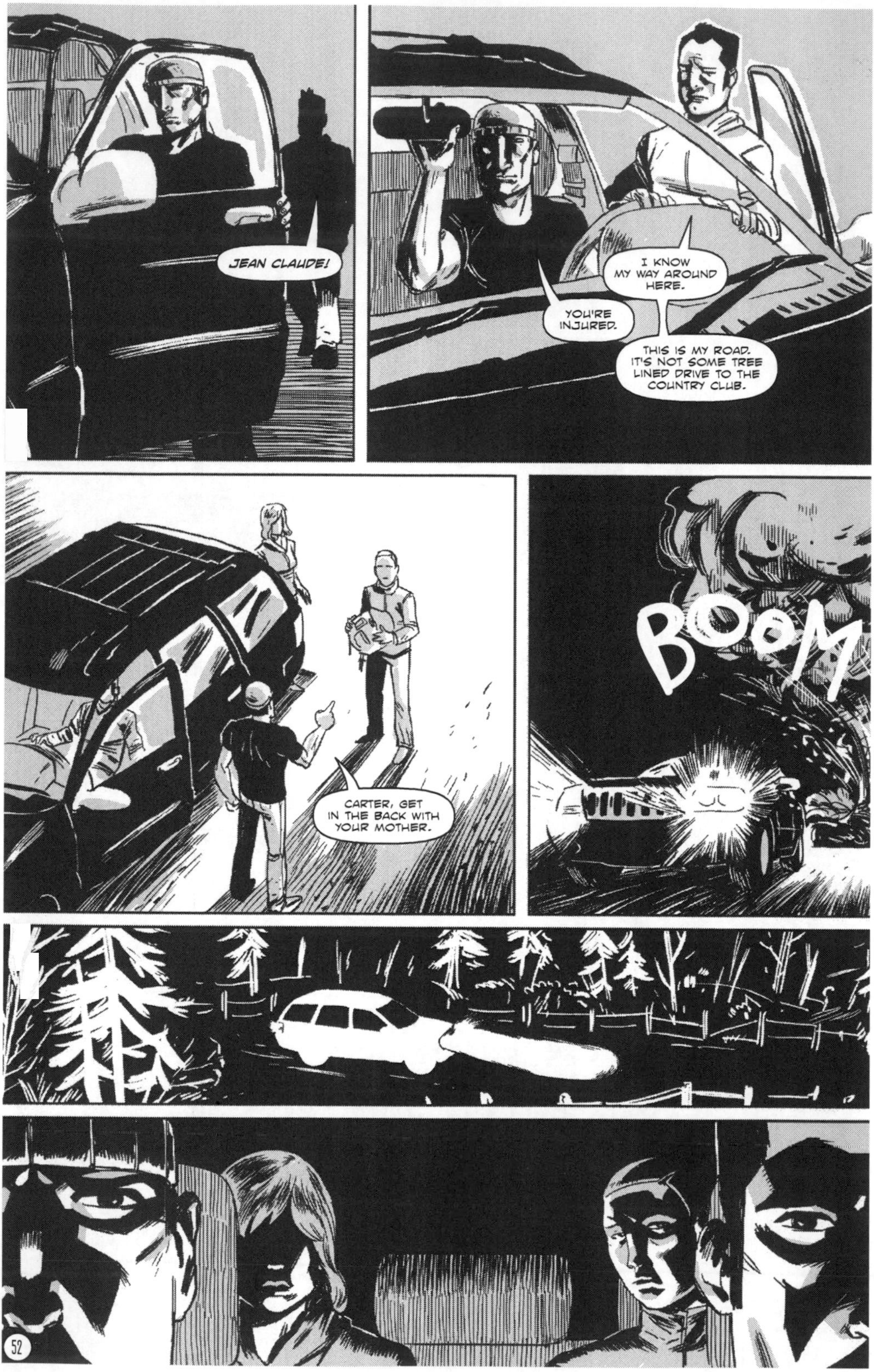
JEAN CLAUDE!
YOU'RE INJURED.
I KNOW MY WAY AROUND HERE.
THIS IS MY ROAD. IT'S NOT SOME TREE LINED DRIVE TO THE COUNTRY CLUB.
CARTER, GET IN THE BACK WITH YOUR MOTHER.
BOOM

NICE TO SEE YOU GOT OFF YOUR *BOURGEOIS DUFF*, J.C.

OH *YES*, I'M A TYPICAL NEWFIE. WHEN IT'S ALL OVER, I'LL JUST GO BACK TO THE *ROCK* AND COLLECT MY POGEY CHECK. AND WHAT ABOUT *YOU?* STILL THROWING MOLOTOV COCKTAILS AT TANKS? YOU'VE GOT YOUR SNOUT *ALL OVER* THE PLACE ON WANTED POSTERS. AT LEAST THEY DON'T KNOW WHAT I *LOOK* LIKE.

IF *YOU* EVER LIVED ON THE ROCK, YOU'D HAVE A REASON TO GET OUT. MY YOUNGER BROTHER, THEY SENT HIM DOWN TO CENT-AM. THE KID HAD NEVER EVEN KILLED A *FISH* AND THEY SENT HIM TO THE FUCKIN' FRONT LINES. HE WAS *DEAD* IN THREE DAYS.

WHY, IT NEARLY *KILLED* ME OLD MOM.

WELL, IF YOU'D *STOP* FOR A WHILE IN THE CITY RATHER THAN BURNING AROUND IT. YES, EVERYONE KNOWS 'THE DRIVER.' DRUG SMUGGLER, ARMS DEALER. AS LONG AS YOU'RE DRIVING. THIS REBEL ACTION IS JUST A *JOB* FOR YOU, JUST A WAY TO COLLECT A PAY CHECK.

THEN THEY SEND THAT ONE MILLION DOLLAR AMALGAMATION REWARD. A *GIFT* TO THE CANADIAN PEOPLE. YOU SHOULD SEE THE ROCK NOW. PEOPLE WHO NEVER OWNED *NOTHING* IN THEIR LIVES. SO MUCH DEBT. THEY GOT THEM *TRAPPED*.

WHEELER? ARE YOU RELATED TO DANNY WHEELER THEN? WORD'S COME DOWN THE LINE HE'S *MISSING*. HAVE YOU HEARD ANYTHING AT ALL?

PARDON ME, MA'AM. WE HAVEN'T MET. I'M NATE.

THIS IS CAROL WHEELER AND HER SON, CARTER.

HE'S GONE.

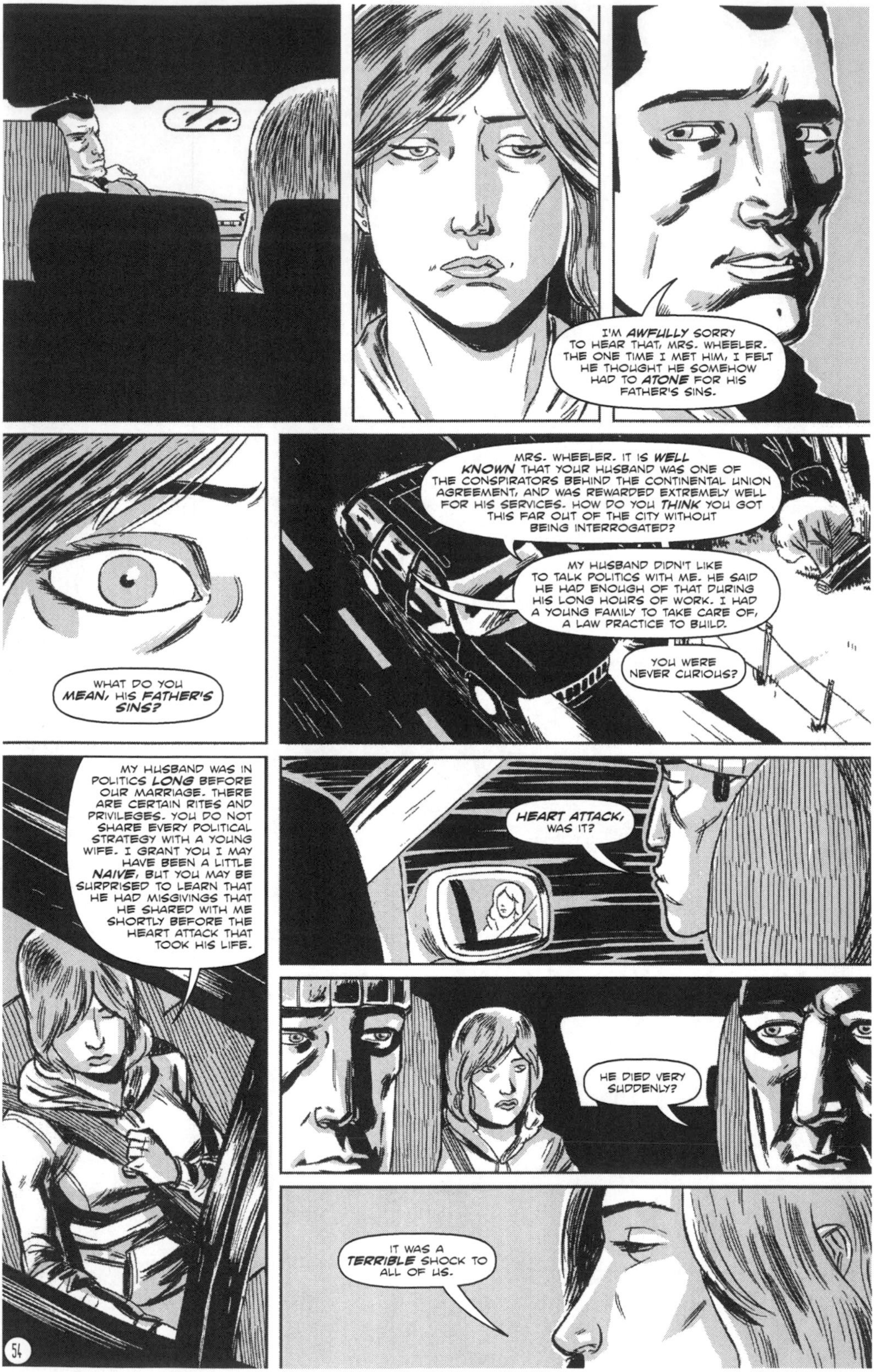
I'M AWFULLY SORRY TO HEAR THAT, MRS. WHEELER. THE ONE TIME I MET HIM, I FELT HE THOUGHT HE SOMEHOW HAD TO ATONE FOR HIS FATHER'S SINS.
WHAT DO YOU MEAN, HIS FATHER'S SINS?
MRS. WHEELER. IT IS WELL KNOWN THAT YOUR HUSBAND WAS ONE OF THE CONSPIRATORS BEHIND THE CONTINENTAL UNION AGREEMENT, AND WAS REWARDED EXTREMELY WELL FOR HIS SERVICES. HOW DO YOU THINK YOU GOT THIS FAR OUT OF THE CITY WITHOUT BEING INTERROGATED?
MY HUSBAND DIDN'T LIKE TO TALK POLITICS WITH ME. HE SAID HE HAD ENOUGH OF THAT DURING HIS LONG HOURS OF WORK. I HAD A YOUNG FAMILY TO TAKE CARE OF, A LAW PRACTICE TO BUILD.
YOU WERE NEVER CURIOUS?
MY HUSBAND WAS IN POLITICS LONG BEFORE OUR MARRIAGE. THERE ARE CERTAIN RITES AND PRIVILEGES. YOU DO NOT SHARE EVERY POLITICAL STRATEGY WITH A YOUNG WIFE. I GRANT YOU I MAY HAVE BEEN A LITTLE NAIVE, BUT YOU MAY BE SURPRISED TO LEARN THAT HE HAD MISGIVINGS THAT HE SHARED WITH ME SHORTLY BEFORE THE HEART ATTACK THAT TOOK HIS LIFE.
HEART ATTACK, WAS IT?
HE DIED VERY SUDDENLY?
IT WAS A TERRIBLE SHOCK TO ALL OF US.

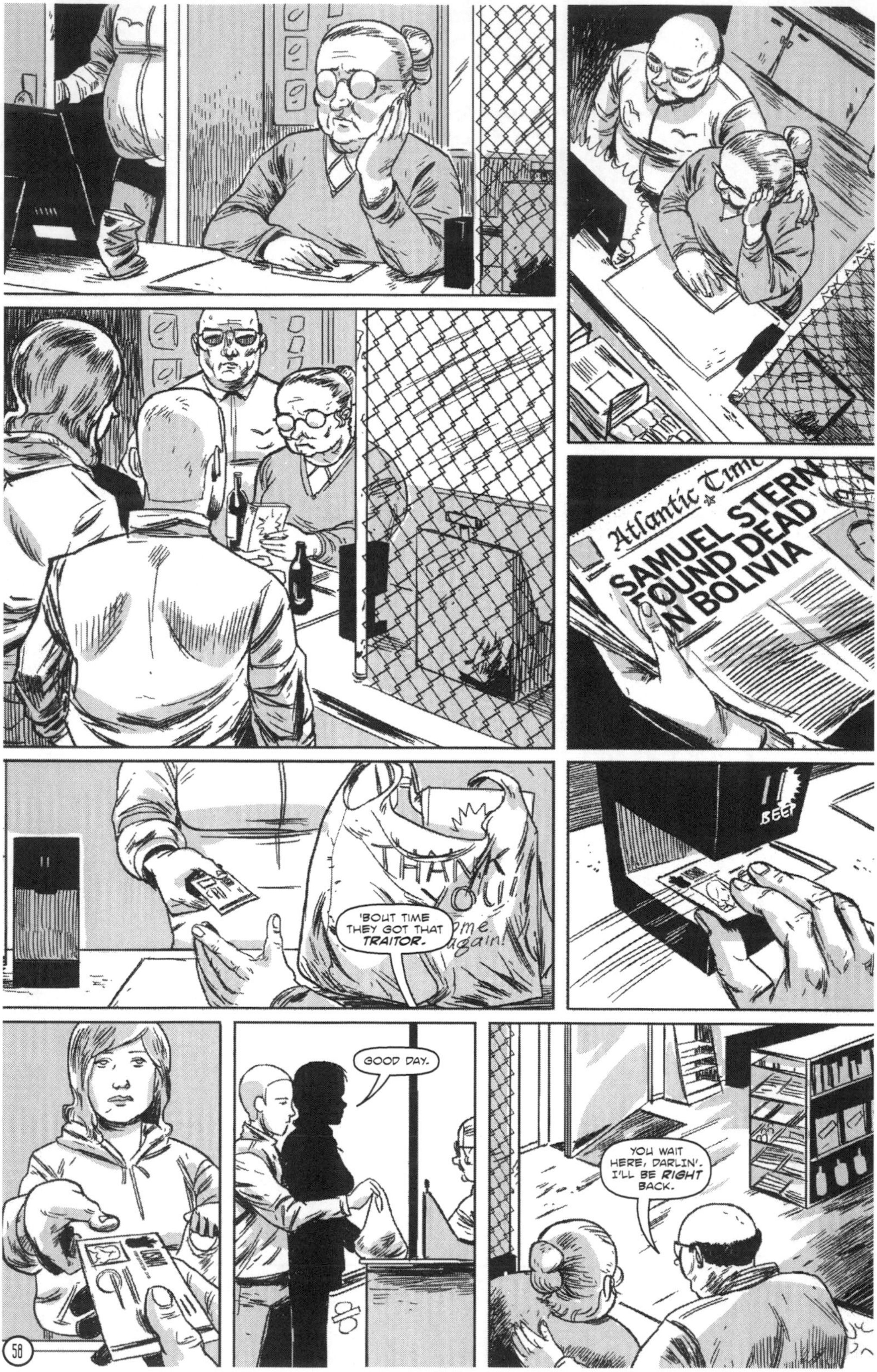

Atlantic Times
SAMUEL STERN FOUND DEAD IN BOLIVIA
THANK YOU! Come again!
'BOUT TIME THEY GOT THAT TRAITOR.
BEEP
GOOD DAY.
YOU WAIT HERE, DARLIN'. I'LL BE RIGHT BACK.

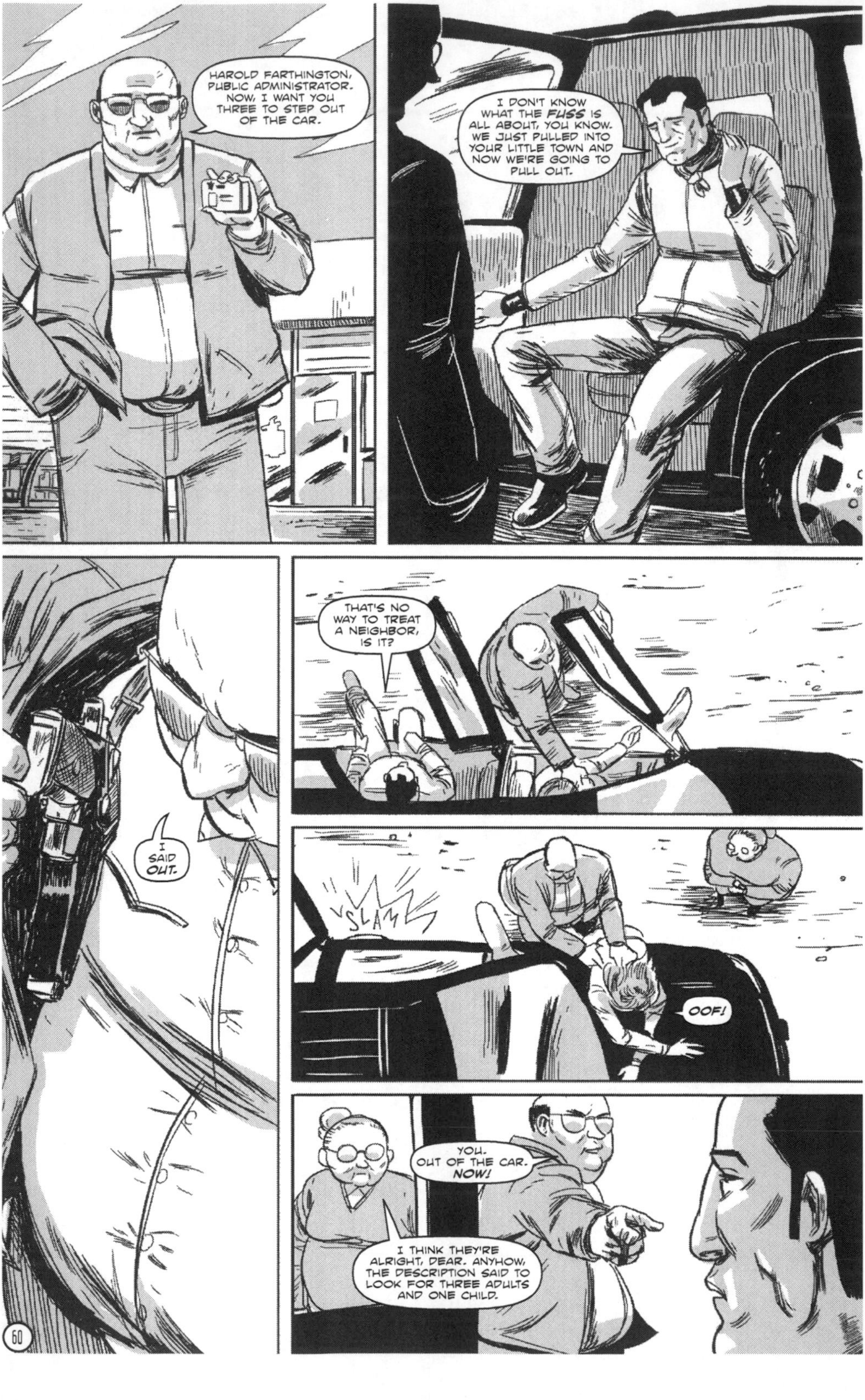
HAROLD FARTHINGTON, PUBLIC ADMINISTRATOR. NOW, I WANT YOU THREE TO STEP OUT OF THE CAR.
I DON'T KNOW WHAT THE FUSS IS ALL ABOUT, YOU KNOW. WE JUST PULLED INTO YOUR LITTLE TOWN AND NOW WE'RE GOING TO PULL OUT.
I SAID OUT.
THAT'S NO WAY TO TREAT A NEIGHBOR, IS IT?
SLAM
OOF!
YOU. OUT OF THE CAR. NOW!
I THINK THEY'RE ALRIGHT, DEAR. ANYHOW, THE DESCRIPTION SAID TO LOOK FOR THREE ADULTS AND ONE CHILD.

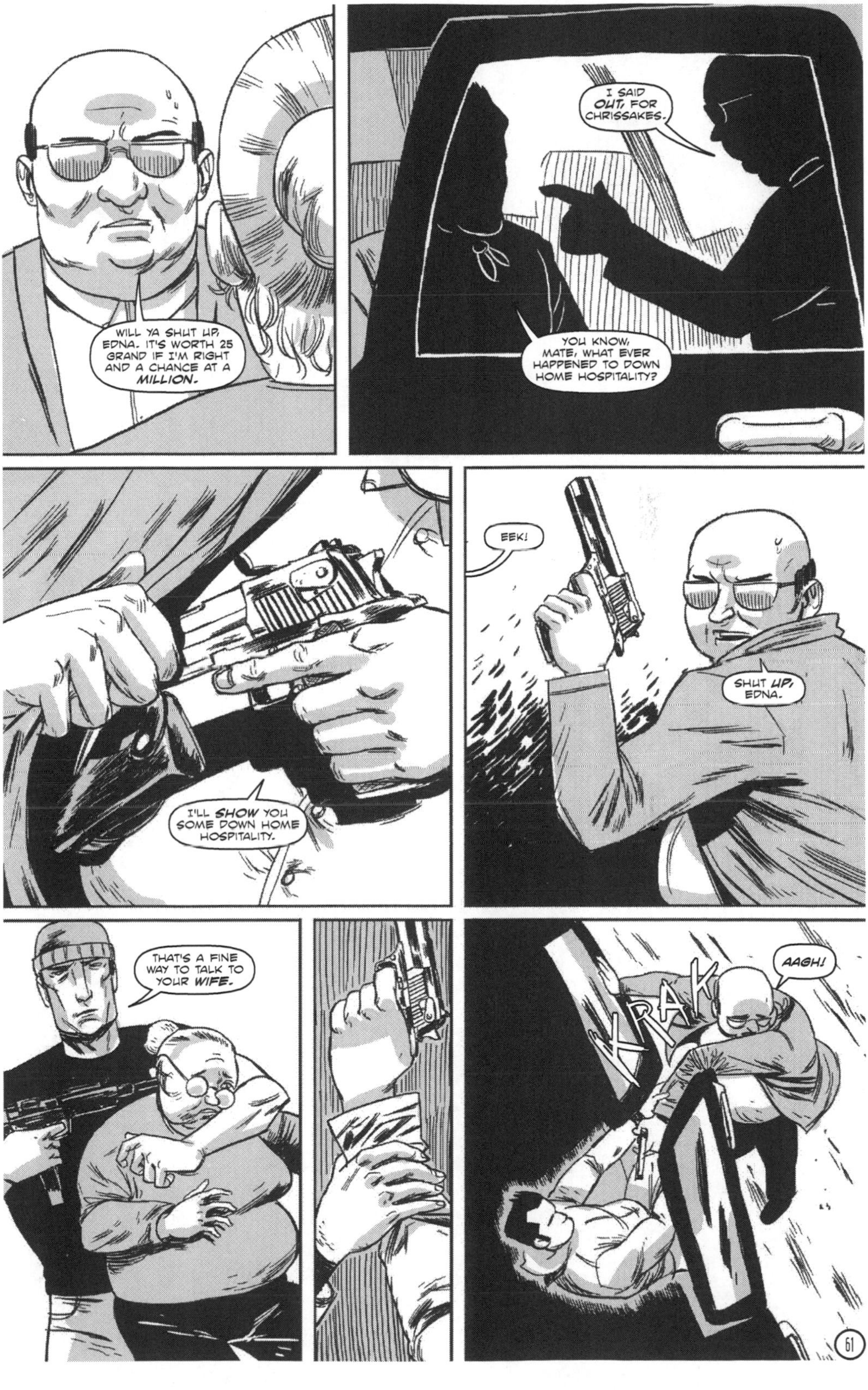
WILL YA SHUT UP, EDNA. IT'S WORTH 25 GRAND IF I'M RIGHT AND A CHANCE AT A MILLION.
I SAID OUT, FOR CHRISSAKES.
YOU KNOW, MATE, WHAT EVER HAPPENED TO DOWN HOME HOSPITALITY?
I'LL SHOW YOU SOME DOWN HOME HOSPITALITY.
EEK!
SHUT UP, EDNA.
THAT'S A FINE WAY TO TALK TO YOUR WIFE.
KRAK
AAGH!

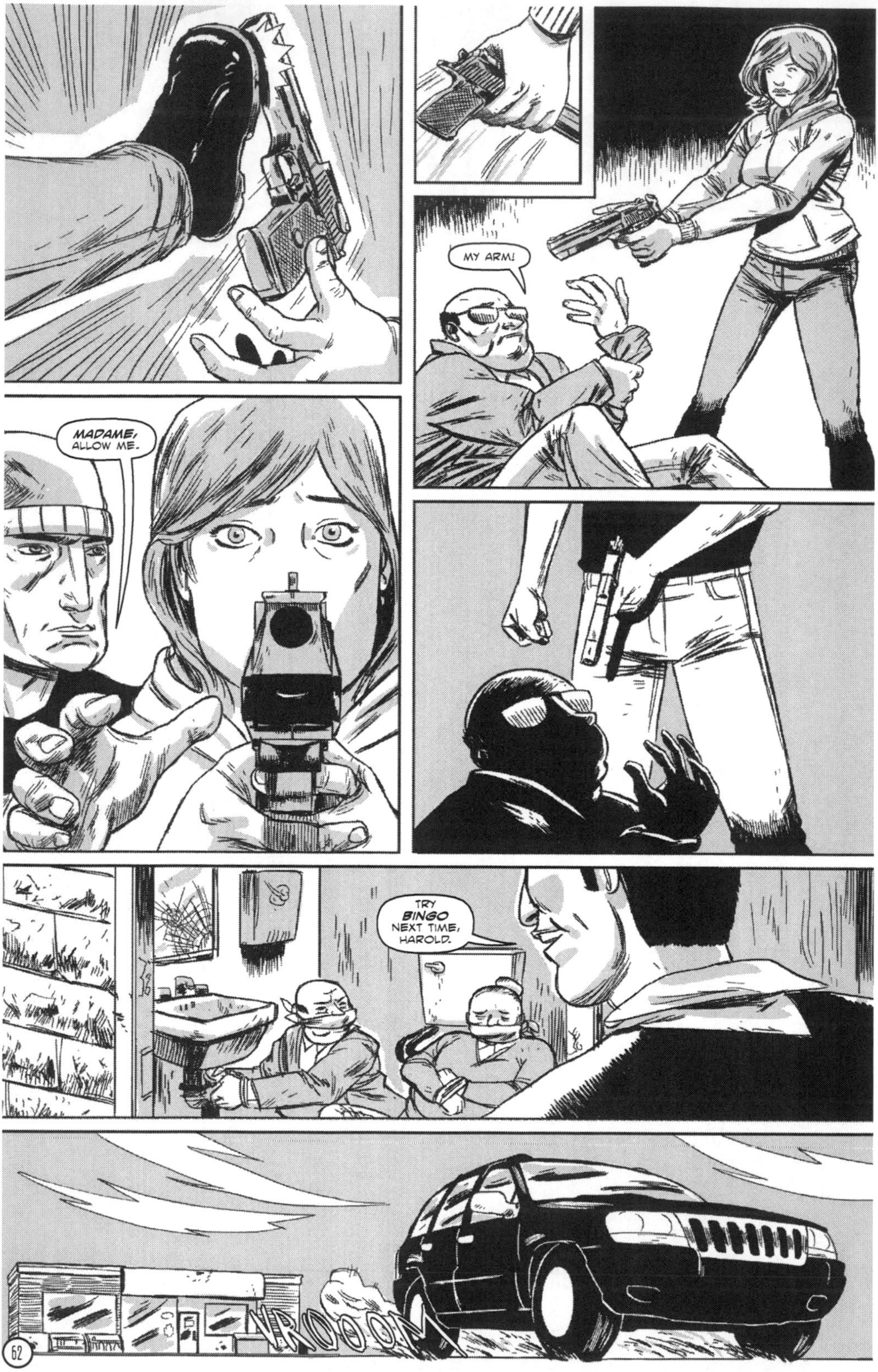
MY ARM!
MADAME, ALLOW ME.
TRY BINGO NEXT TIME, HAROLD.
VROOOM

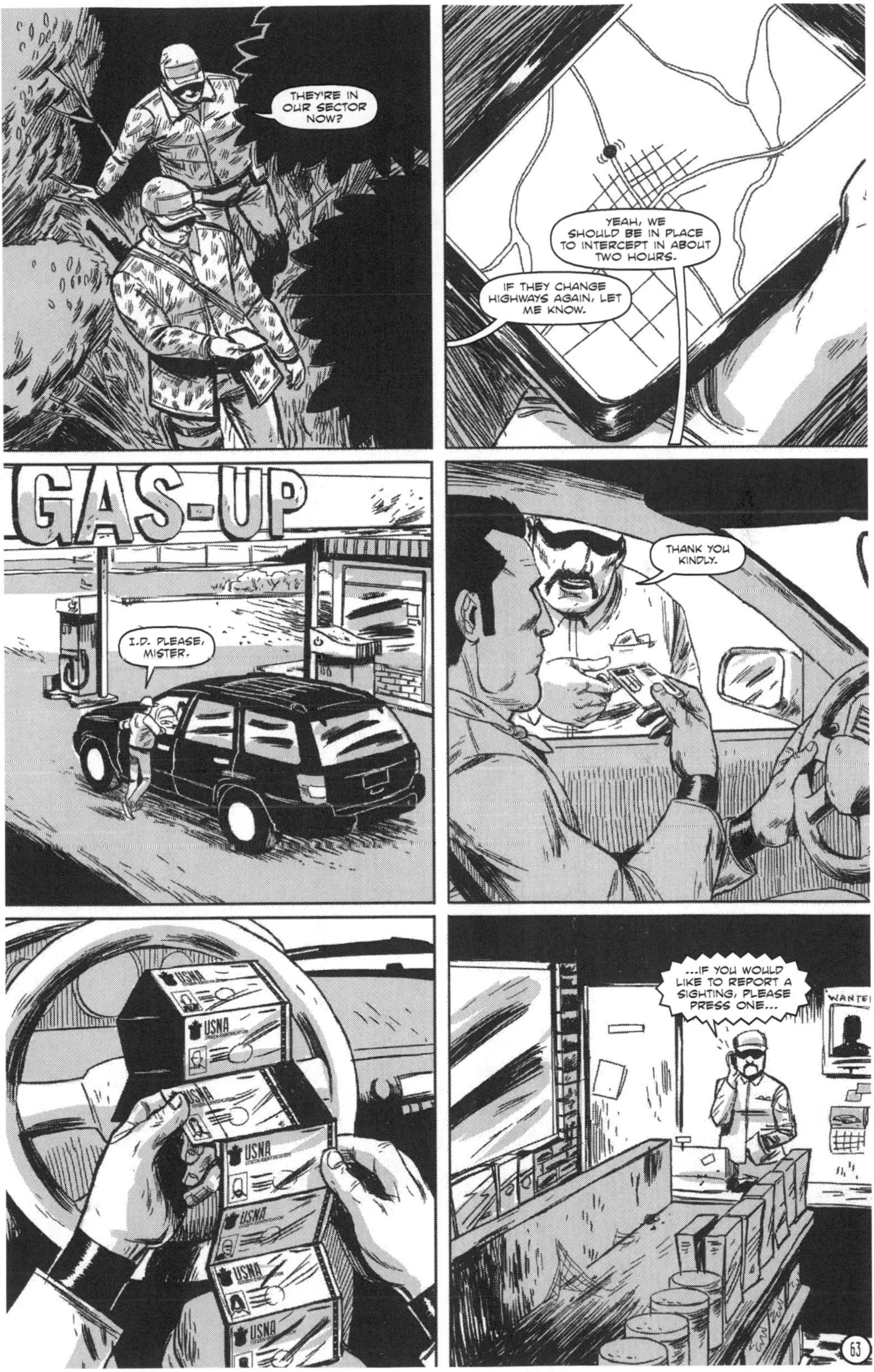
THEY'RE IN OUR SECTOR NOW?
YEAH, WE SHOULD BE IN PLACE TO INTERCEPT IN ABOUT TWO HOURS.
IF THEY CHANGE HIGHWAYS AGAIN, LET ME KNOW.
GAS-UP
I.D. PLEASE, MISTER.
THANK YOU KINDLY.
USNA
...IF YOU WOULD LIKE TO REPORT A SIGHTING, PLEASE PRESS ONE...

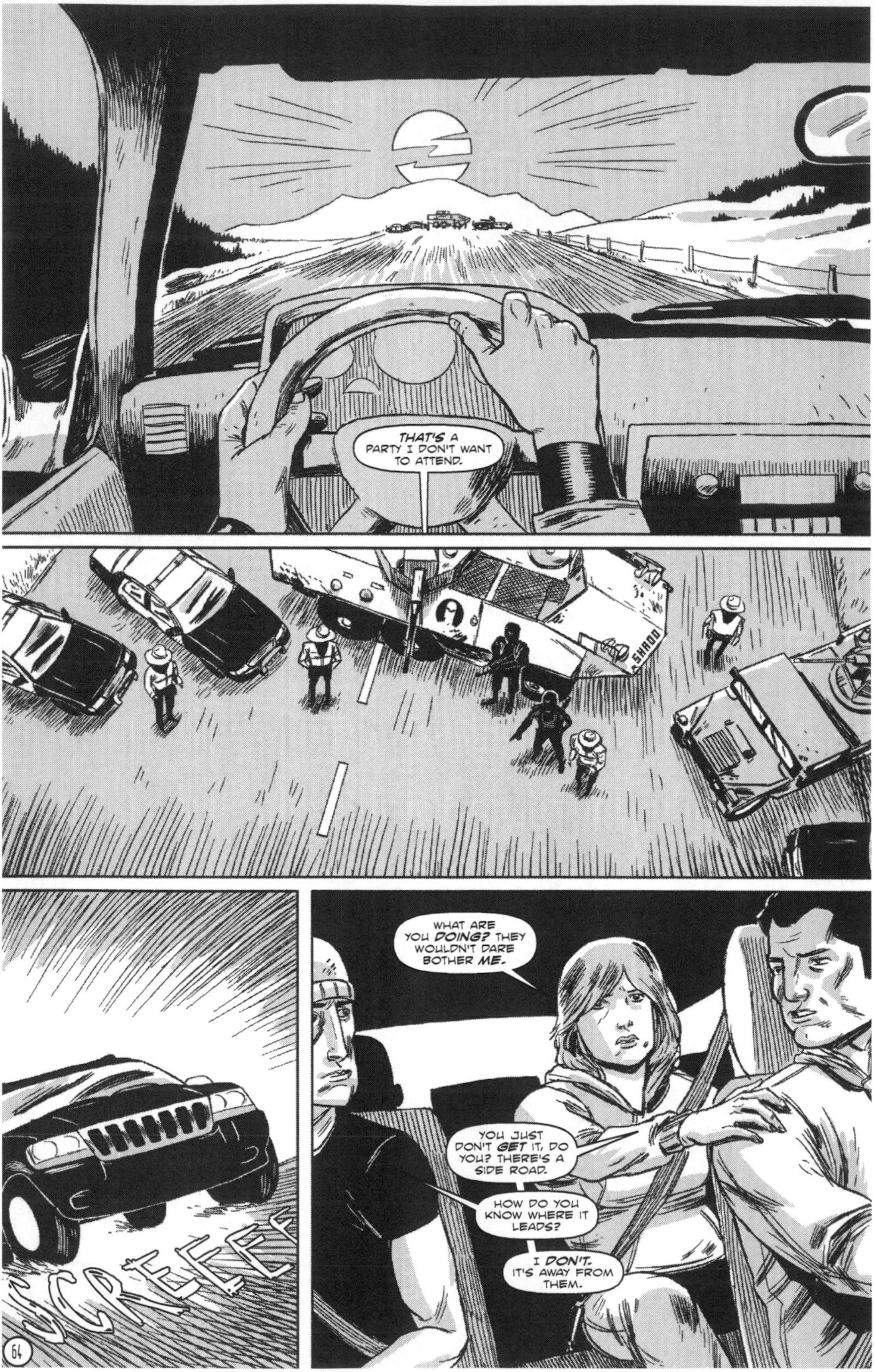
THAT'S A PARTY I DON'T WANT TO ATTEND.
SHADO
SCREEE
WHAT ARE YOU DOING? THEY WOULDN'T DARE BOTHER ME.
YOU JUST DON'T GET IT, DO YOU? THERE'S A SIDE ROAD.
HOW DO YOU KNOW WHERE IT LEADS?
I DON'T. IT'S AWAY FROM THEM.

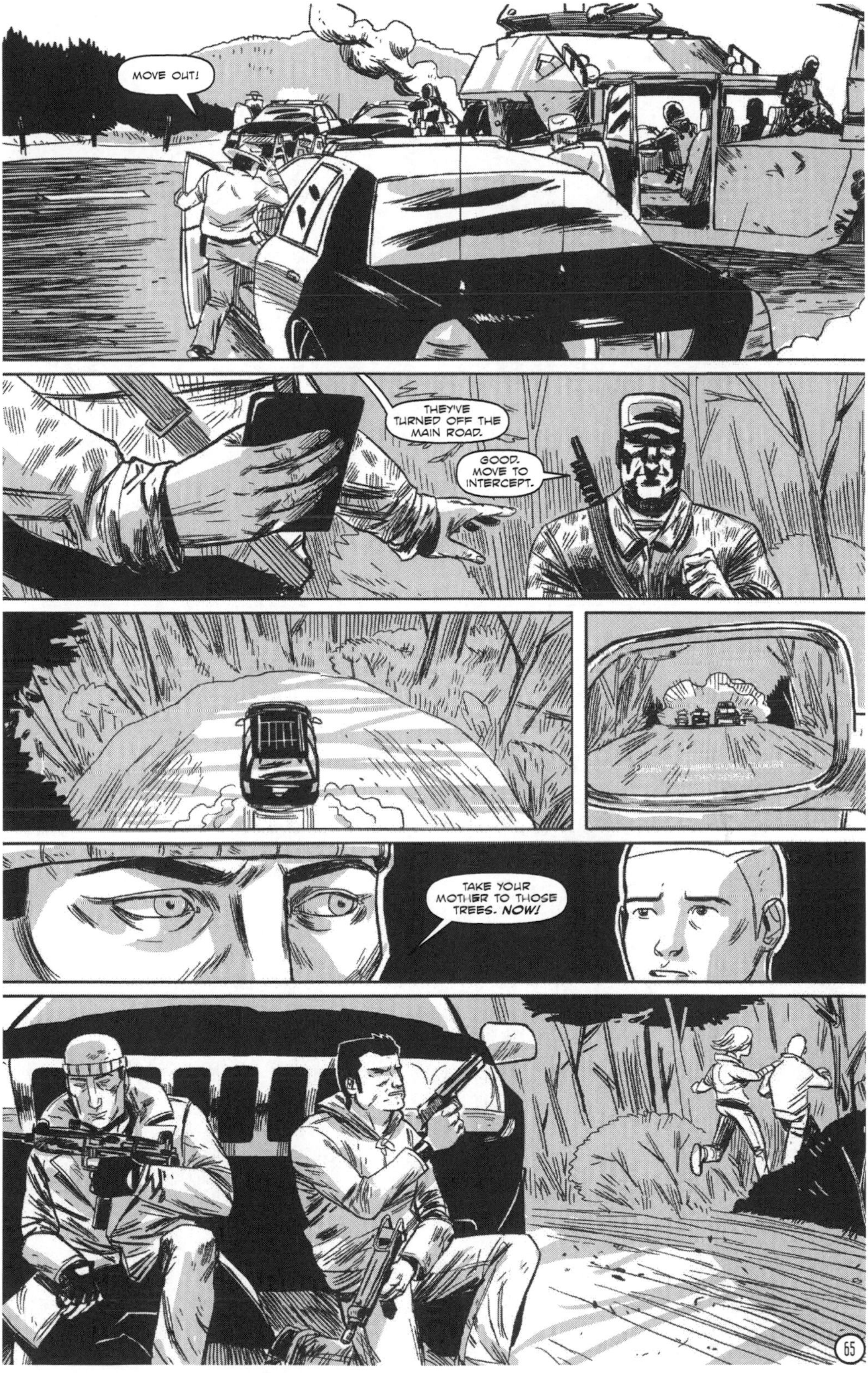
MOVE OUT!
THEY'VE TURNED OFF THE MAIN ROAD.
GOOD. MOVE TO INTERCEPT.
TAKE YOUR MOTHER TO THOSE TREES. NOW!

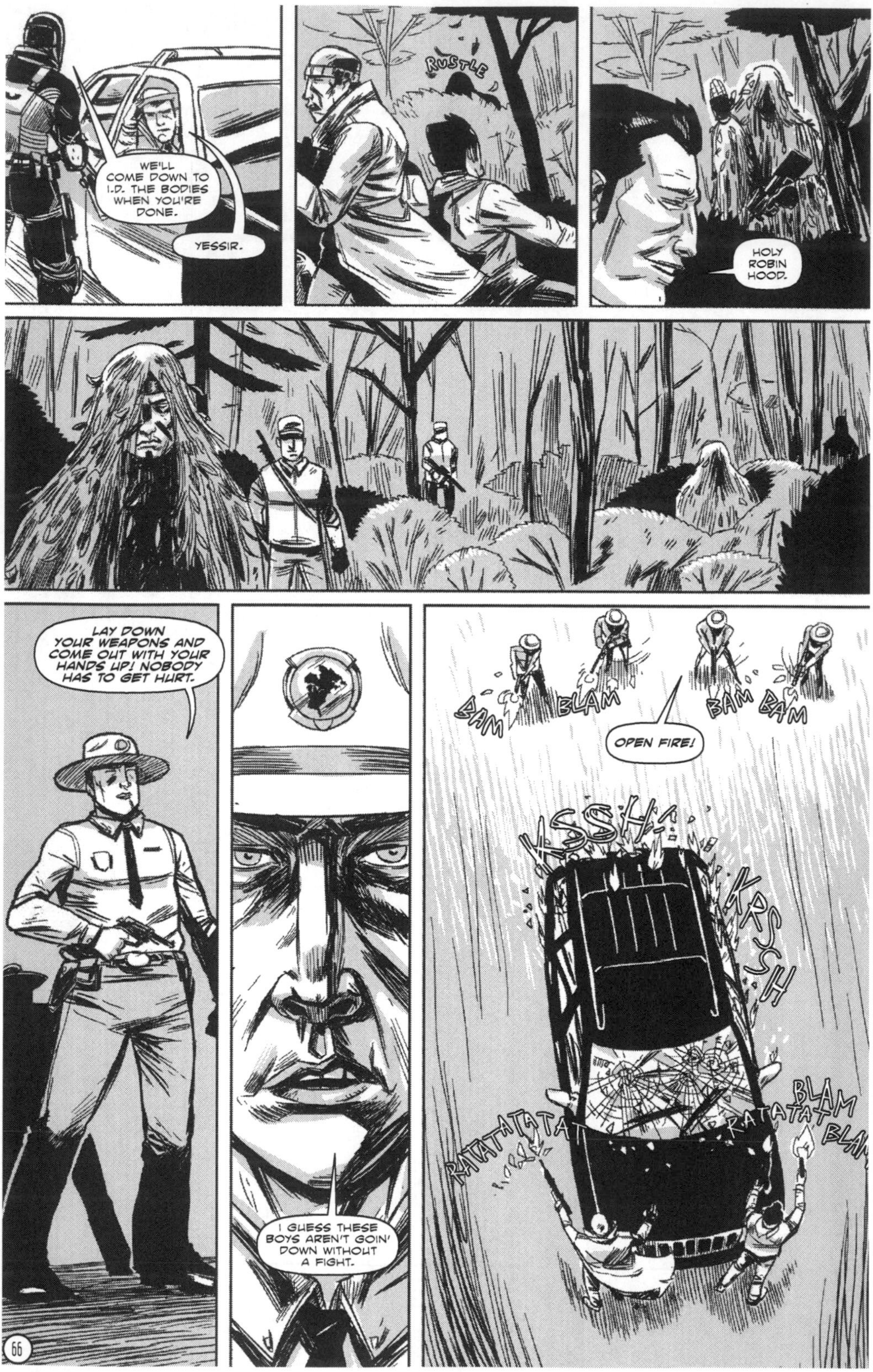
WE'LL COME DOWN TO I.D. THE BODIES WHEN YOU'RE DONE.
YESSIR.
RUSTLE
HOLY ROBIN HOOD.
LAY DOWN YOUR WEAPONS AND COME OUT WITH YOUR HANDS UP! NOBODY HAS TO GET HURT.
I GUESS THESE BOYS AREN'T GOIN' DOWN WITHOUT A FIGHT.
BAM
BLAM
BAM BAM
OPEN FIRE!
KSSH!
KRSSH
RATATATATAT
RATATATAT
BLAM

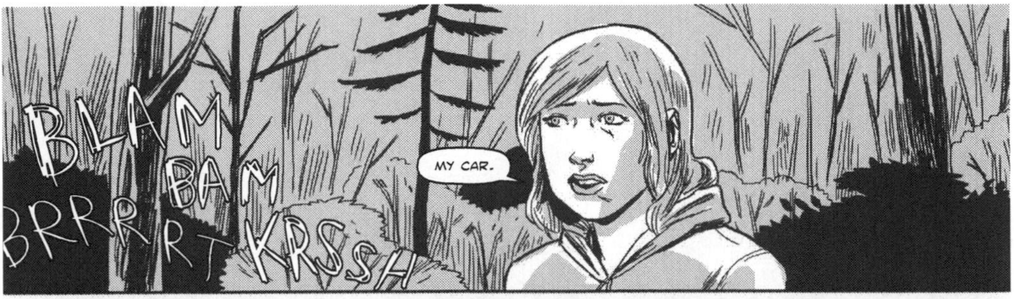
BLAM
BAM
BRRRRRT
KRSSH
MY CAR.

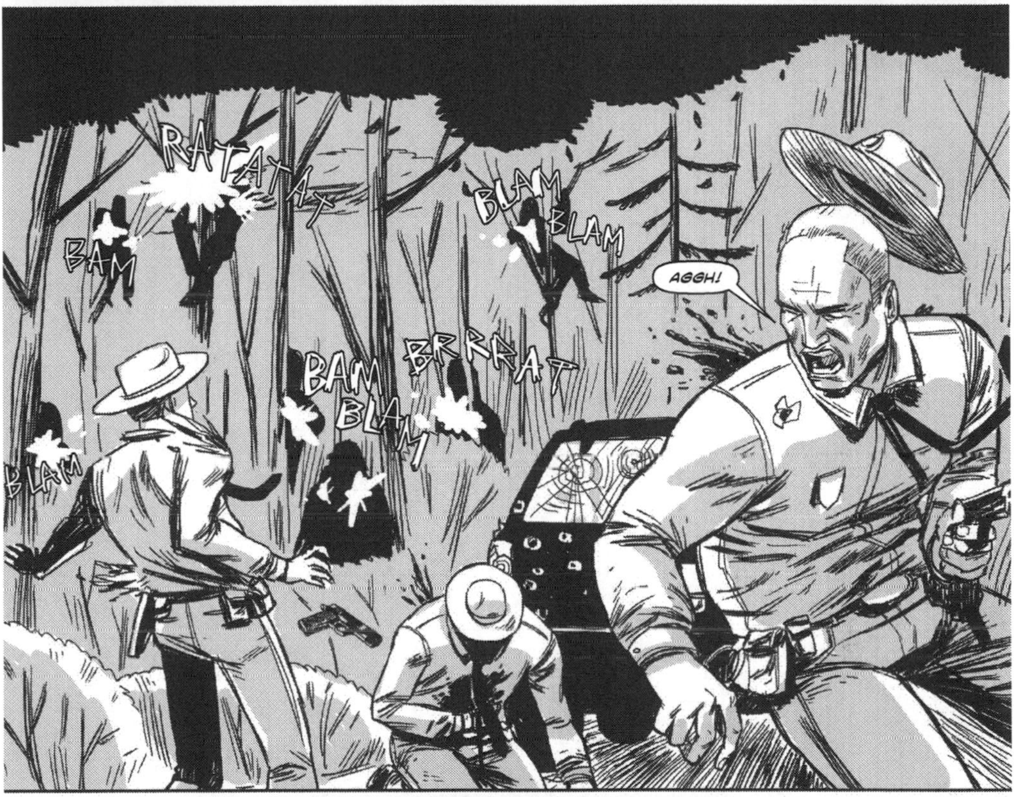
RATATATAT
BAM
BLAM
BLAM
AGGH!
BAM
BLAM
BRRRRAT
BLAM

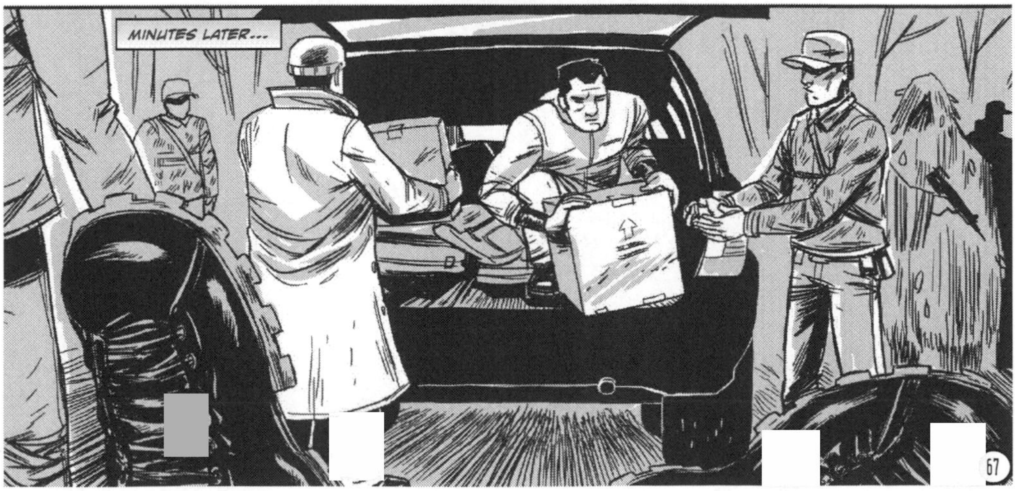
MINUTES LATER...

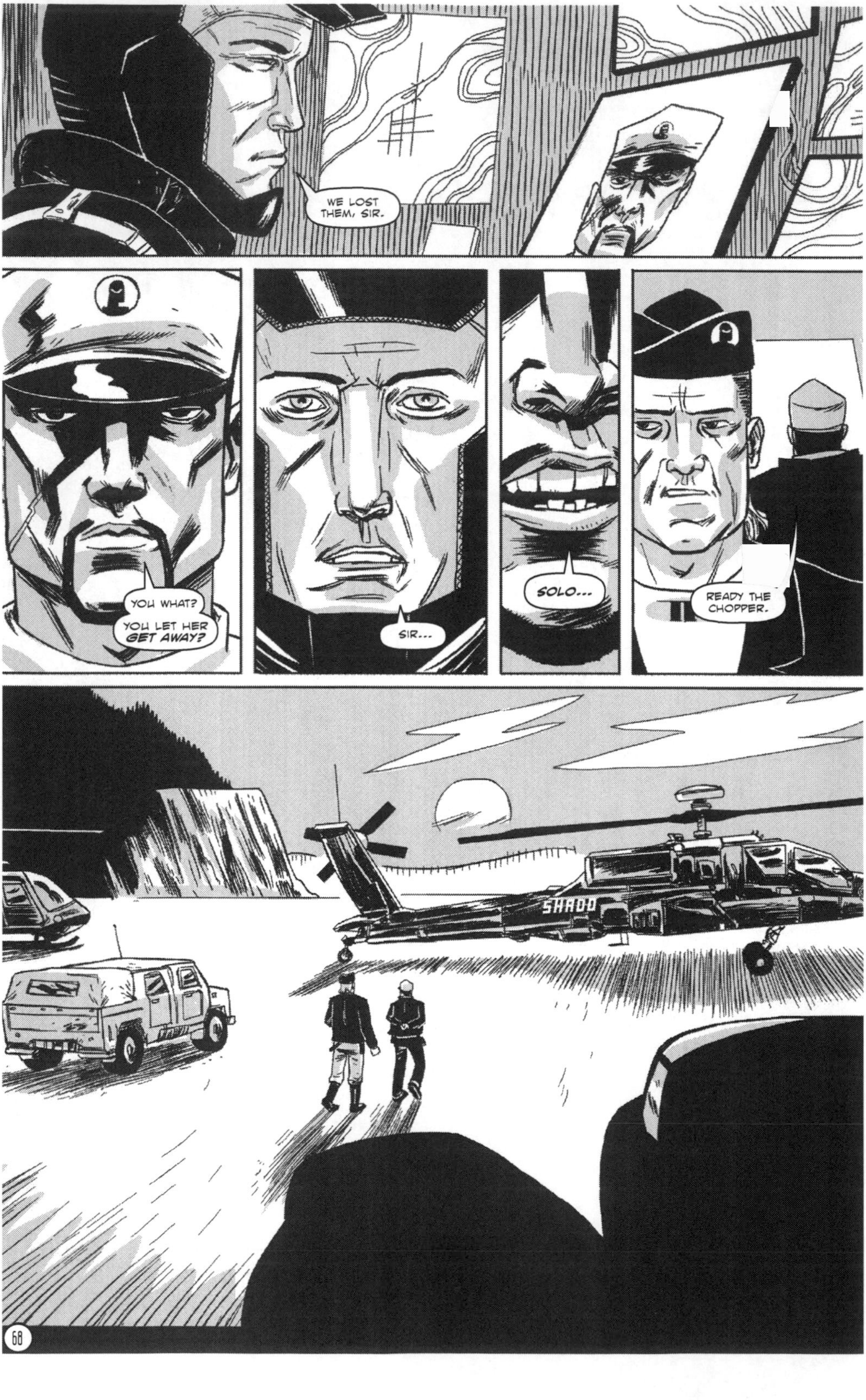
WE LOST THEM, SIR.
YOU WHAT?
YOU LET HER GET AWAY?
SIR...
SOLO...
READY THE CHOPPER.
SHADO

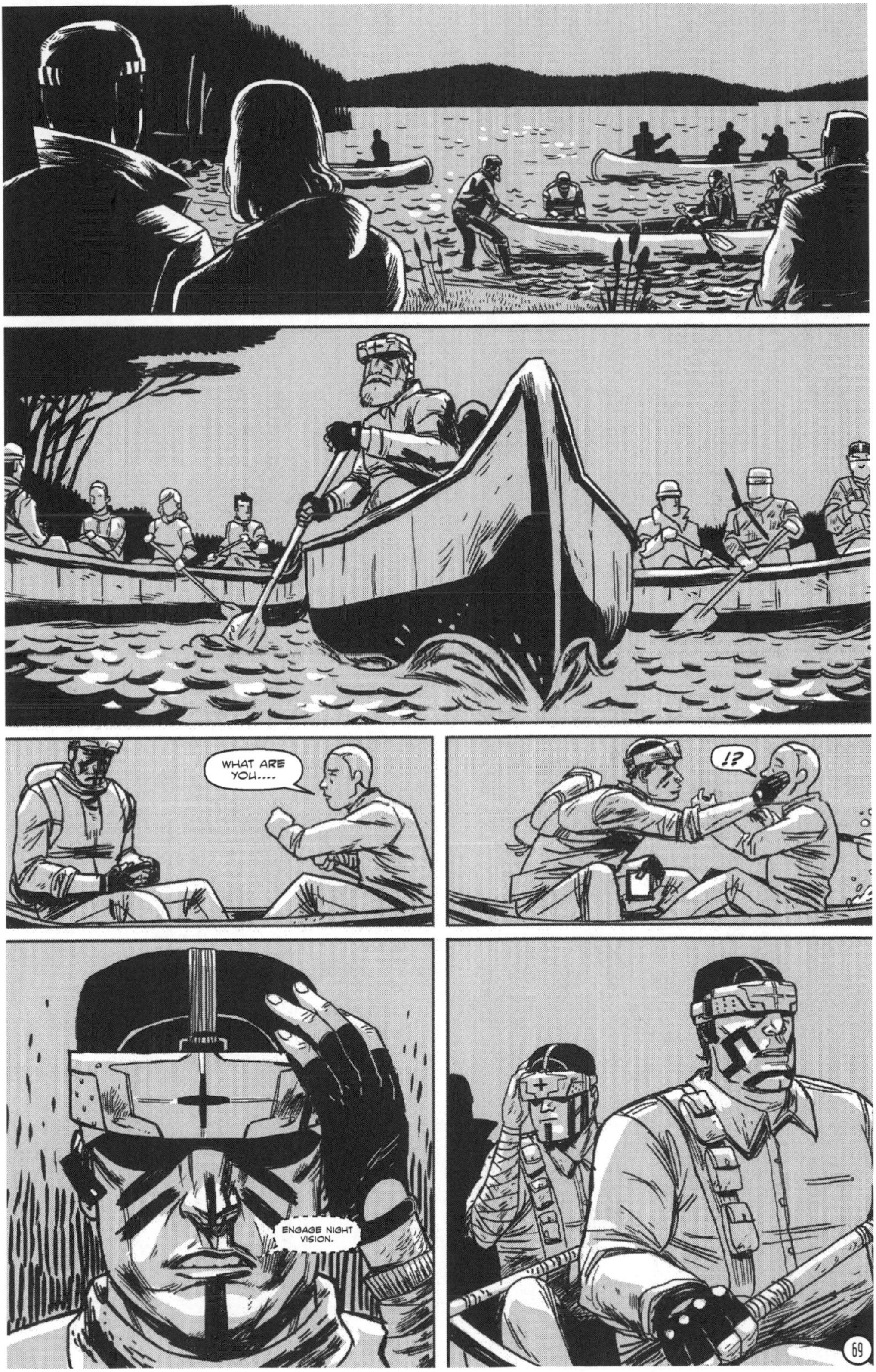
WHAT ARE YOU....
!?
ENGAGE NIGHT VISION.

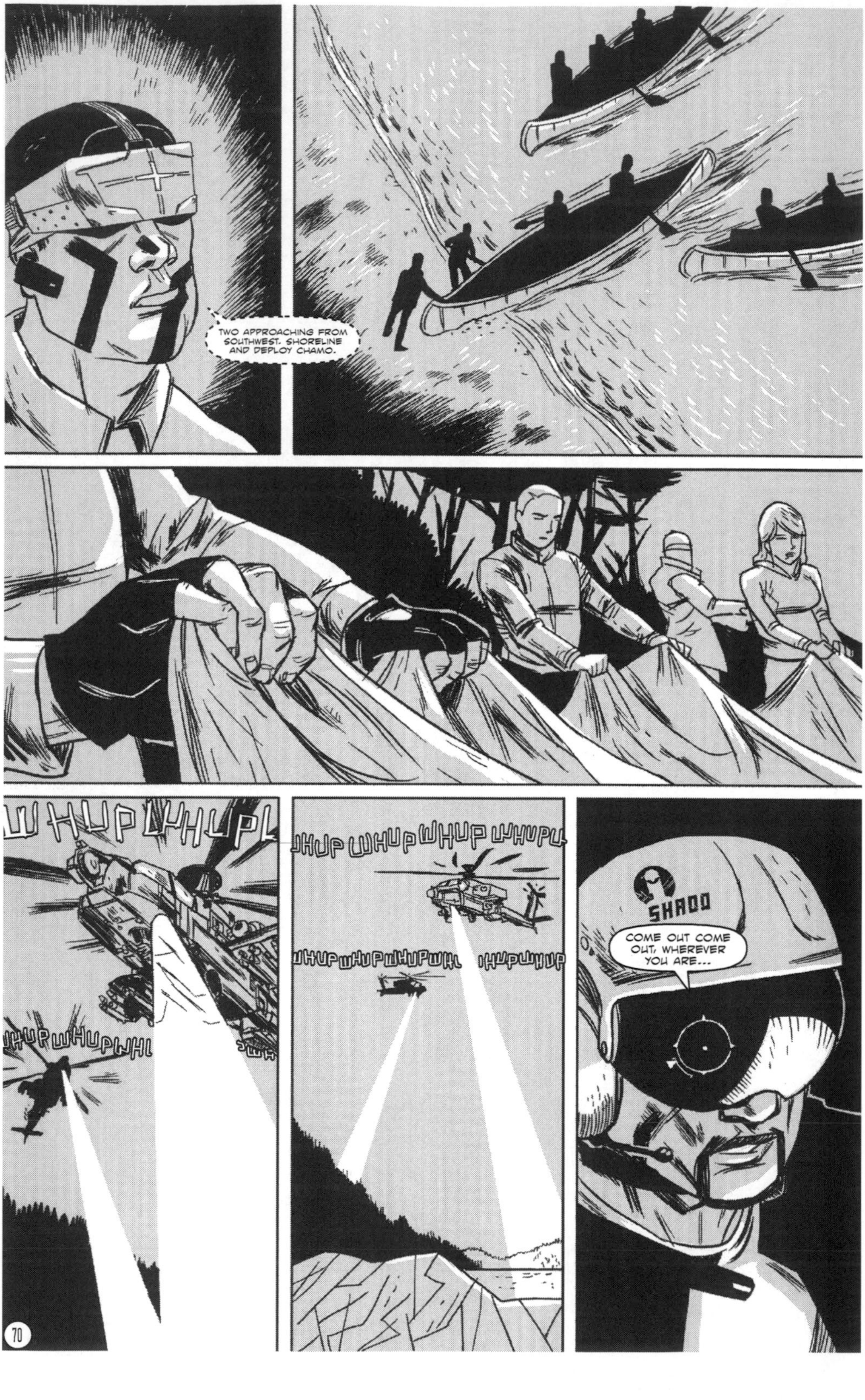
TWO APPROACHING FROM SOUTHWEST. SHORELINE AND DEPLOY CHAMO.
WHUPWHUP
WHUPWHUPWHUPWHUP
WHUPWHUPWHUPWHUP
SHADO
COME OUT COME OUT, WHEREVER YOU ARE...

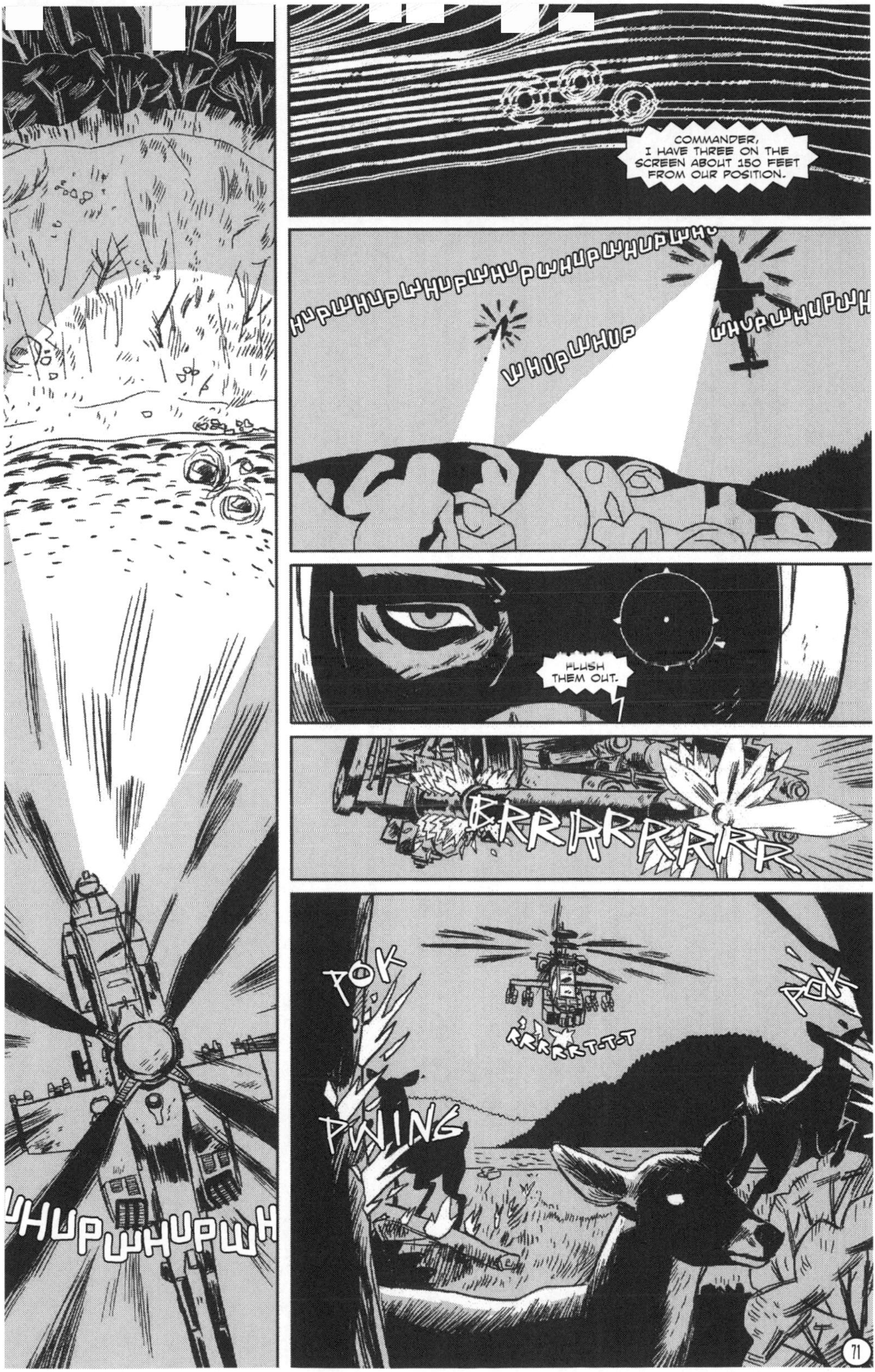
WHUPWHUPWH
COMMANDER, I HAVE THREE ON THE SCREEN ABOUT 150 FEET FROM OUR POSITION.
WHUPWHUPWHUPWHU PWHUPWHUPWHU
WHUPWHUP
WHUPWHUPWH
FLUSH THEM OUT.
BRRRRRRRR
POK
RRRRRT-T-T
POK
PWING

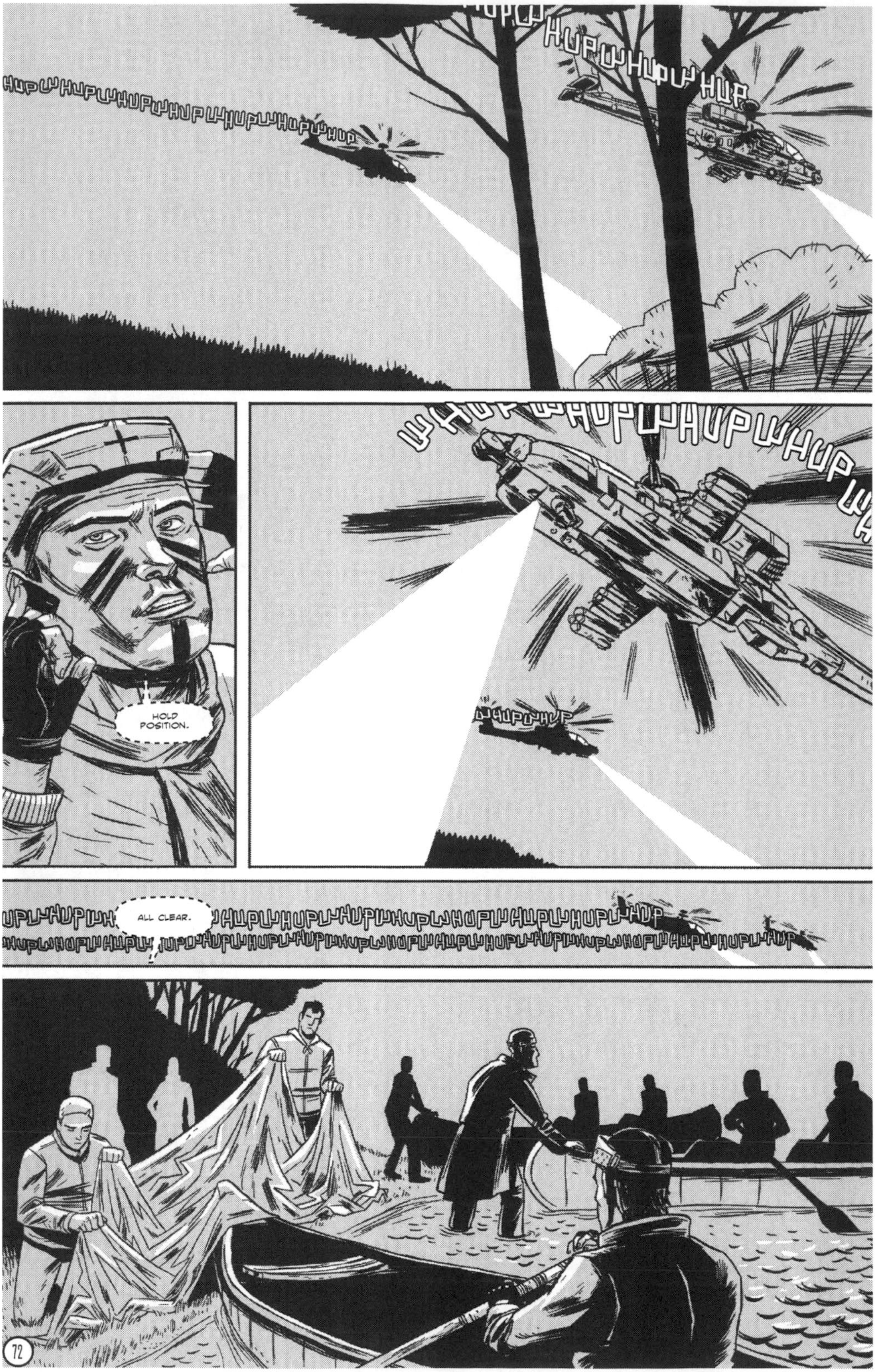
HOLD POSITION.
ALL CLEAR.

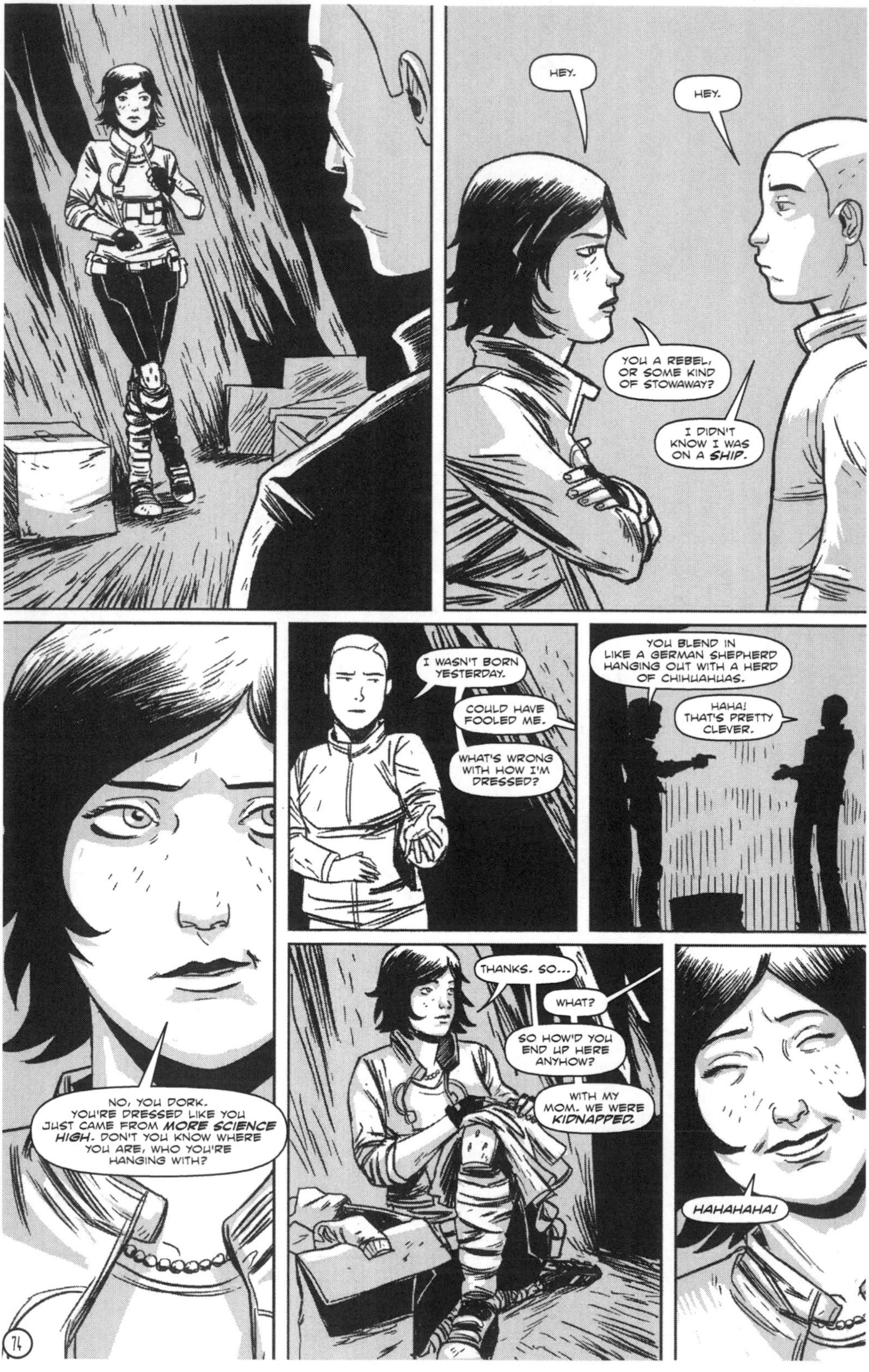
HEY.
HEY.
YOU A REBEL, OR SOME KIND OF STOWAWAY?
I DIDN'T KNOW I WAS ON A SHIP.
NO, YOU DORK. YOU'RE DRESSED LIKE YOU JUST CAME FROM MORE SCIENCE HIGH. DON'T YOU KNOW WHERE YOU ARE, WHO YOU'RE HANGING WITH?
I WASN'T BORN YESTERDAY.
COULD HAVE FOOLED ME.
WHAT'S WRONG WITH HOW I'M DRESSED?
YOU BLEND IN LIKE A GERMAN SHEPHERD HANGING OUT WITH A HERD OF CHIHUAHUAS.
HAHA! THAT'S PRETTY CLEVER.
THANKS. SO...
WHAT?
SO HOW'D YOU END UP HERE ANYHOW?
WITH MY MOM. WE WERE KIDNAPPED.
HAHAHAHA!

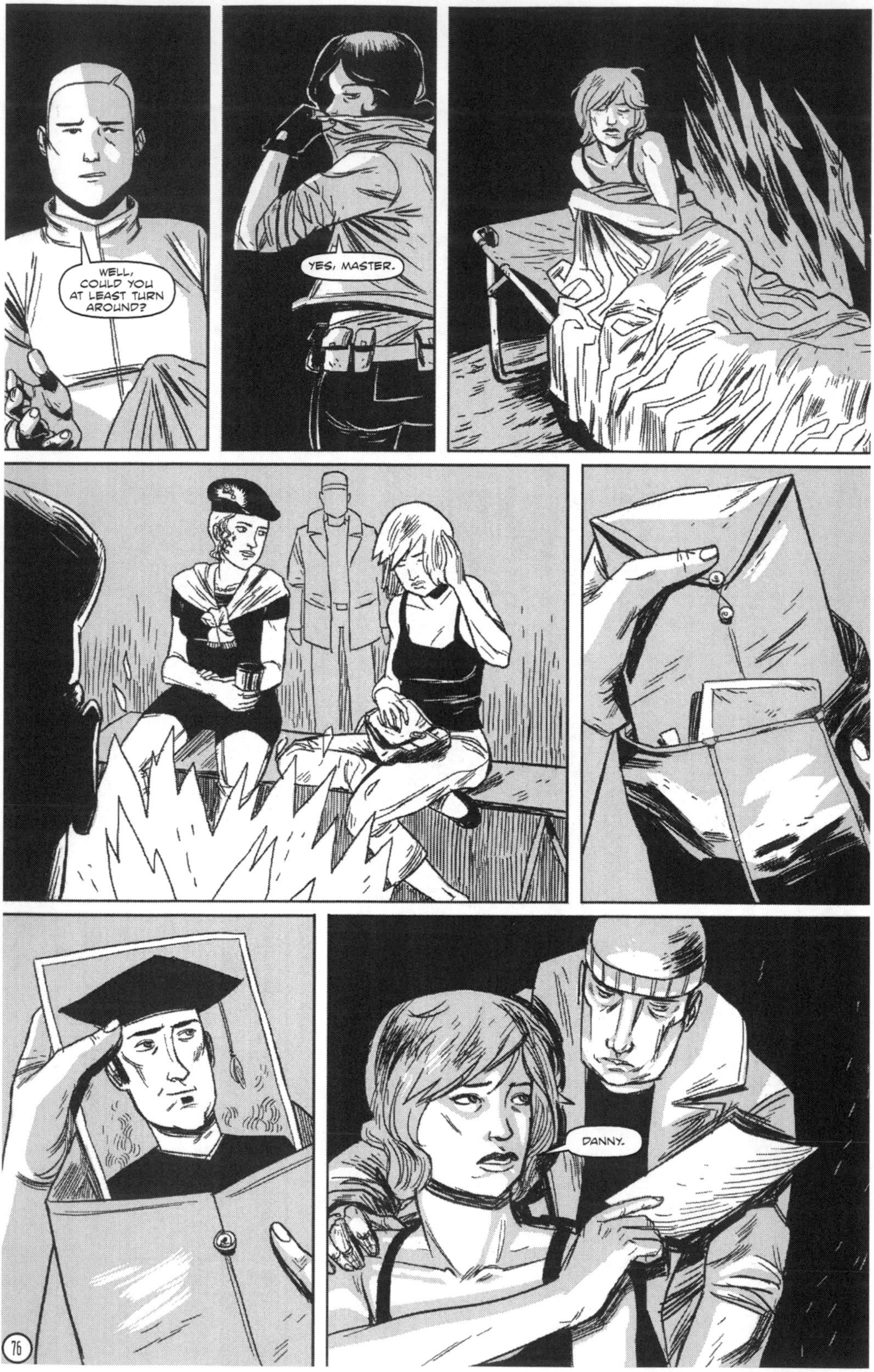
WELL, COULD YOU AT LEAST TURN AROUND?
YES, MASTER.
DANNY.

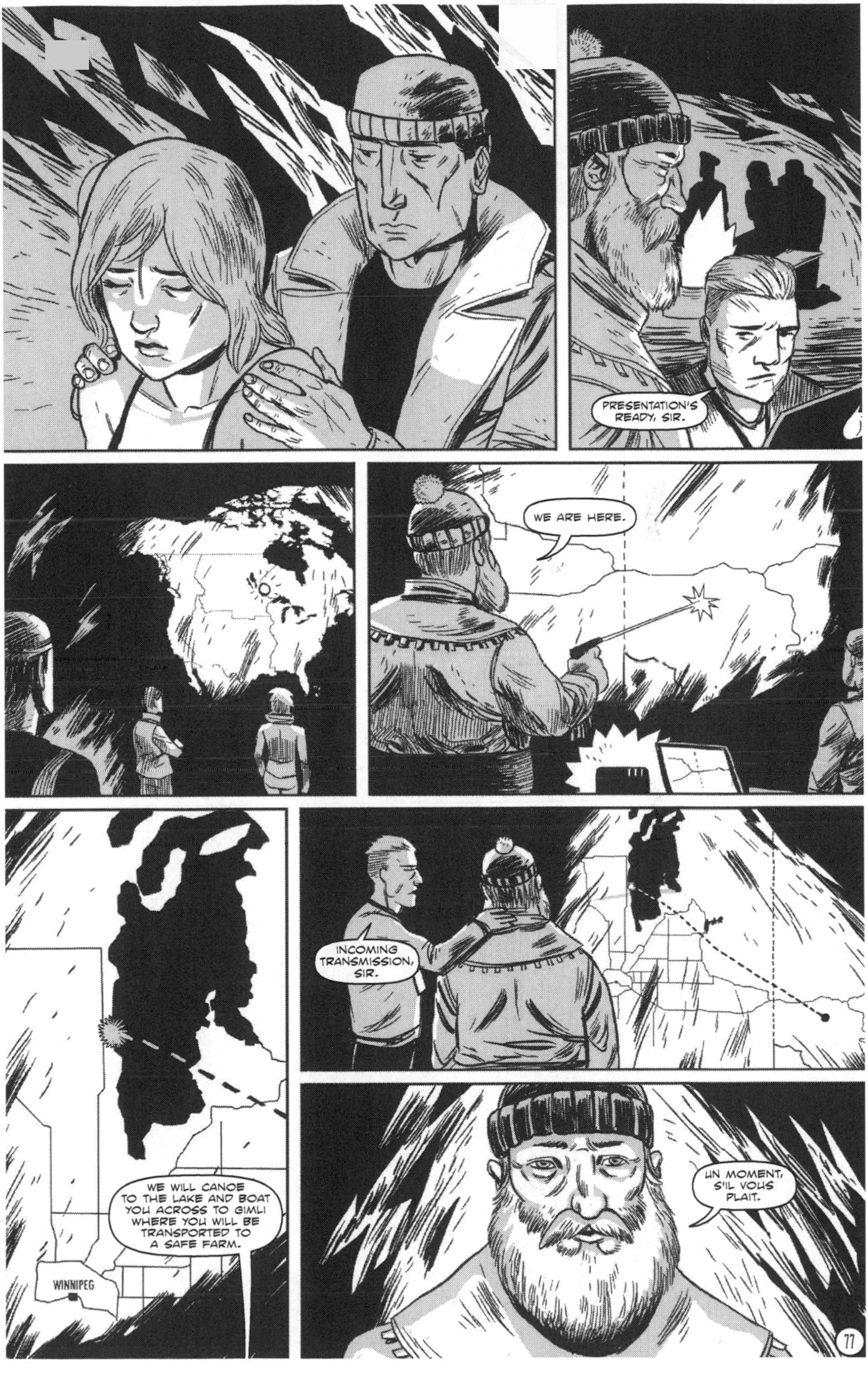
PRESENTATION'S READY, SIR.
WE ARE HERE.
INCOMING TRANSMISSION, SIR.
WE WILL CANOE TO THE LAKE AND BOAT YOU ACROSS TO GIMLI WHERE YOU WILL BE TRANSPORTED TO A SAFE FARM.
WINNIPEG
UN MOMENT, S'IL VOUS PLAIT.

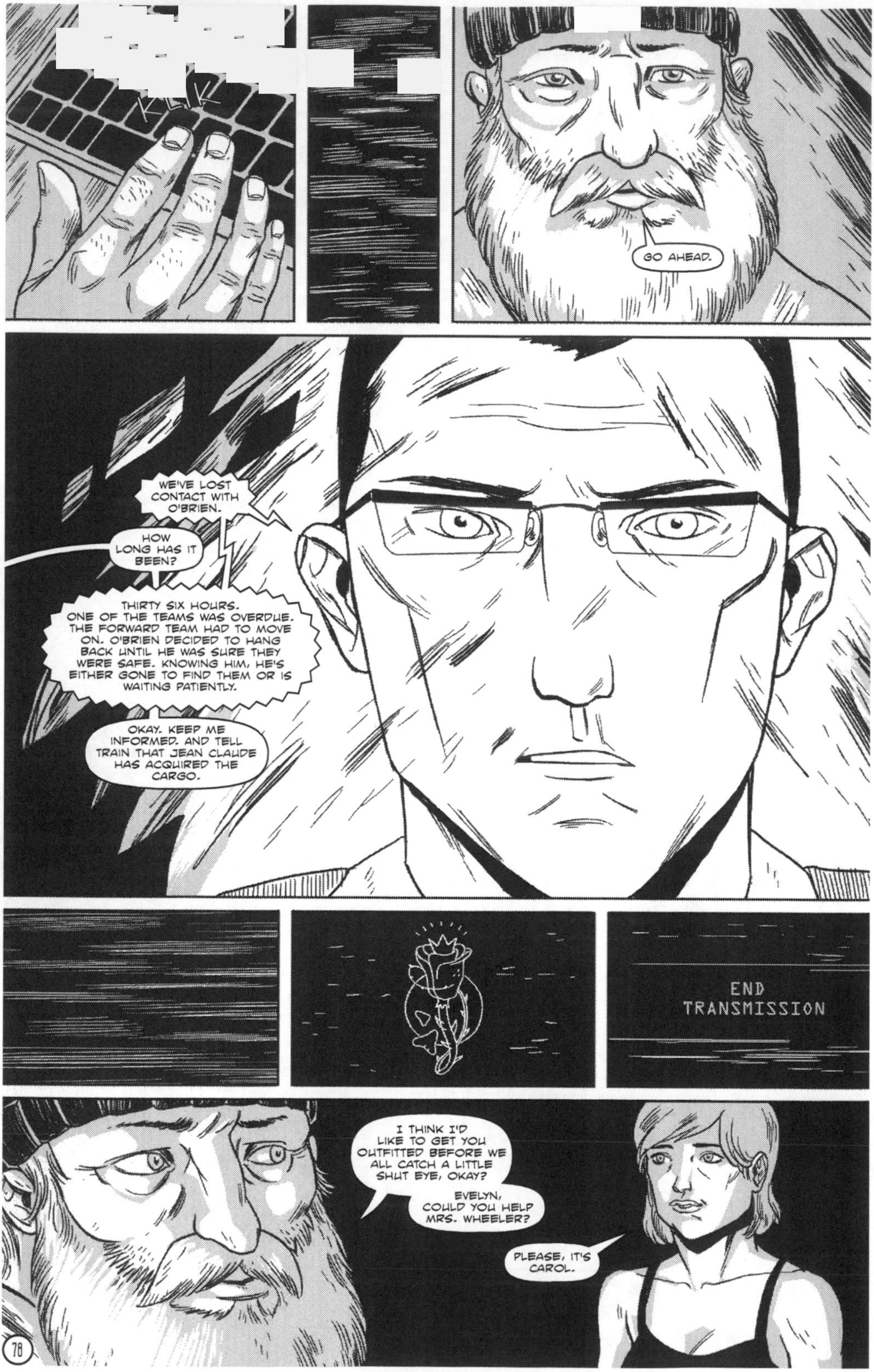
GO AHEAD.
WE'VE LOST CONTACT WITH O'BRIEN.
HOW LONG HAS IT BEEN?
THIRTY SIX HOURS. ONE OF THE TEAMS WAS OVERDUE. THE FORWARD TEAM HAD TO MOVE ON. O'BRIEN DECIDED TO HANG BACK UNTIL HE WAS SURE THEY WERE SAFE. KNOWING HIM, HE'S EITHER GONE TO FIND THEM OR IS WAITING PATIENTLY.
OKAY. KEEP ME INFORMED. AND TELL TRAIN THAT JEAN CLAUDE HAS ACQUIRED THE CARGO.
END TRANSMISSION
I THINK I'D LIKE TO GET YOU OUTFITTED BEFORE WE ALL CATCH A LITTLE SHUT EYE, OKAY?
EVELYN, COULD YOU HELP MRS. WHEELER?
PLEASE, IT'S CAROL.

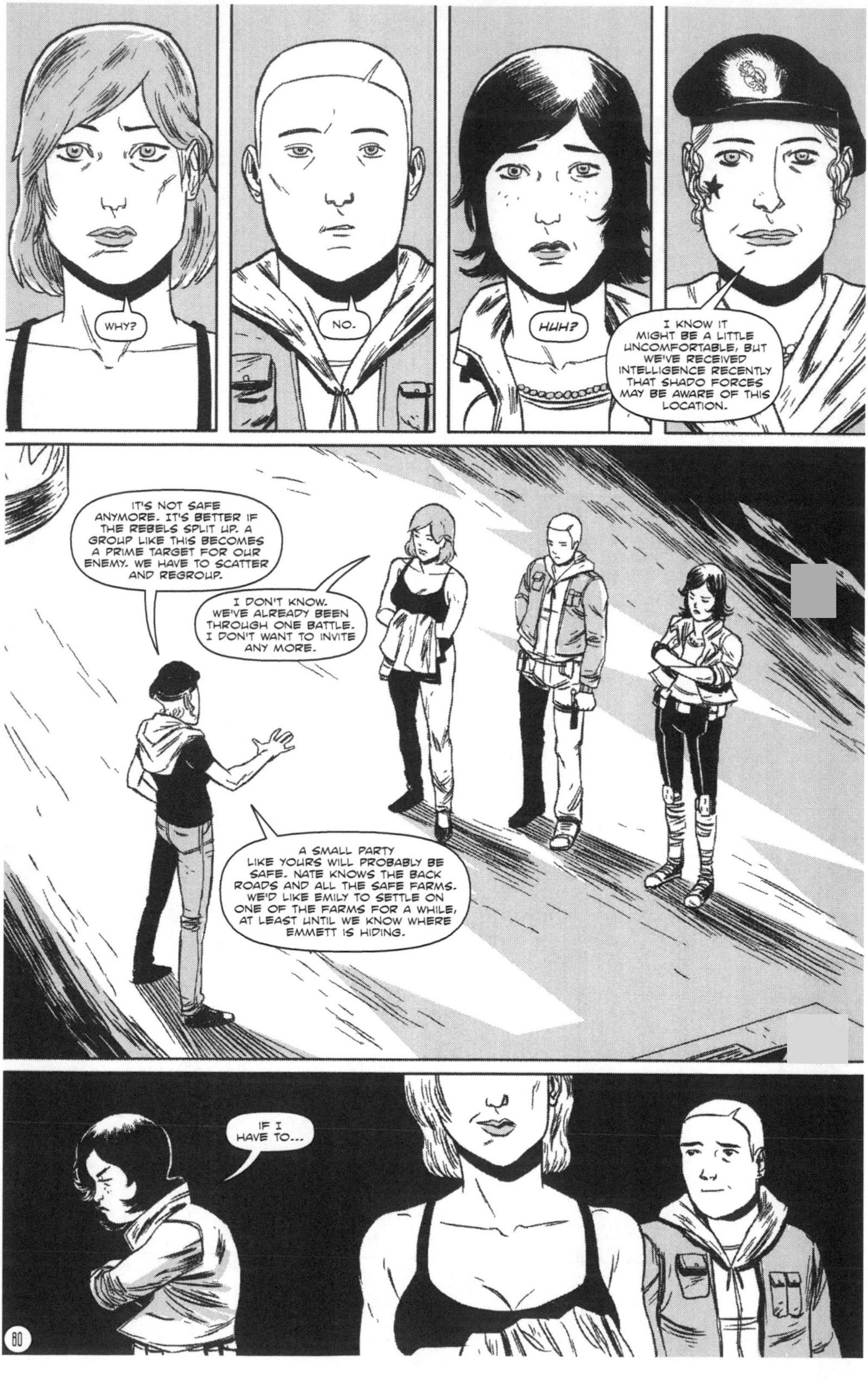
WHY?
NO.
HUH?
I KNOW IT MIGHT BE A LITTLE UNCOMFORTABLE, BUT WE'VE RECEIVED INTELLIGENCE RECENTLY THAT SHADO FORCES MAY BE AWARE OF THIS LOCATION.
IT'S NOT SAFE ANYMORE. IT'S BETTER IF THE REBELS SPLIT UP. A GROUP LIKE THIS BECOMES A PRIME TARGET FOR OUR ENEMY. WE HAVE TO SCATTER AND REGROUP.
I DON'T KNOW. WE'VE ALREADY BEEN THROUGH ONE BATTLE. I DON'T WANT TO INVITE ANY MORE.
A SMALL PARTY LIKE YOURS WILL PROBABLY BE SAFE. NATE KNOWS THE BACK ROADS AND ALL THE SAFE FARMS. WE'D LIKE EMILY TO SETTLE ON ONE OF THE FARMS FOR A WHILE, AT LEAST UNTIL WE KNOW WHERE EMMETT IS HIDING.
IF I HAVE TO...

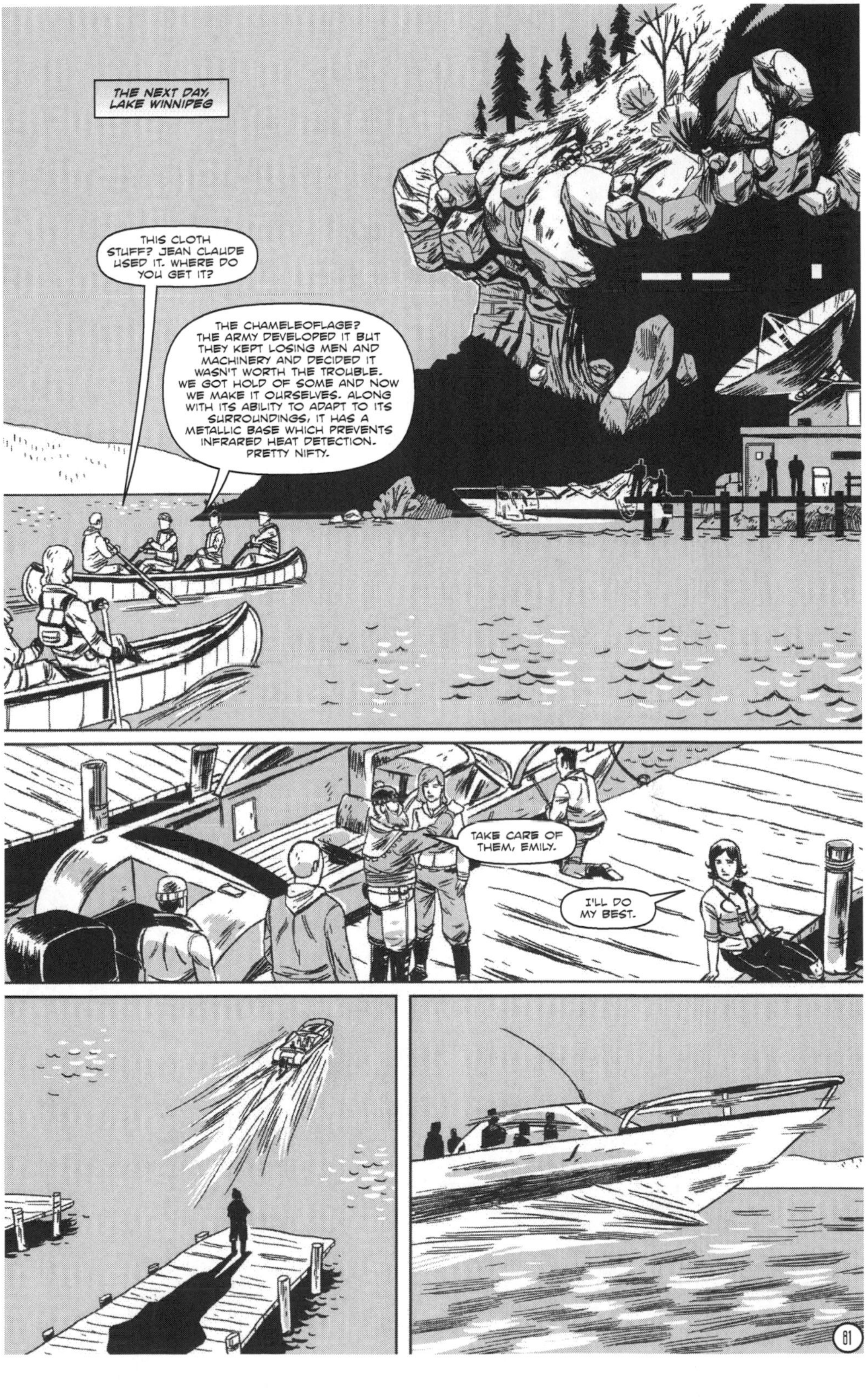
THE NEXT DAY, LAKE WINNIPEG
THIS CLOTH STUFF? JEAN CLAUDE USED IT. WHERE DO YOU GET IT?
THE CHAMELEOFLAGE? THE ARMY DEVELOPED IT BUT THEY KEPT LOSING MEN AND MACHINERY AND DECIDED IT WASN'T WORTH THE TROUBLE. WE GOT HOLD OF SOME AND NOW WE MAKE IT OURSELVES. ALONG WITH ITS ABILITY TO ADAPT TO ITS SURROUNDINGS, IT HAS A METALLIC BASE WHICH PREVENTS INFRARED HEAT DETECTION. PRETTY NIFTY.
TAKE CARE OF THEM, EMILY.
I'LL DO MY BEST.

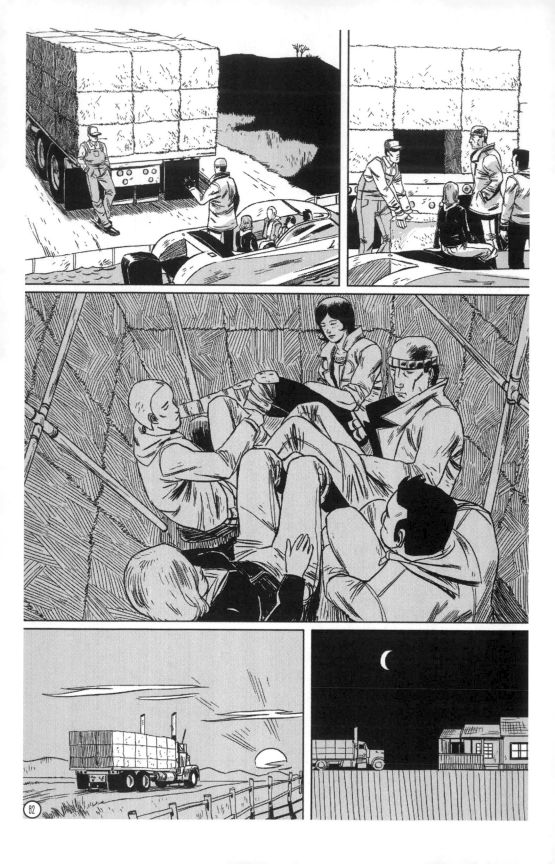

```
-----------------------------------

hey dad,

where r u?
there u go again. doin the disappearing act. don't you think it's getting
kinda....old.  so things are okay with my crew. jacques tries to keep an eye on
me and evelyn has been alright. i kinda miss having kids around.
btw  this woman and a dorky kid named carter showed up today with j.c. and that
driver guy, you know, from newfoundland. forget his name. sorry.
anyhow, this carter is pretty out of touch with what we're doing. he thinks it's
some kind of game, like we're playing rebels. he just doesn't get it. his mom
is some lawyer chick from toronto. kinda stuck up, city trash. thinks she knows
what's going on 'cause she watches the news. she's sure in for some surprises...
lol. i can't wait. she's upset 'cause her suv is doa from a firefight. would have
loved to c that!
seems the shados were tracking that driver guy and j.c. but jacques and his men
came to the rescue. cue the cavalry.
g2g we're heading out soon. the firefight alerted them to our presence in the area.
anyhow, can't u just send us a short message. let us know ur alright.
miss you,

    lol
    18r
    em

-----------------------------------
```

SHADO

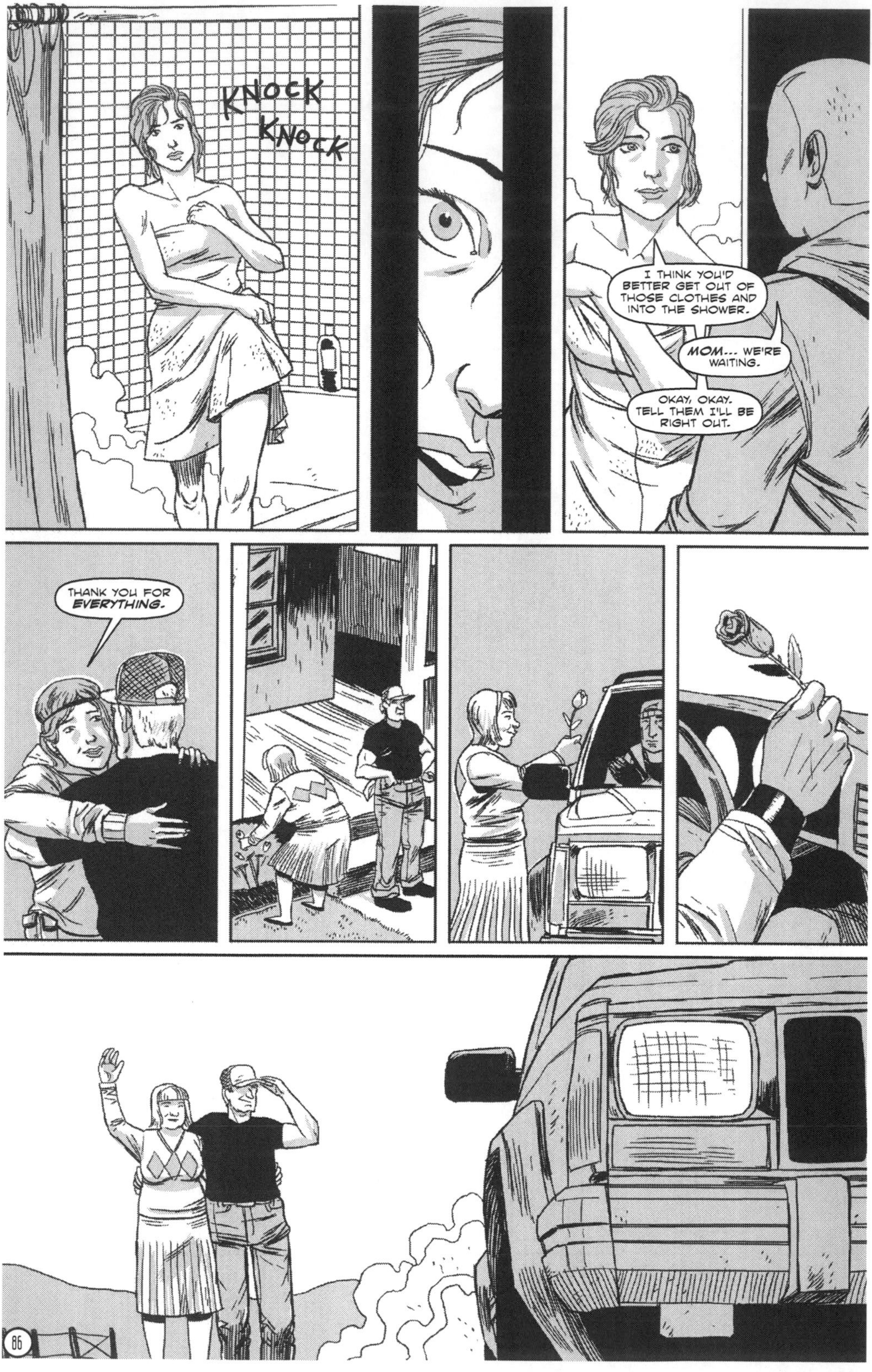
KNOCK
KNOCK
I THINK YOU'D BETTER GET OUT OF THOSE CLOTHES AND INTO THE SHOWER.
MOM... WE'RE WAITING.
OKAY, OKAY. TELL THEM I'LL BE RIGHT OUT.
THANK YOU FOR EVERYTHING.

INTERVIEW WITH PROFESSOR SAMUEL STERN

by Matt Clement
USNA News Services
Filed 04.09.12

Professor Samuel Stern is one of the people of whom the ruling elite wishes
would just teach his seminars and be quiet. From his office at McGill University
in Montreal, he has been a consistent voice of dissent against the perceived
blunders of the governments of both the United States and Canada. Despite the
assassination attempt last year, Professor Stern remains as vocal and passionate
as ever. I spoke to him in his office, amidst the chaos of books, papers and
computers.

Clement: I don't think it's particularly insulting to say that you have a rather
messy office, Professor Stern.

Stern: (laughs) Well, I suppose the cadence of life rises from the mists of
chaos.

Clement: Cadence is actually an important word in your lexicon.

Stern: If you study patterns, repeated sequences of events, you will find the
heart of history. For example, if you dig back into the early years of the lives
of most dictators, you find the same story, the same sequence of events. Usually
a lonely or misunderstood young man who finds a home or family or community
amongst a group of people with ideas that are far from any sense of natural
order or justice. He may not subscribe to this set of beliefs but the need
to belong supersedes any desire to follow a more humane path, especially
when the leadership, or, more appropriately, becoming the father of the
organization, becomes attainable.

Clement: Your recently published book, 'The Ascent of the Military' details what
you call the 'overt takeover of the civilian authority.' Do you find similar
cadence or patterns in what is happening now?

Stern: (laughs) Yeah, that book hasn't made me the most popular academic in
North America. The border has, in some ways, protected me from some of my more
vocal and passionate opponents from down south. There are, in a sense, two
parallel patterns at play. What I call the external and internal. The
external is the deteriorating economic conditions, the collapse of the
European economic Union, the weather disasters, the west coast earthquakes
and the central American unrest. All have lead to a destabilization of
established order and the opportunity to use fear as a weapon. This enhances
the opportunity for a tighter, smaller group to take over the power
structures and political mechanisms of government. The floundering presidency
of Jonathan Reed, a nice man, a smart man, but a man who, much like George W.
Bush, exhibits all the characteristics of a prop or puppet, led to the
Proclamation of Suspension, the so-called temporary suspension of government
allowing the forces of the military and the secret police to govern without
civilian oversight during this period of unrest and uncertainty. The internal
pattern is the combination of the weak leadership of President Reed and the
ascendency of General Karol Klusinsky. Klusinsky is the kind of aggressive,
chest thumping leader that appeals to the people who do no analysis but
accept the image and story presented to them.

Clement: His early life fits the pattern you presented earlier.

Stern: His mother was an alcoholic who looked after the boy until his 6th
birthday. His father, ex-military, was also an alcoholic and disappeared shortly
after the death of his wife. There is much speculation as to whether her death
was self induced alcoholic poisoning or something more sinister. Klusinksi
grew up in foster homes until his early teens when, in a desperate plan
to cure his chronic law breaking and drug induced violence, he was sent to
military boarding school. It was here that he found his collective family and
a place where his aggressiveness and anti-social behaviour was accepted and
nurtured.

Clement: What do you make of the rumors flying around Ottawa about secret amalgamation talks?

Stern: Let me deal with this question in two parts. First of all, the process to accepting amalgamation would require the change to our constitution and would require the acceptance of all provinces and territories plus, the government would be wise to hold a national plebiscite to insure the people were actually in support of the idea. That process would take years to organize, debate and carry out. This present government exhibits the arrogance to believe that they know what the people want and are going to give it to them. I do not put it past them to drive it down the throats of the Canadian people using fear and bullying as the tools of persuasion.

Clement: And the second?

Stern: It would be a colossal mistake. It's certainly a situation where if it actually happened, there would be no turning back, short of armed revolution. An amalgamation would lead to a more militarized society, and, I fear, a more aggressive military stance on the world stage. The United States has everything to gain, as has been pointed out many times: labour, access to market, access to natural resources, access to the Canadian north. Canada will be sold on the free flow of money, access to the US market, that sort of nonsense. Mostly, Canadians will be sold on the idea of increased personal wealth. They will also be sold on the idea of more security from outside forces. I wouldn't be surprised if there was some kind of horrific so-called terrorist incident to fuel the pro-amalgamation fires.

Clement: It's obvious that you are passionate about this issue.

Stern: As a political scientist, there is none more urgent to consider.

Clement: You have the reputation of your seminars becoming the training ground for future political talent. Any of your students worth mentioning?

Stern: Gosh, I hate to jinx my students. Well, yes there are a few worth keeping an eye on. Emmett O'Brien, who led the school's debating team at the world's this year has that rare combination of intellectual curiosity and humanity. He's much like I was 30 years ago. I'm fascinated by Jean Claude Boisvert because of his family connections in Montreal and his keen sense of timing. He just seems to know when to lay low and when to strike. A political animal who has his feet planted firmly in academia. He may not escape the cushioned university life, but if he does, watch out. Joseph A. Conrad is another. He's a wily, clever kid whose achilles' heel may be his predilection to quick decisions without complete analysis. That kind of crapshoot is effective but can also backfire in unexpected ways. He's ambitious and formidable. The one woman who shines is a gal named Judy Taylor from Sudbury who has used her physical attractiveness as a weapon against weak men who do not sense her extraordinary intellectual abilities and simple common sense. If she runs for office, as she's indicated throughout her academic career, she's a force to consider.

Clement: The leadership of the Liberal Democrat Party is coming up soon. As a former cabinet member, you are being heavily recruited to run for the leadership of the party. Are you willing to go on record and announce your candidacy?

Stern: Matt, I enjoy our chats and would love for you to have the scoop of the year, but I cannot commit at this time.

Clement: So you're literally sitting on the fence?

Stern: I cannot confirm nor deny at this time.

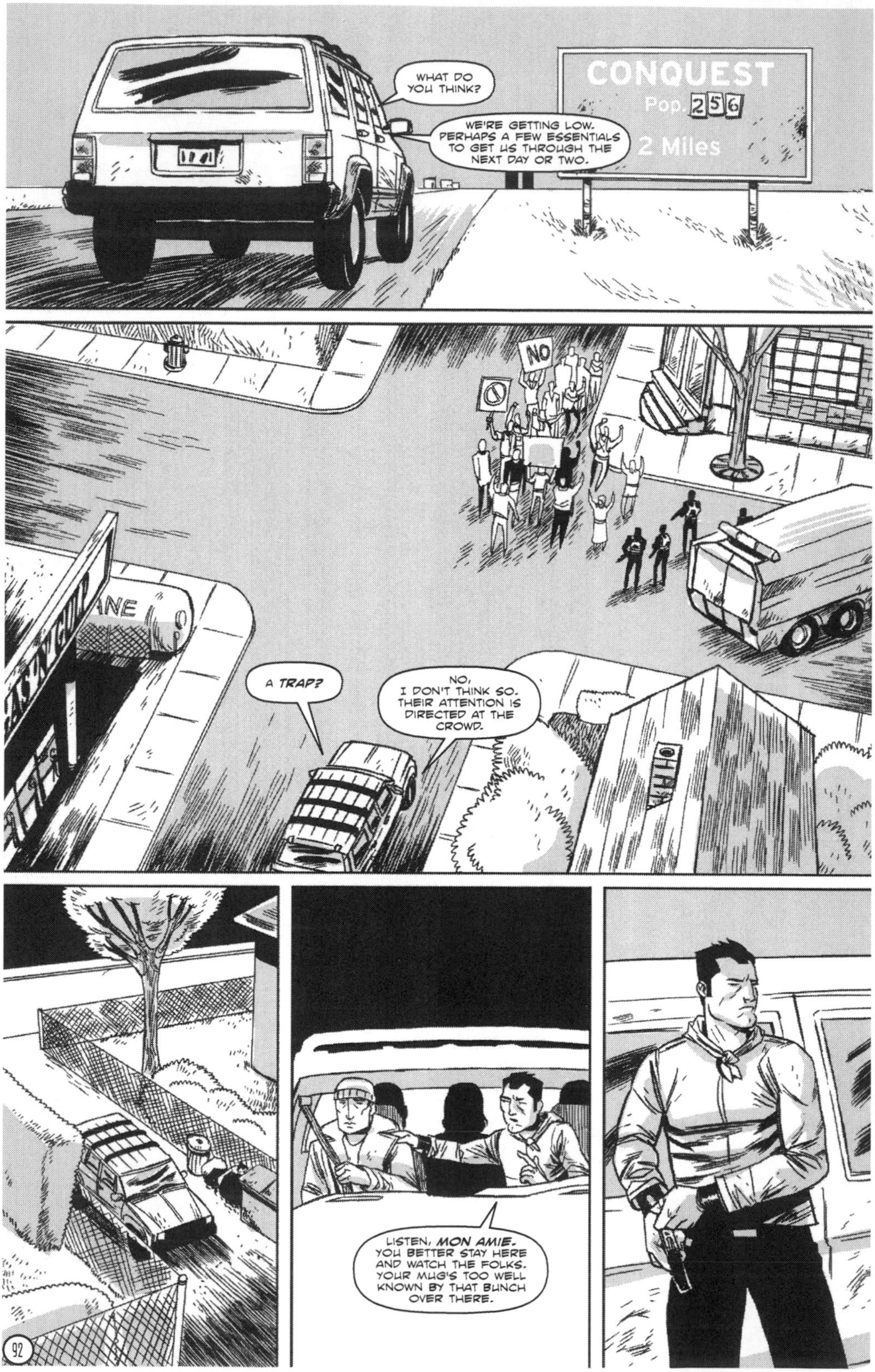
WHAT DO YOU THINK?
WE'RE GETTING LOW. PERHAPS A FEW ESSENTIALS TO GET US THROUGH THE NEXT DAY OR TWO.
CONQUEST
Pop. 256
2 Miles
NO
A *TRAP?*
NO, I DON'T THINK SO. THEIR ATTENTION IS DIRECTED AT THE CROWD.
LISTEN, ***MON AMIE.*** YOU BETTER STAY HERE AND WATCH THE FOLKS. YOUR MUG'S TOO WELL KNOWN BY THAT BUNCH OVER THERE.

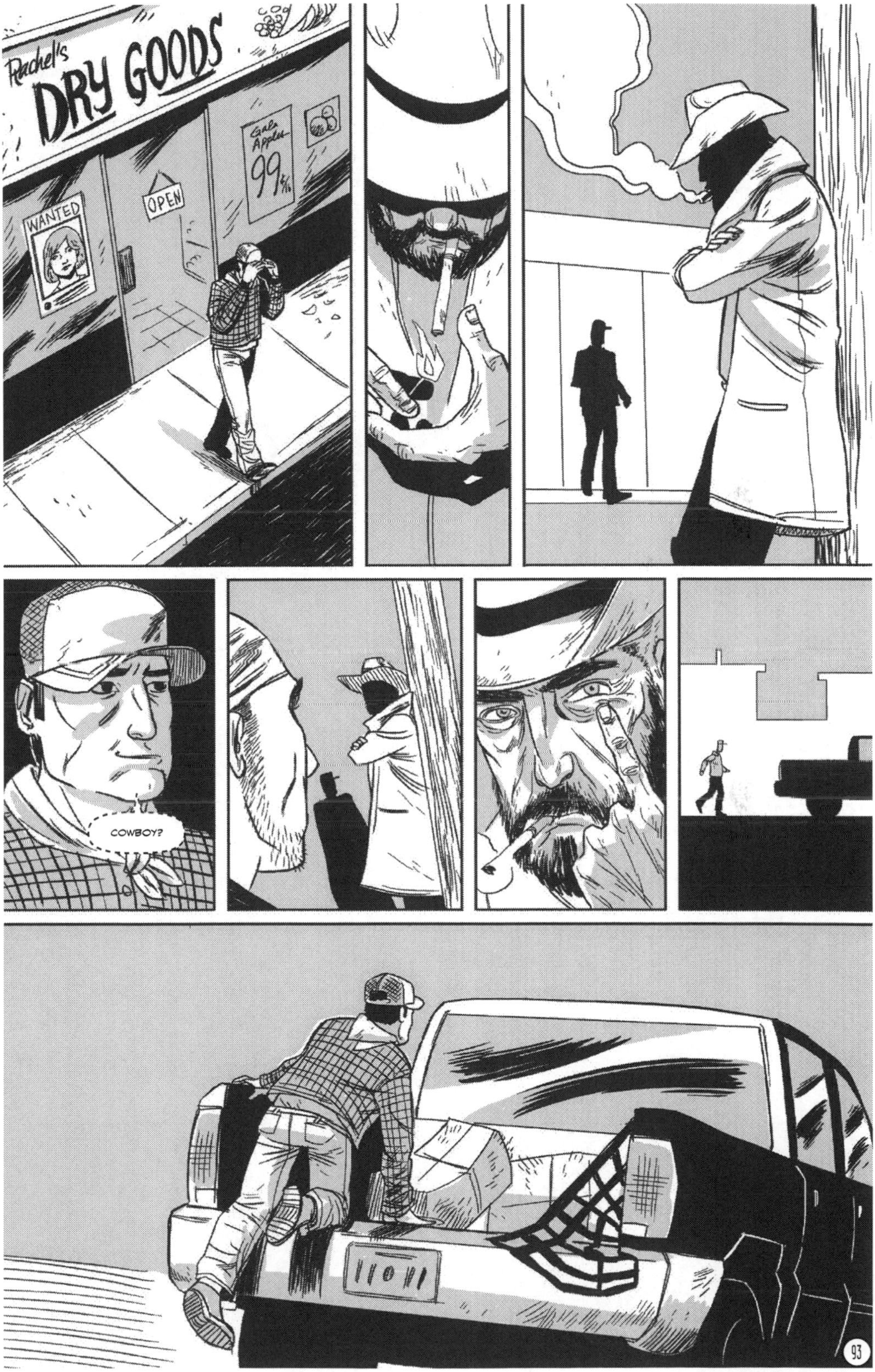
Rachel's
DRY GOODS
WANTED
OPEN
Gala Apples 99¢/lb
COWBOY?

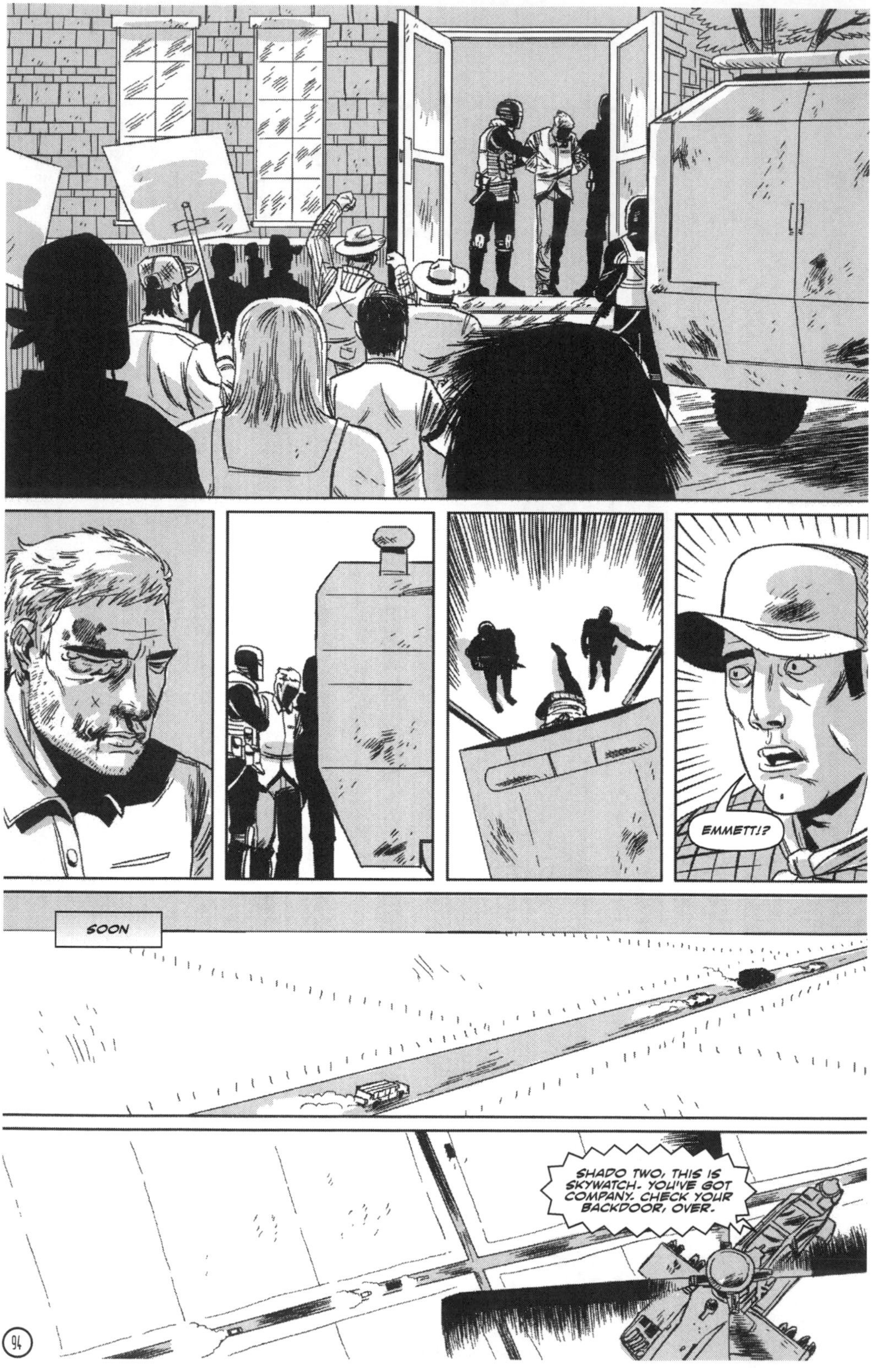
EMMETT!?
SOON
SHADO TWO, THIS IS SKYWATCH- YOU'VE GOT COMPANY. CHECK YOUR BACKDOOR, OVER.

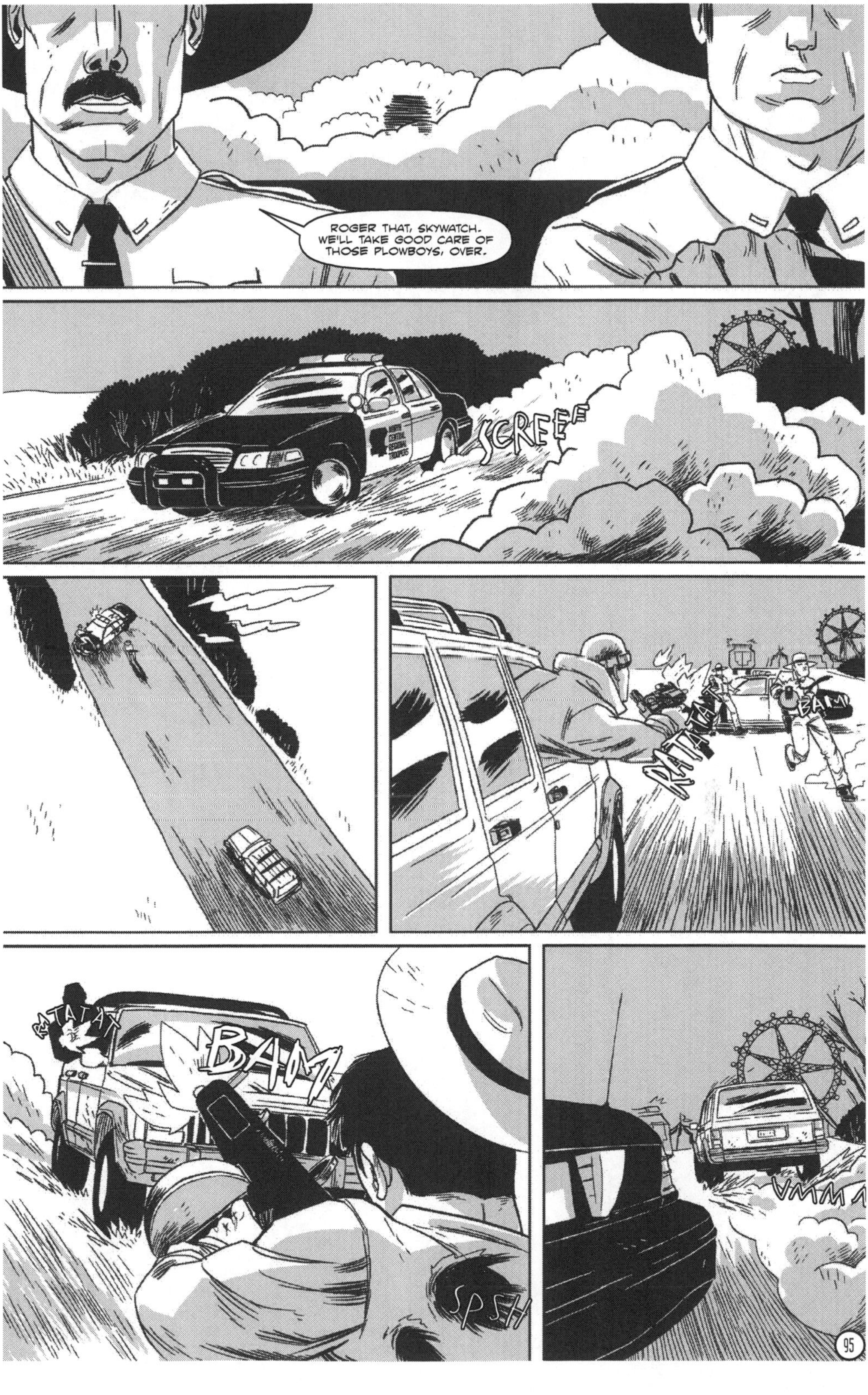
ROGER THAT, SKYWATCH. WE'LL TAKE GOOD CARE OF THOSE PLOWBOYS, OVER.
SCREEE
RATATAT
BAM
RATATAT
BAM
SPSH

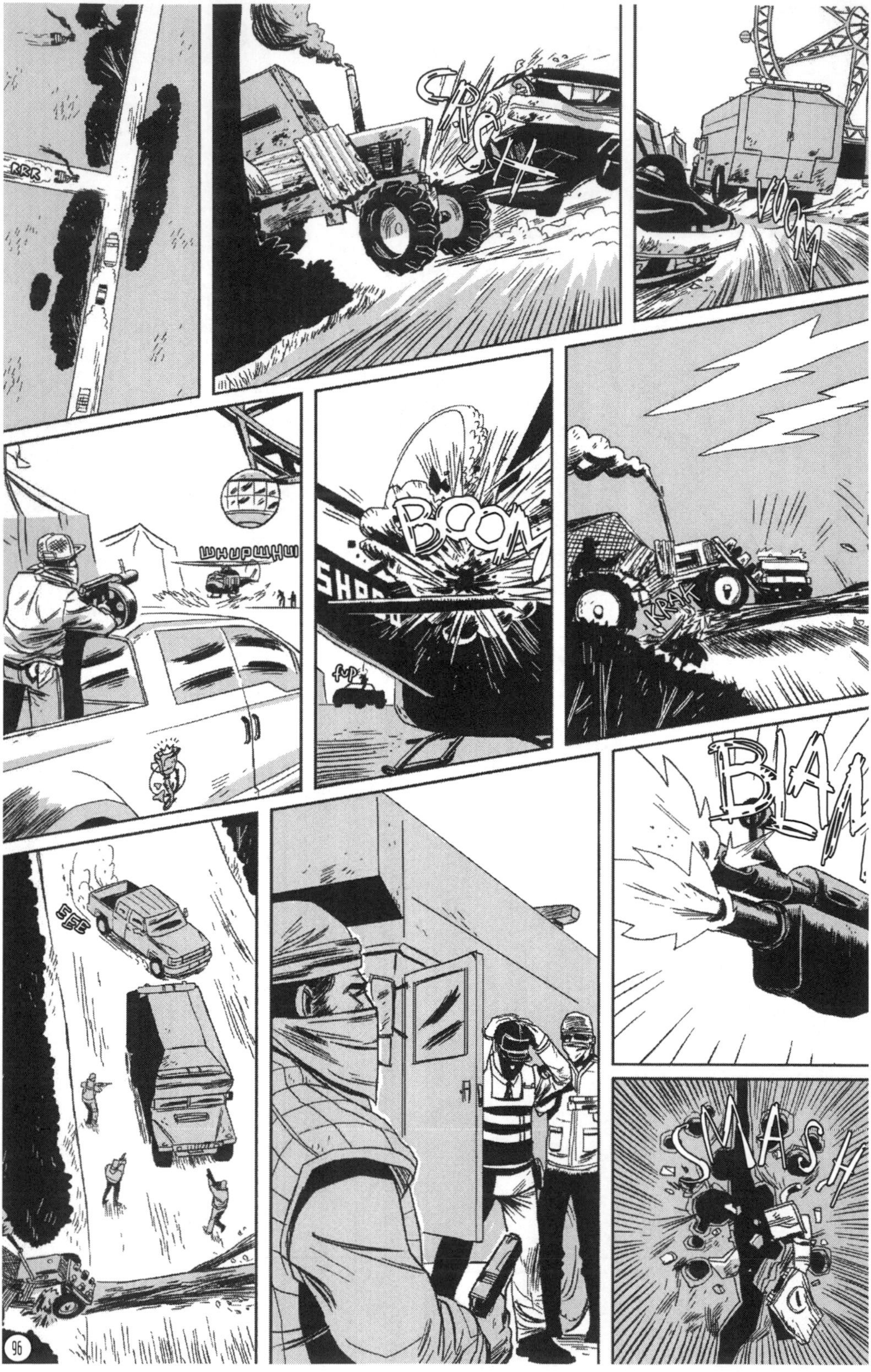
RRR
CRSH
VOOM
WHUPWHU
BOOM
SHO
fup
KRAK
BLAM
SEE
SMASH

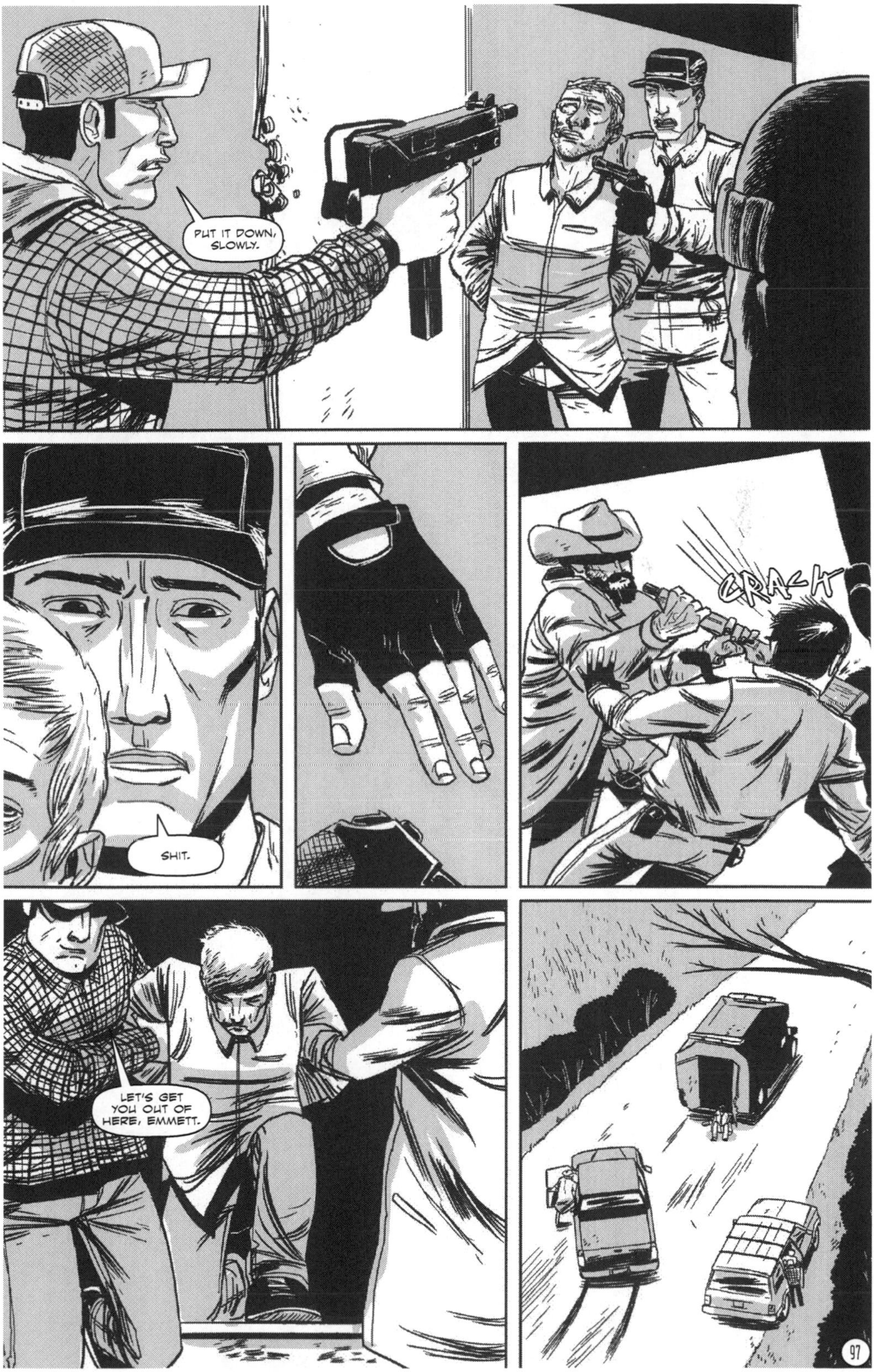
PUT IT DOWN, SLOWLY.
SHIT.
CRACK
LET'S GET YOU OUT OF HERE, EMMETT.

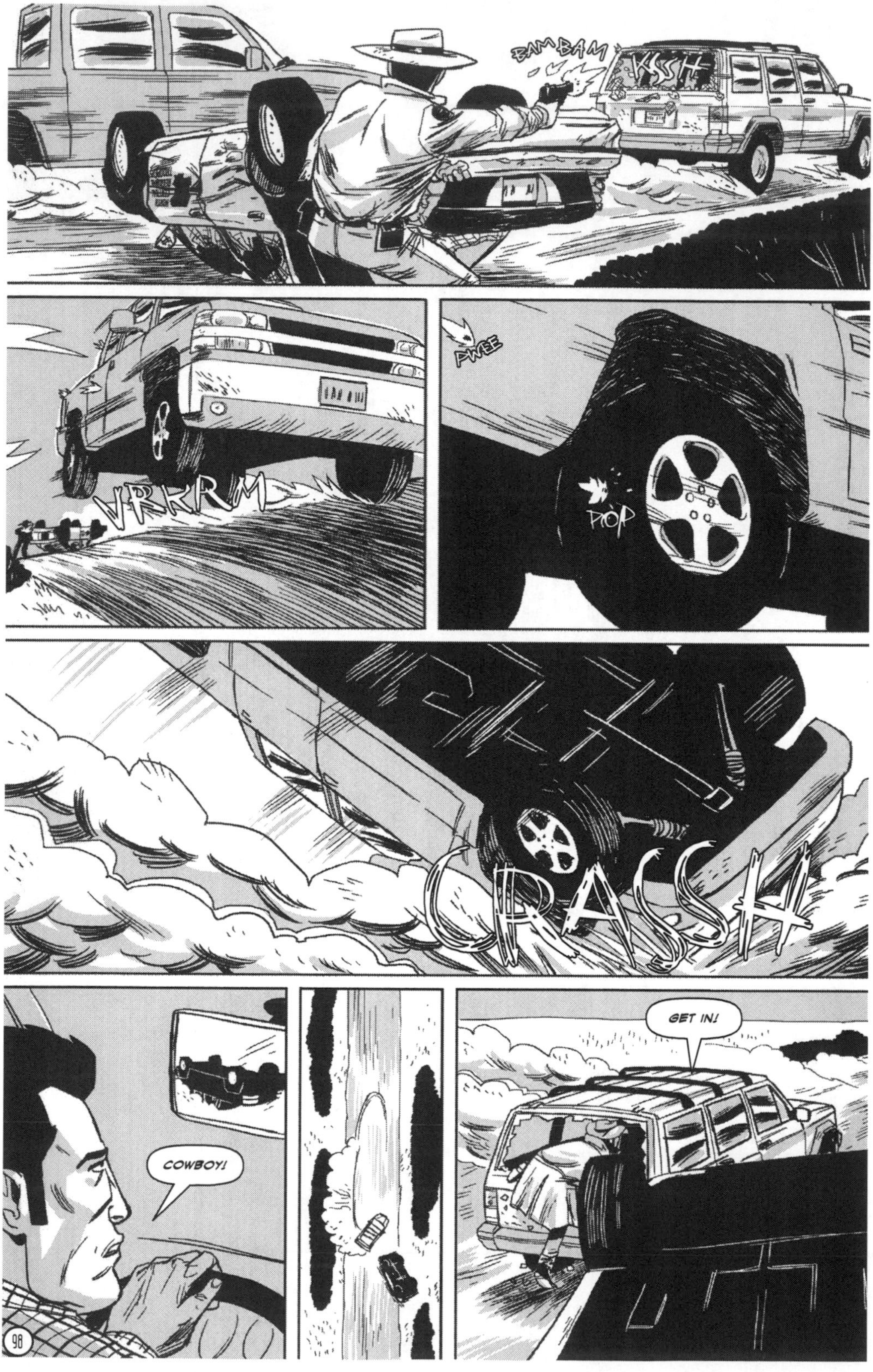
BAM BAM
KSSH
VRKRM
PWEE
POP
CRASSH
COWBOY!
GET IN!

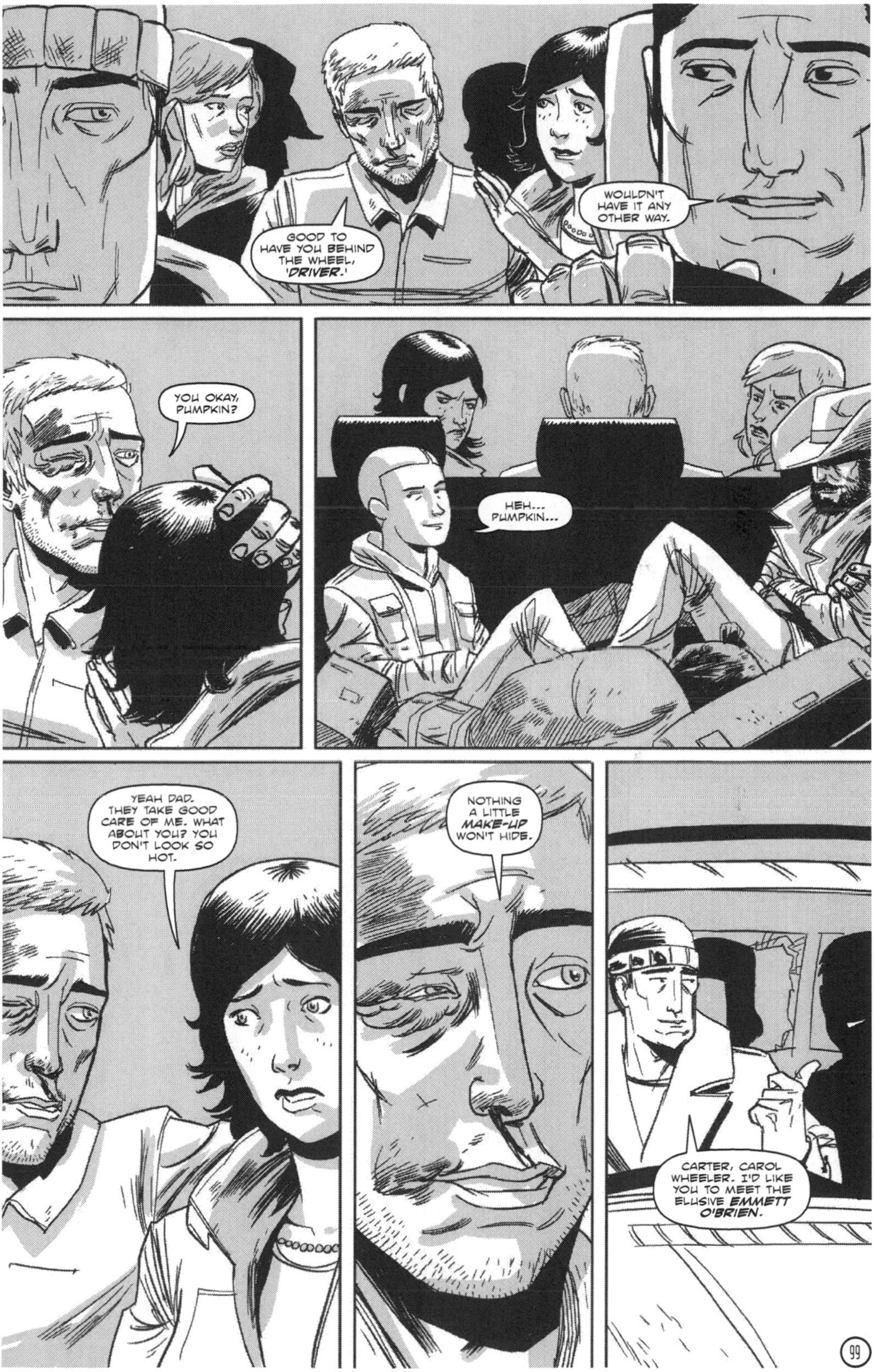
GOOD TO HAVE YOU BEHIND THE WHEEL, 'DRIVER.'
WOULDN'T HAVE IT ANY OTHER WAY.
YOU OKAY, PUMPKIN?
HEH... PUMPKIN...
YEAH DAD. THEY TAKE GOOD CARE OF ME. WHAT ABOUT YOU? YOU DON'T LOOK SO HOT.
NOTHING A LITTLE MAKE-UP WON'T HIDE.
CARTER, CAROL WHEELER. I'D LIKE YOU TO MEET THE ELUSIVE EMMETT O'BRIEN.

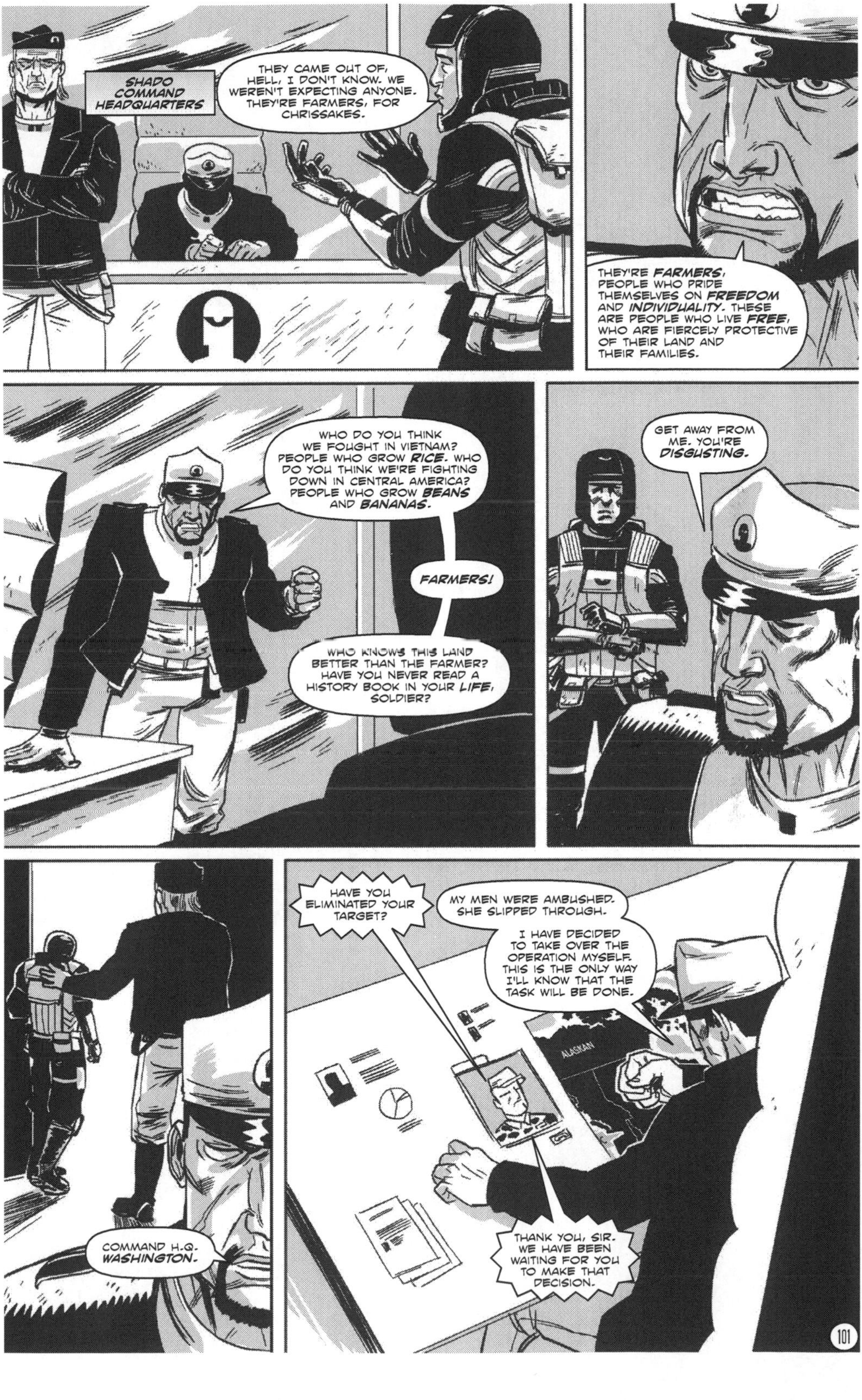
SHADO COMMAND HEADQUARTERS
THEY CAME OUT OF, HELL, I DON'T KNOW. WE WEREN'T EXPECTING ANYONE. THEY'RE FARMERS, FOR CHRISSAKES.
THEY'RE FARMERS, PEOPLE WHO PRIDE THEMSELVES ON FREEDOM AND INDIVIDUALITY. THESE ARE PEOPLE WHO LIVE FREE, WHO ARE FIERCELY PROTECTIVE OF THEIR LAND AND THEIR FAMILIES.
WHO DO YOU THINK WE FOUGHT IN VIETNAM? PEOPLE WHO GROW RICE. WHO DO YOU THINK WE'RE FIGHTING DOWN IN CENTRAL AMERICA? PEOPLE WHO GROW BEANS AND BANANAS.
FARMERS!
WHO KNOWS THIS LAND BETTER THAN THE FARMER? HAVE YOU NEVER READ A HISTORY BOOK IN YOUR LIFE, SOLDIER?
GET AWAY FROM ME. YOU'RE DISGUSTING.
COMMAND H.Q. WASHINGTON.
HAVE YOU ELIMINATED YOUR TARGET?
MY MEN WERE AMBUSHED. SHE SLIPPED THROUGH.
I HAVE DECIDED TO TAKE OVER THE OPERATION MYSELF. THIS IS THE ONLY WAY I'LL KNOW THAT THE TASK WILL BE DONE.
ALASKAN
THANK YOU, SIR. WE HAVE BEEN WAITING FOR YOU TO MAKE THAT DECISION.

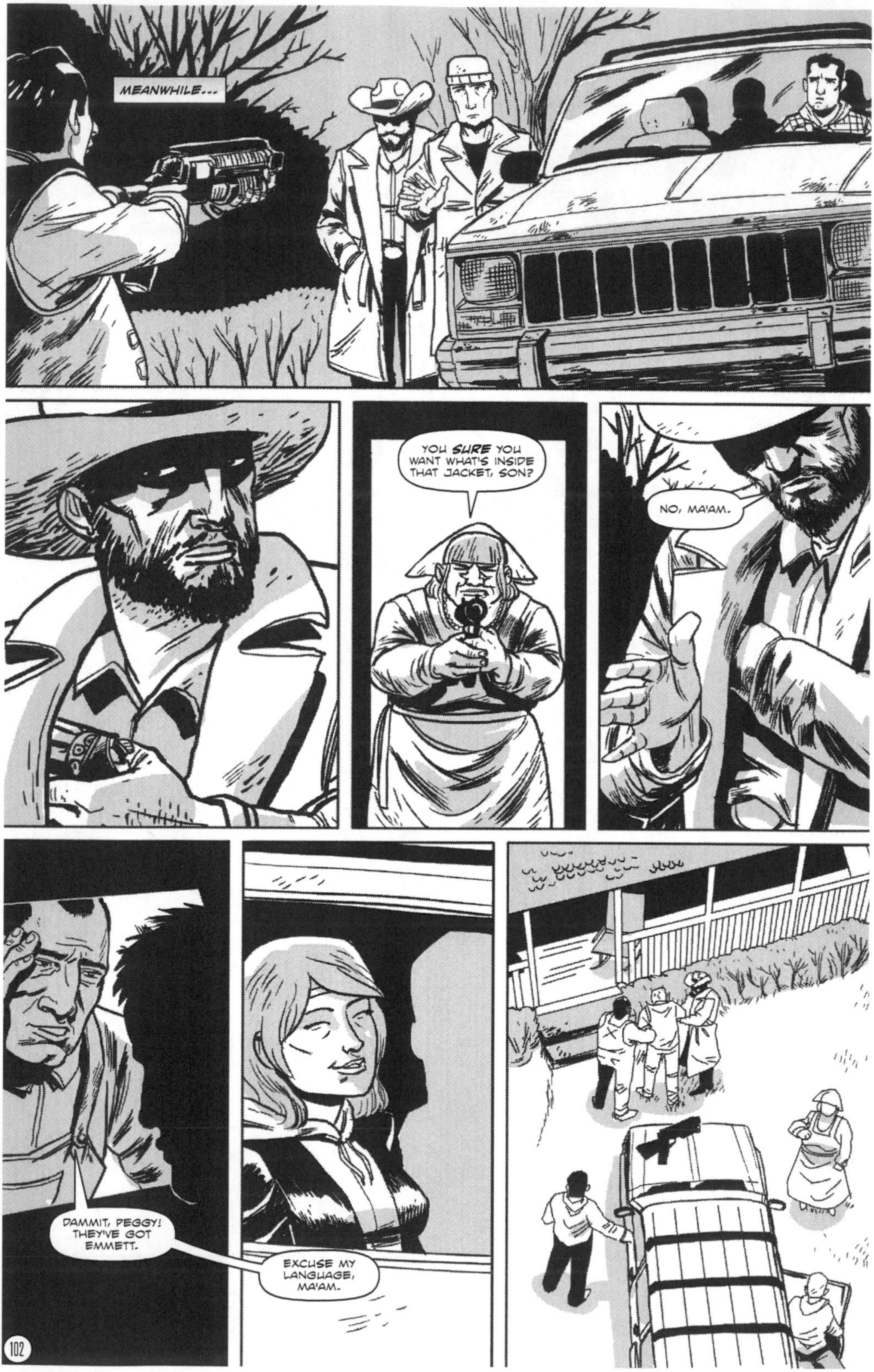

MEANWHILE...
YOU SURE YOU WANT WHAT'S INSIDE THAT JACKET, SON?
NO, MA'AM.
DAMMIT, PEGGY! THEY'VE GOT EMMETT.
EXCUSE MY LANGUAGE, MA'AM.

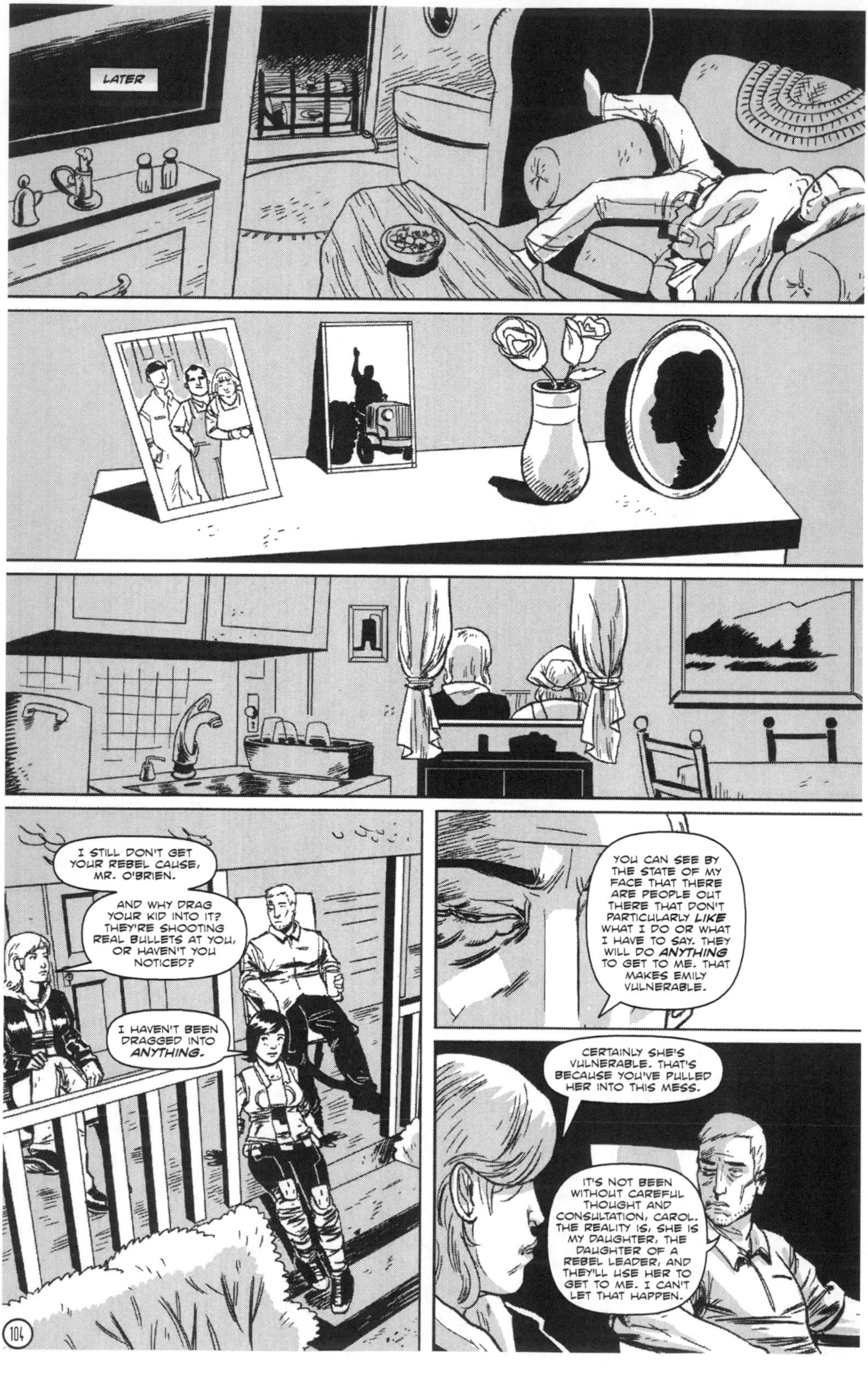

LATER
I STILL DON'T GET YOUR REBEL CAUSE, MR. O'BRIEN.
AND WHY DRAG YOUR KID INTO IT? THEY'RE SHOOTING REAL BULLETS AT YOU, OR HAVEN'T YOU NOTICED?
I HAVEN'T BEEN DRAGGED INTO *ANYTHING*.
YOU CAN SEE BY THE STATE OF MY FACE THAT THERE ARE PEOPLE OUT THERE THAT DON'T PARTICULARLY *LIKE* WHAT I DO OR WHAT I HAVE TO SAY. THEY WILL DO *ANYTHING* TO GET TO ME. THAT MAKES EMILY VULNERABLE.
CERTAINLY SHE'S VULNERABLE. THAT'S BECAUSE YOU'VE PULLED HER INTO THIS MESS.
IT'S NOT BEEN WITHOUT CAREFUL THOUGHT AND CONSULTATION, CAROL. THE REALITY IS, SHE IS MY DAUGHTER, THE DAUGHTER OF A REBEL LEADER, AND THEY'LL USE HER TO GET TO ME. I CAN'T LET THAT HAPPEN.

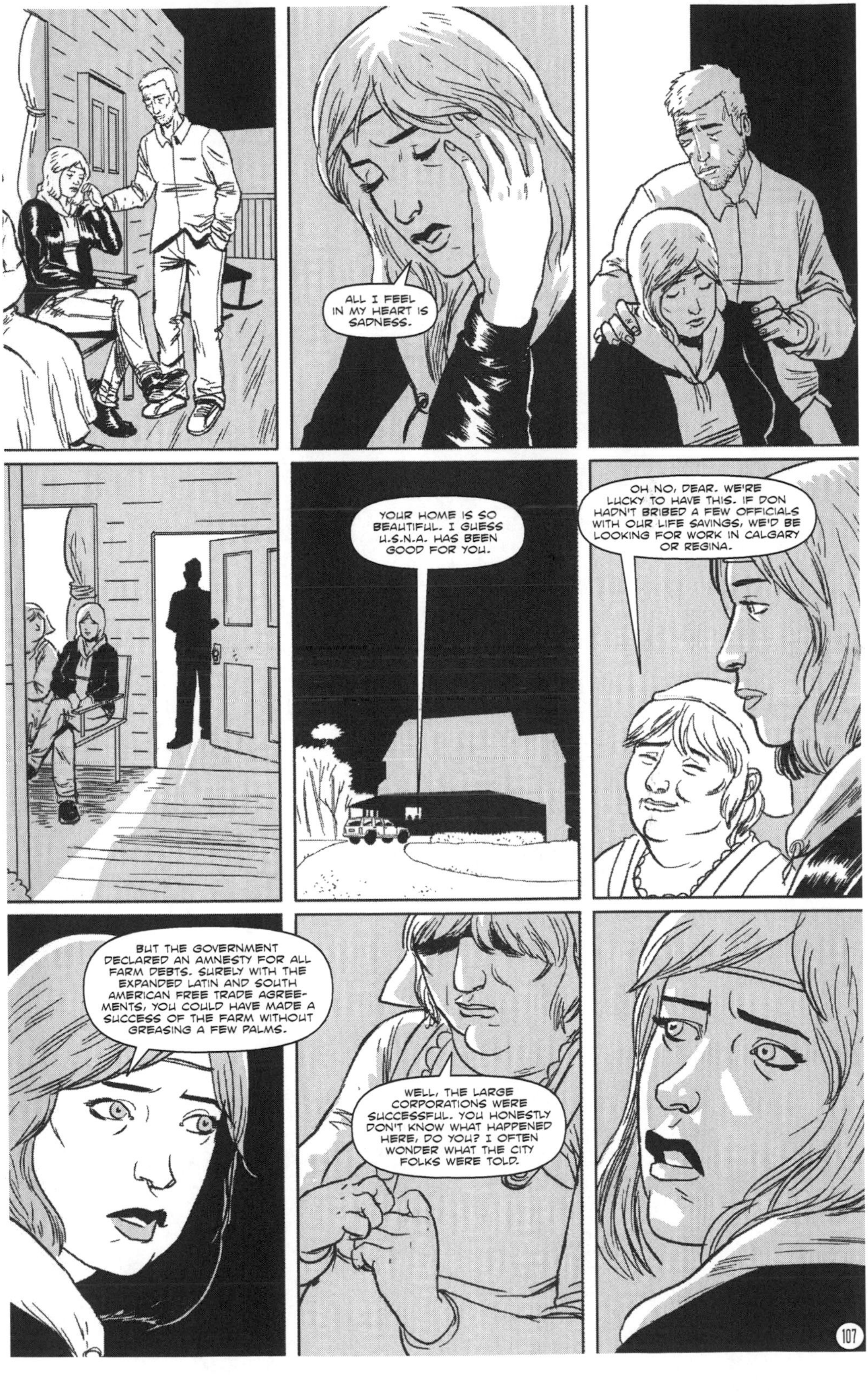
ALL I FEEL IN MY HEART IS SADNESS.
YOUR HOME IS SO BEAUTIFUL. I GUESS U.S.N.A. HAS BEEN GOOD FOR YOU.
OH NO, DEAR. WE'RE LUCKY TO HAVE THIS. IF DON HADN'T BRIBED A FEW OFFICIALS WITH OUR LIFE SAVINGS, WE'D BE LOOKING FOR WORK IN CALGARY OR REGINA.
BUT THE GOVERNMENT DECLARED AN AMNESTY FOR ALL FARM DEBTS. SURELY WITH THE EXPANDED LATIN AND SOUTH AMERICAN FREE TRADE AGREEMENTS, YOU COULD HAVE MADE A SUCCESS OF THE FARM WITHOUT GREASING A FEW PALMS.
WELL, THE LARGE CORPORATIONS WERE SUCCESSFUL. YOU HONESTLY DON'T KNOW WHAT HAPPENED HERE, DO YOU? I OFTEN WONDER WHAT THE CITY FOLKS WERE TOLD.

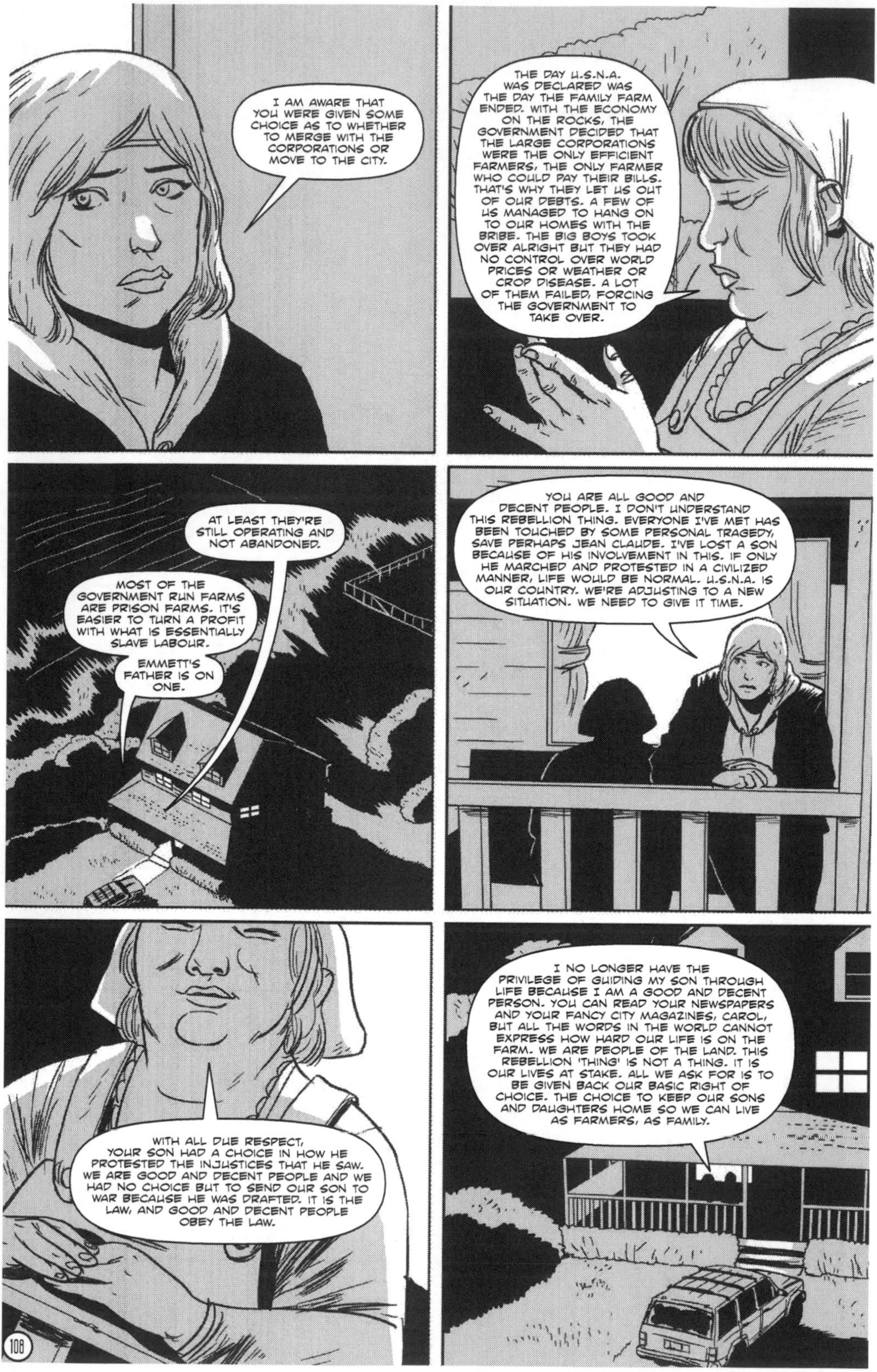
I AM AWARE THAT YOU WERE GIVEN SOME CHOICE AS TO WHETHER TO MERGE WITH THE CORPORATIONS OR MOVE TO THE CITY.
THE DAY U.S.N.A. WAS DECLARED WAS THE DAY THE FAMILY FARM ENDED. WITH THE ECONOMY ON THE ROCKS, THE GOVERNMENT DECIDED THAT THE LARGE CORPORATIONS WERE THE ONLY EFFICIENT FARMERS, THE ONLY FARMER WHO COULD PAY THEIR BILLS. THAT'S WHY THEY LET US OUT OF OUR DEBTS. A FEW OF US MANAGED TO HANG ON TO OUR HOMES WITH THE BRIBE. THE BIG BOYS TOOK OVER ALRIGHT BUT THEY HAD NO CONTROL OVER WORLD PRICES OR WEATHER OR CROP DISEASE. A LOT OF THEM FAILED, FORCING THE GOVERNMENT TO TAKE OVER.
AT LEAST THEY'RE STILL OPERATING AND NOT ABANDONED.
MOST OF THE GOVERNMENT RUN FARMS ARE PRISON FARMS. IT'S EASIER TO TURN A PROFIT WITH WHAT IS ESSENTIALLY SLAVE LABOUR.
EMMETT'S FATHER IS ON ONE.
YOU ARE ALL GOOD AND DECENT PEOPLE. I DON'T UNDERSTAND THIS REBELLION THING. EVERYONE I'VE MET HAS BEEN TOUCHED BY SOME PERSONAL TRAGEDY, SAVE PERHAPS JEAN CLAUDE. I'VE LOST A SON BECAUSE OF HIS INVOLVEMENT IN THIS. IF ONLY HE MARCHED AND PROTESTED IN A CIVILIZED MANNER, LIFE WOULD BE NORMAL. U.S.N.A. IS OUR COUNTRY. WE'RE ADJUSTING TO A NEW SITUATION. WE NEED TO GIVE IT TIME.
WITH ALL DUE RESPECT, YOUR SON HAD A CHOICE IN HOW HE PROTESTED THE INJUSTICES THAT HE SAW. WE ARE GOOD AND DECENT PEOPLE AND WE HAD NO CHOICE BUT TO SEND OUR SON TO WAR BECAUSE HE WAS DRAFTED. IT IS THE LAW, AND GOOD AND DECENT PEOPLE OBEY THE LAW.
I NO LONGER HAVE THE PRIVILEGE OF GUIDING MY SON THROUGH LIFE BECAUSE I AM A GOOD AND DECENT PERSON. YOU CAN READ YOUR NEWSPAPERS AND YOUR FANCY CITY MAGAZINES, CAROL, BUT ALL THE WORDS IN THE WORLD CANNOT EXPRESS HOW HARD OUR LIFE IS ON THE FARM. WE ARE PEOPLE OF THE LAND. THIS REBELLION 'THING' IS NOT A THING. IT IS OUR LIVES AT STAKE. ALL WE ASK FOR IS TO BE GIVEN BACK OUR BASIC RIGHT OF CHOICE. THE CHOICE TO KEEP OUR SONS AND DAUGHTERS HOME SO WE CAN LIVE AS FARMERS, AS FAMILY.

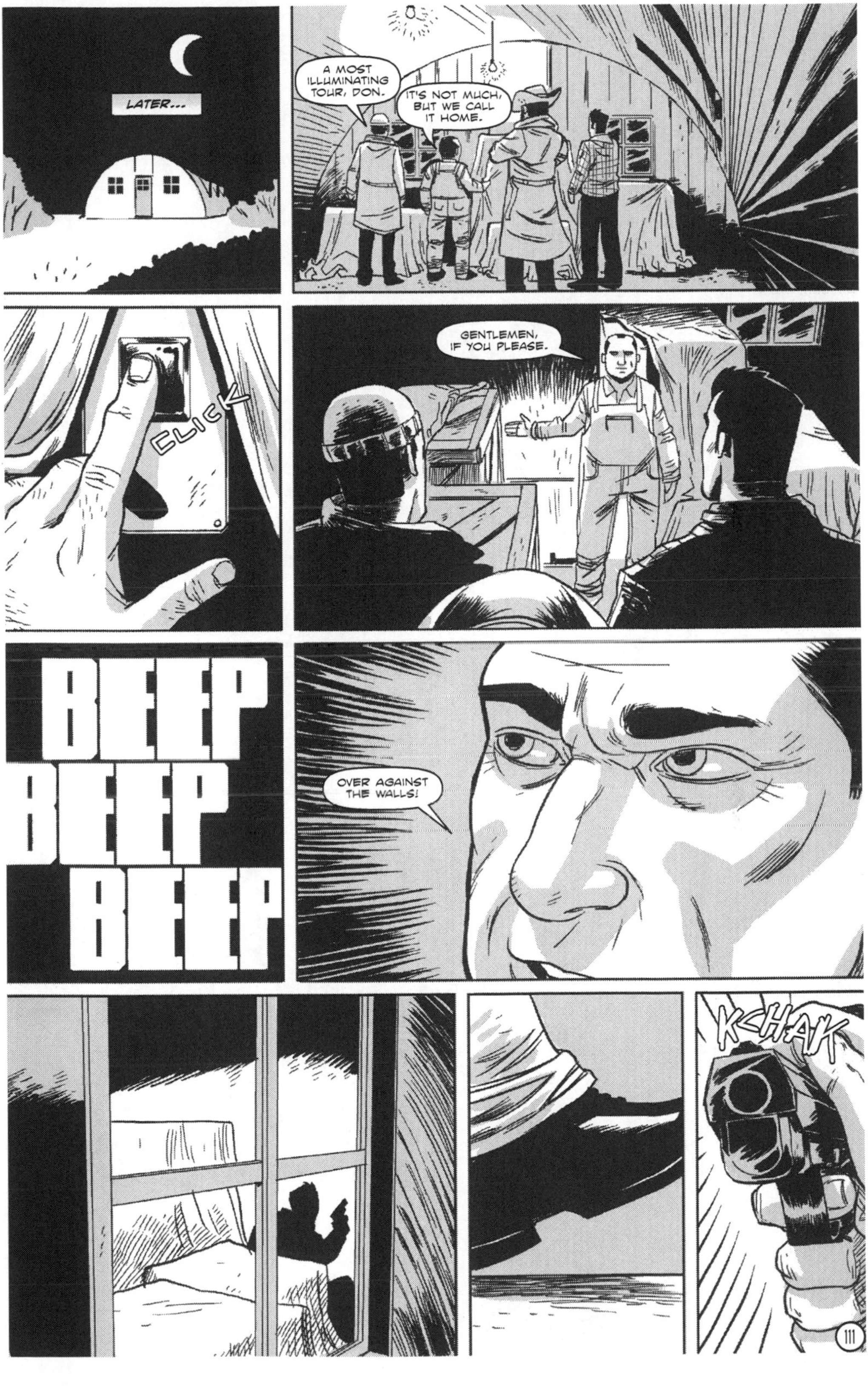
LATER...
A MOST ILLUMINATING TOUR, DON.
IT'S NOT MUCH, BUT WE CALL IT HOME.
CLICK
GENTLEMEN, IF YOU PLEASE.
BEEP BEEP BEEP
OVER AGAINST THE WALLS!
KCHAK

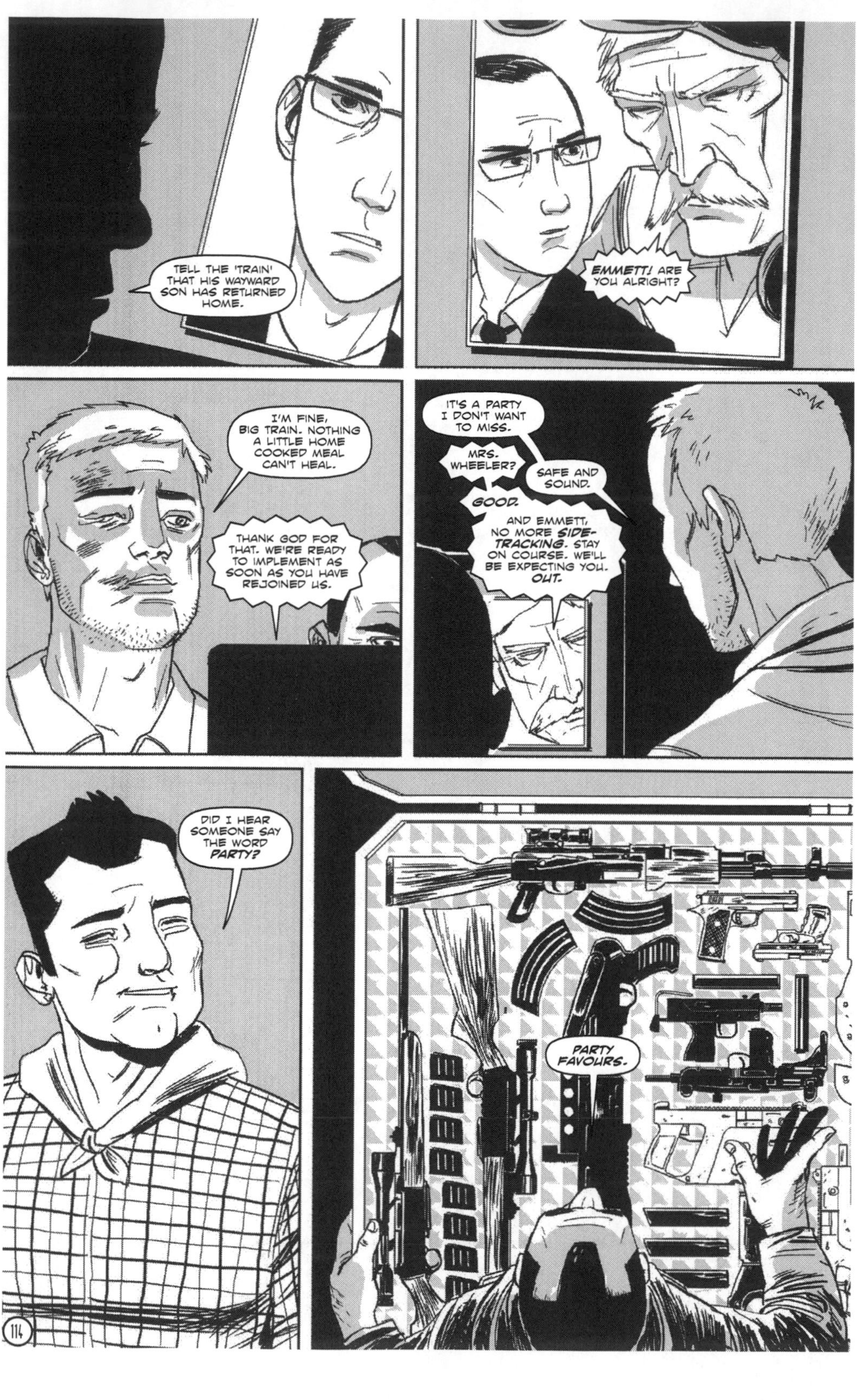
TELL THE 'TRAIN' THAT HIS WAYWARD SON HAS RETURNED HOME.
EMMETT! ARE YOU ALRIGHT?
I'M FINE, BIG TRAIN. NOTHING A LITTLE HOME COOKED MEAL CAN'T HEAL.
THANK GOD FOR THAT. WE'RE READY TO IMPLEMENT AS SOON AS YOU HAVE REJOINED US.
IT'S A PARTY I DON'T WANT TO MISS.
MRS. WHEELER?
SAFE AND SOUND.
GOOD.
AND EMMETT, NO MORE SIDE-TRACKING. STAY ON COURSE. WE'LL BE EXPECTING YOU. OUT.
DID I HEAR SOMEONE SAY THE WORD PARTY?
PARTY FAVOURS.

PEGGY?

HMM?

MY SON IS ONLY SIXTEEN. HE NEEDS A *HOME*. EVERYTHING IS HAPPENING SO QUICKLY. WE NEED A PLACE TO STAY FOR A WHILE, A PLACE FOR A YOUNG MAN TO *GROW UP*.

NOT HERE, CAROL.

BUT...

LISTEN TO ME. YOU'LL BE *SAFEST* WITH EMMETT AND THE MEN. TRUST THEM AS IF YOUR LIFE DEPENDS ON IT... BECAUSE IT *DOES*.

OUR HOME IS *NOT SAFE* FOR YOUR SON, CAROL. THIS PLACE IS LIKE A LIGHT BULB. IT'S BEEN BURNING BRIGHT FOR A LONG TIME AND FOR THAT WE ARE THANKFUL. BUT IT'S GOING TO *BURN OUT*, MAYBE SOON. DON'T MAKE THE MISTAKE OF JUDGING THIS PLACE BY ITS SUGAR COATING. THERE IS *MORE* TO ALL OF THIS THAN YOU HAVE BEEN LED TO BELIEVE. BE THANKFUL OF YOUR *IGNORANCE*. IT MAY SAVE YOUR LIFE.

OH, SORRY. DID YOU NEED A MOMENT ALONE?

NO, IT'S OKAY.

I'M JUST GOING TO CURL UP IN THE CORNER BY THE FIRE. YOU TAKE THE GUEST ROOM. YOU'LL BE MORE COMFORTABLE.

I'M SORRY EMMETT. THIS IS ALL SO NEW, SO STRANGE.

NO NEED TO APOLOGIZE, CAROL. WHEN I THINK OF ALL YOU AND CARTER HAVE BEEN THROUGH THE LAST FEW WEEKS... YOU SHOULD GET SOME SLEEP.

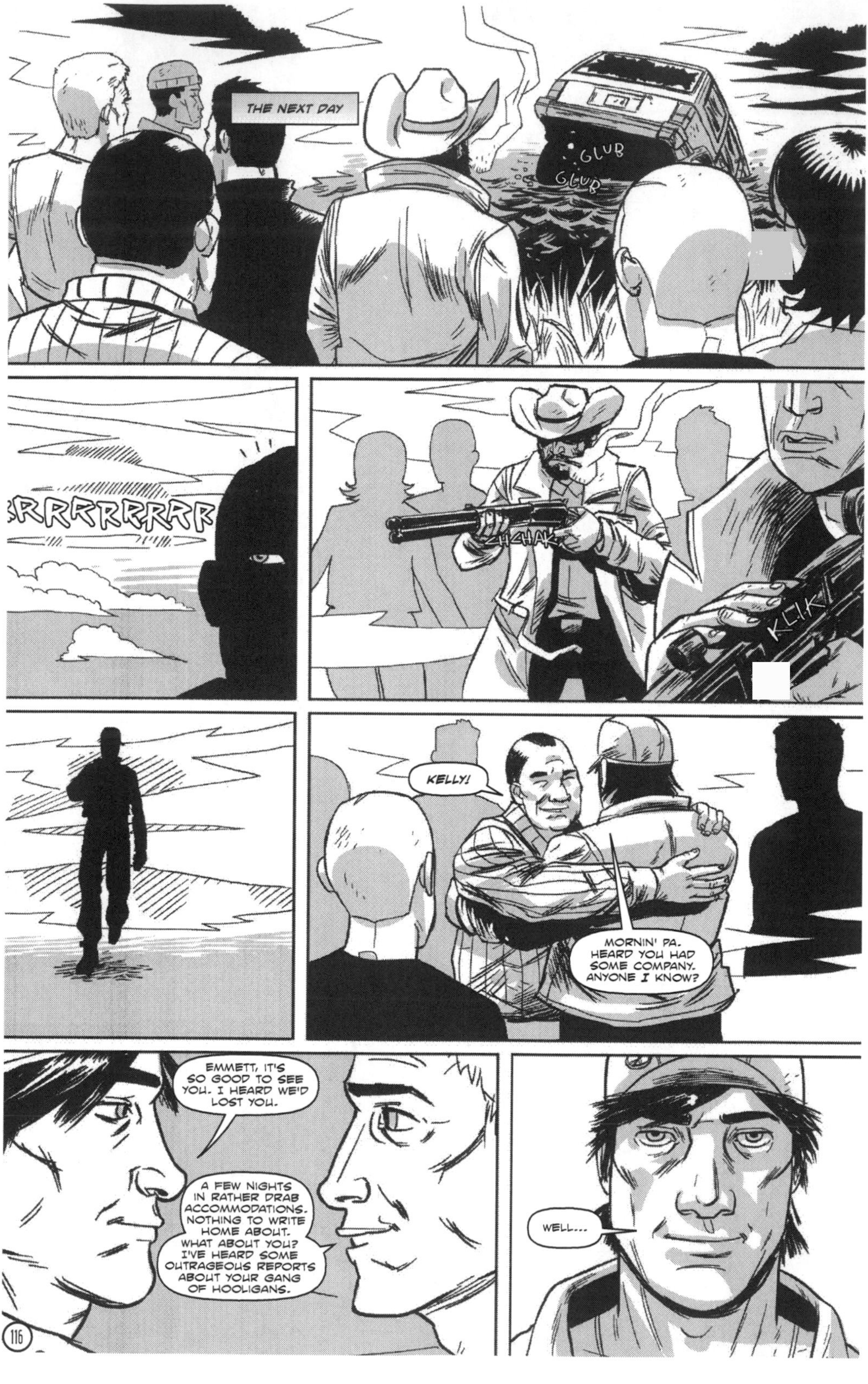
THE NEXT DAY
GLUB
GLUB
RRRRRRRRRRR
ZHCHAK
KLIK
KELLY!
MORNIN' PA. HEARD YOU HAD SOME COMPANY. ANYONE I KNOW?
EMMETT, IT'S SO GOOD TO SEE YOU. I HEARD WE'D LOST YOU.
A FEW NIGHTS IN RATHER DRAB ACCOMMODATIONS. NOTHING TO WRITE HOME ABOUT. WHAT ABOUT YOU? I'VE HEARD SOME OUTRAGEOUS REPORTS ABOUT YOUR GANG OF HOOLIGANS.
WELL...

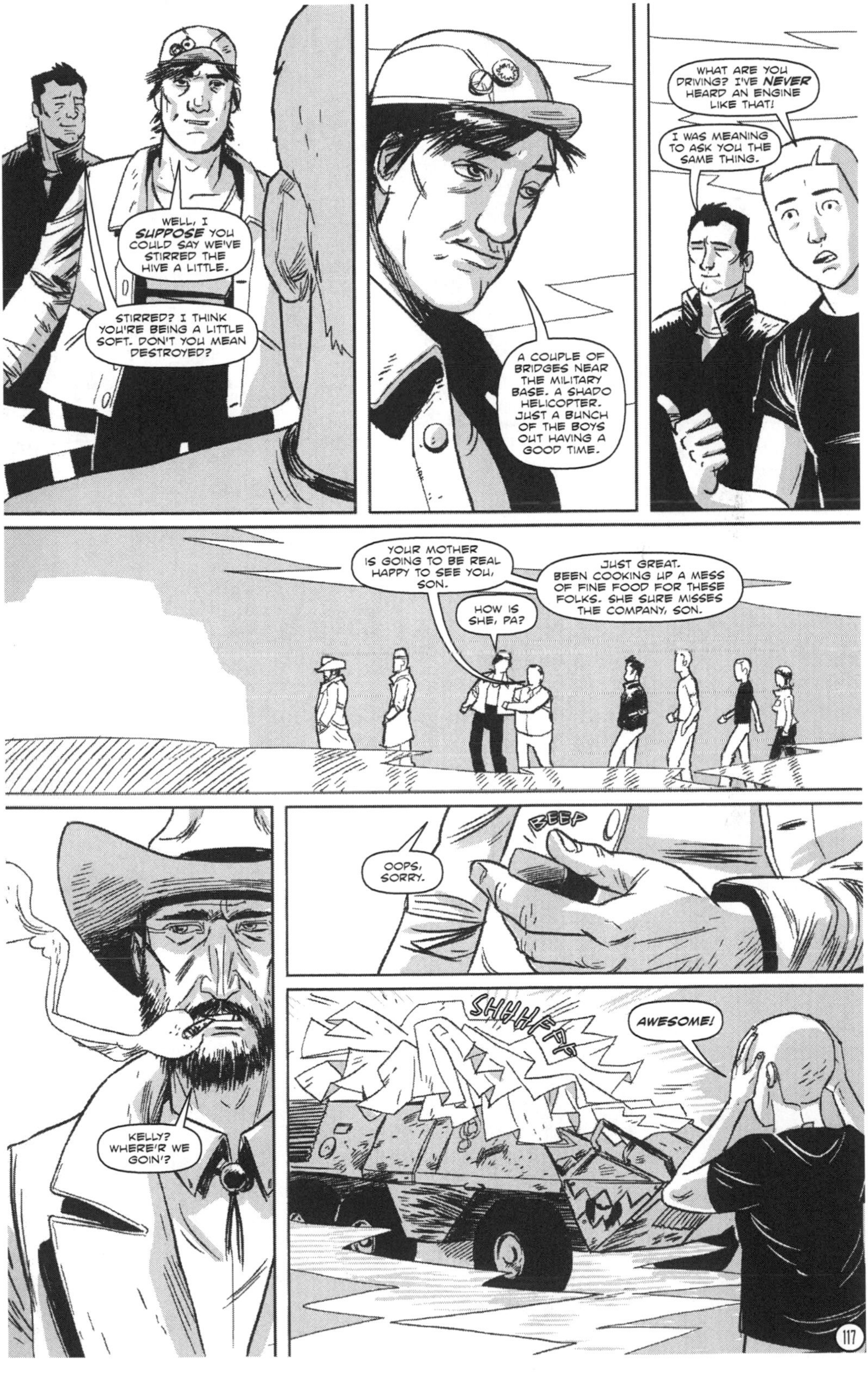
WELL, I SUPPOSE YOU COULD SAY WE'VE STIRRED THE HIVE A LITTLE.
STIRRED? I THINK YOU'RE BEING A LITTLE SOFT. DON'T YOU MEAN DESTROYED?
A COUPLE OF BRIDGES NEAR THE MILITARY BASE. A SHADO HELICOPTER. JUST A BUNCH OF THE BOYS OUT HAVING A GOOD TIME.
WHAT ARE YOU DRIVING? I'VE NEVER HEARD AN ENGINE LIKE THAT!
I WAS MEANING TO ASK YOU THE SAME THING.
YOUR MOTHER IS GOING TO BE REAL HAPPY TO SEE YOU, SON.
HOW IS SHE, PA?
JUST GREAT. BEEN COOKING UP A MESS OF FINE FOOD FOR THESE FOLKS. SHE SURE MISSES THE COMPANY, SON.
KELLY? WHERE'R WE GOIN'?
BEEP
OOPS, SORRY.
SHHHFFT
AWESOME!

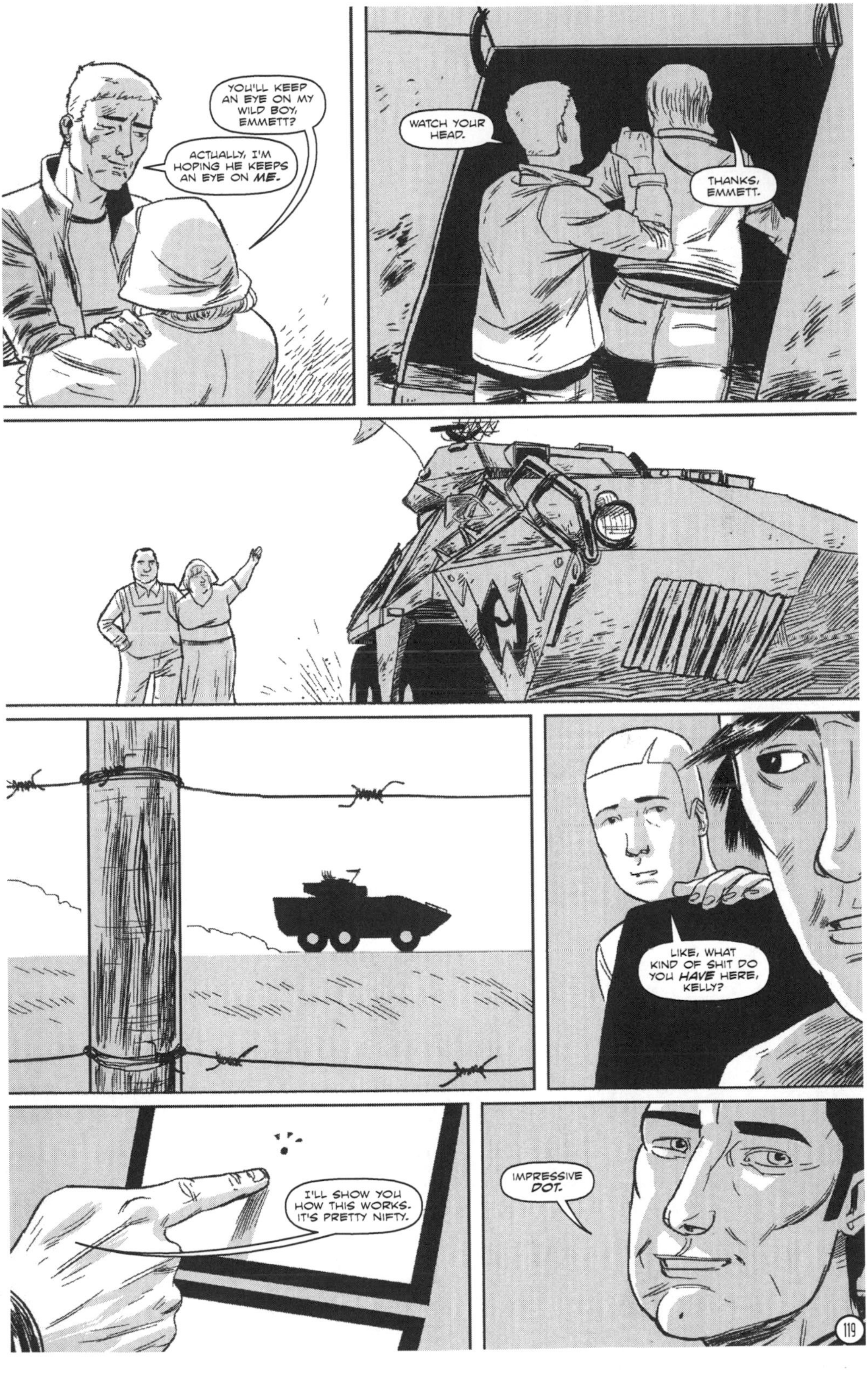
YOU'LL KEEP AN EYE ON MY WILD BOY, EMMETT?
ACTUALLY, I'M HOPING HE KEEPS AN EYE ON *ME*.
WATCH YOUR HEAD.
THANKS, EMMETT.
LIKE, WHAT KIND OF SHIT DO YOU *HAVE* HERE, KELLY?
I'LL SHOW YOU HOW THIS WORKS. IT'S PRETTY NIFTY.
IMPRESSIVE *DOT*.

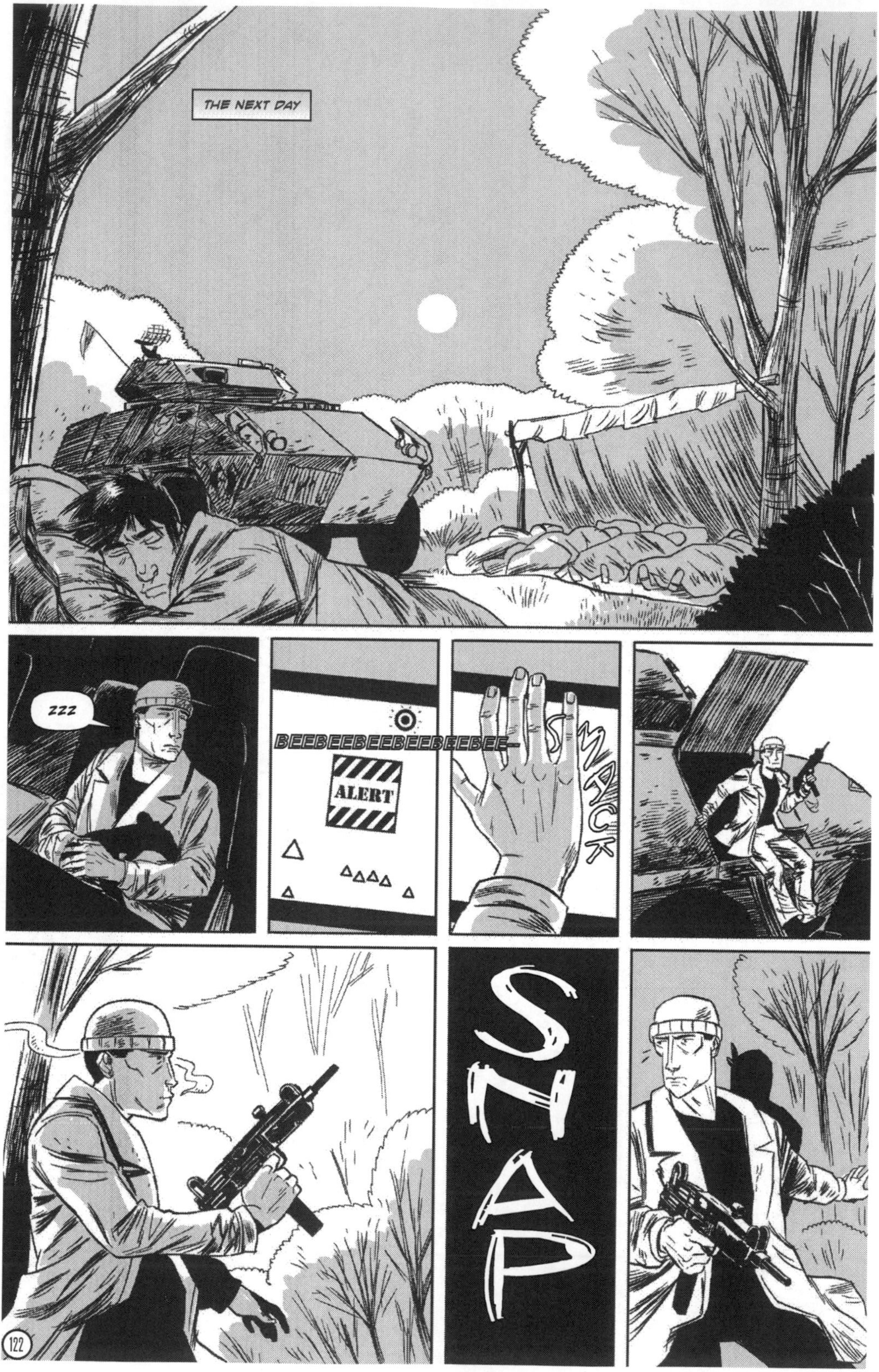
THE NEXT DAY
ZZZ
BEEBEEBEEBEEBEEBEE—
ALERT
SMACK
SNAP

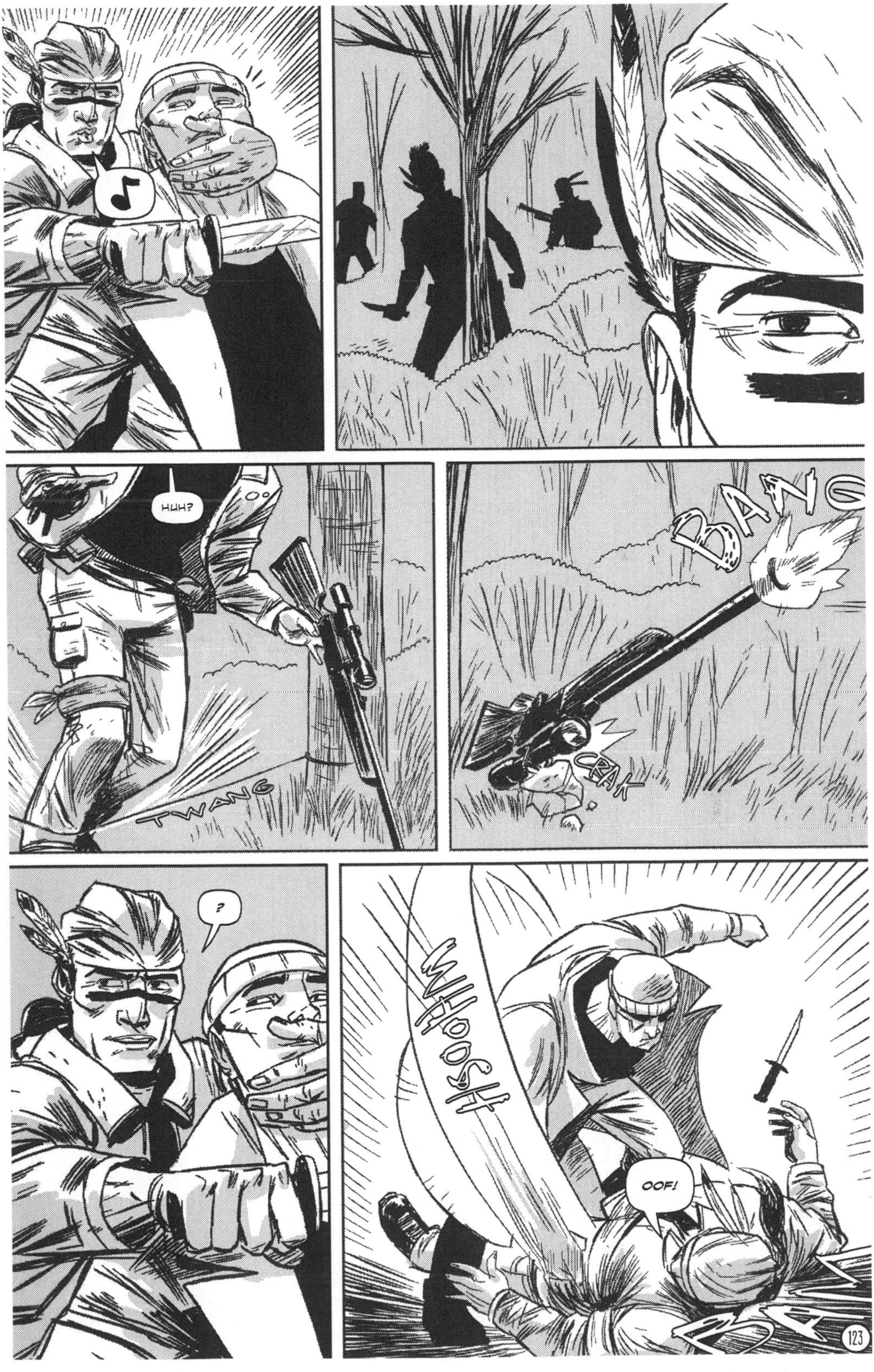
♪
HUH?
TWANG
BANG
CRAK
?
WHOOSH
OOF!

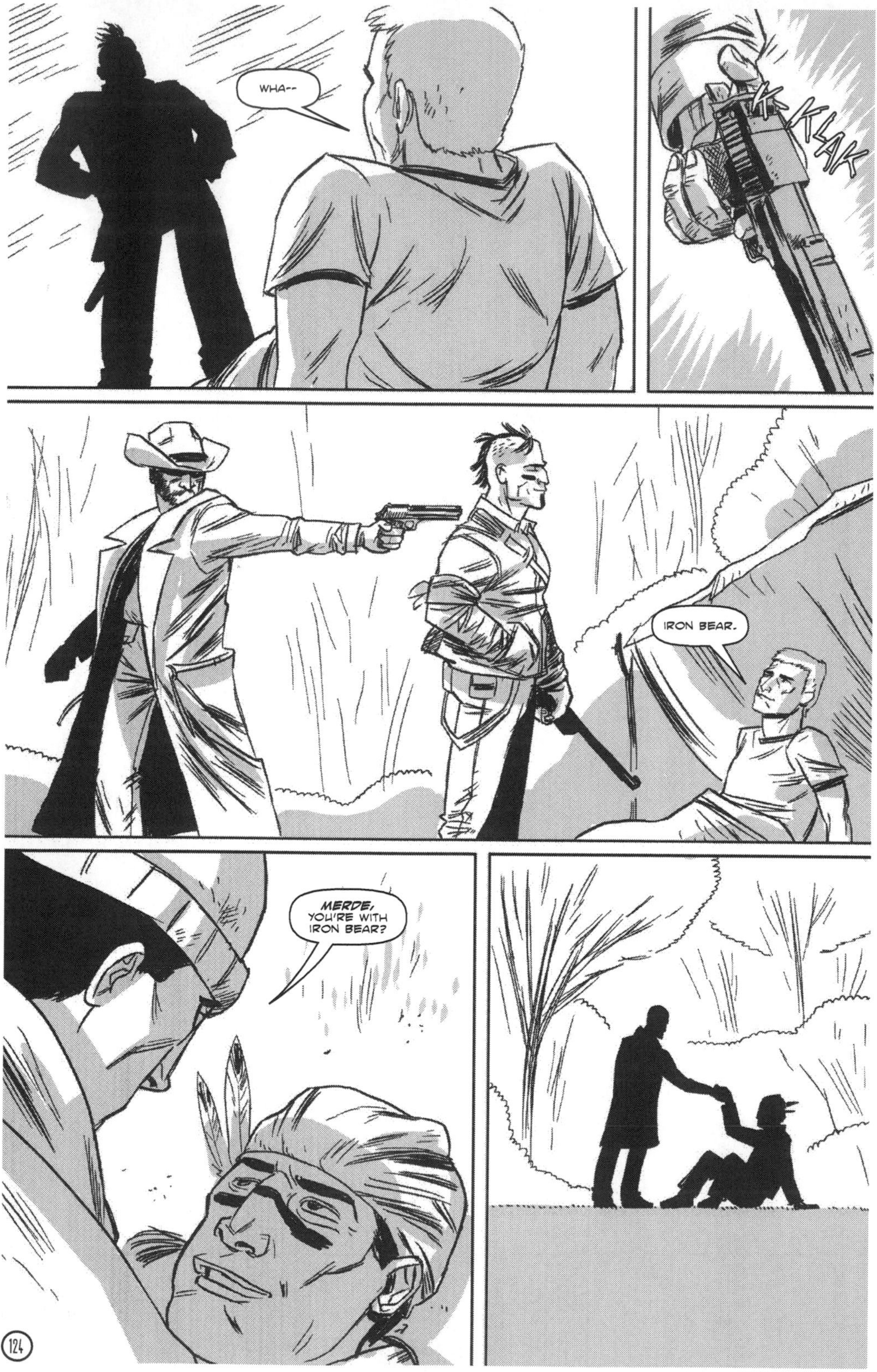
WHA--
K-KLAK
IRON BEAR.
MERDE, YOU'RE WITH IRON BEAR?

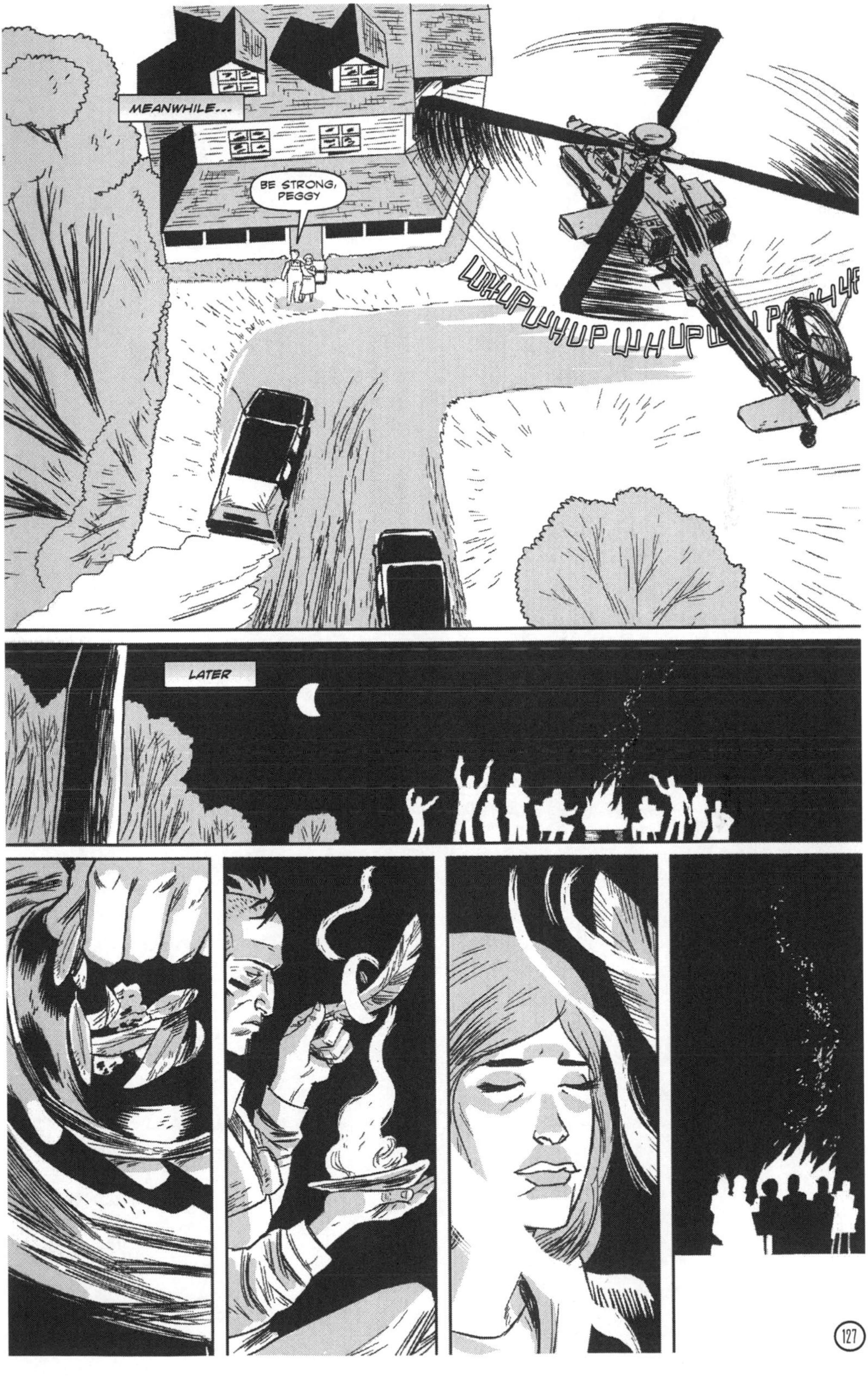
MEANWHILE...
BE STRONG, PEGGY
WHUPWHUPWHUP
LATER

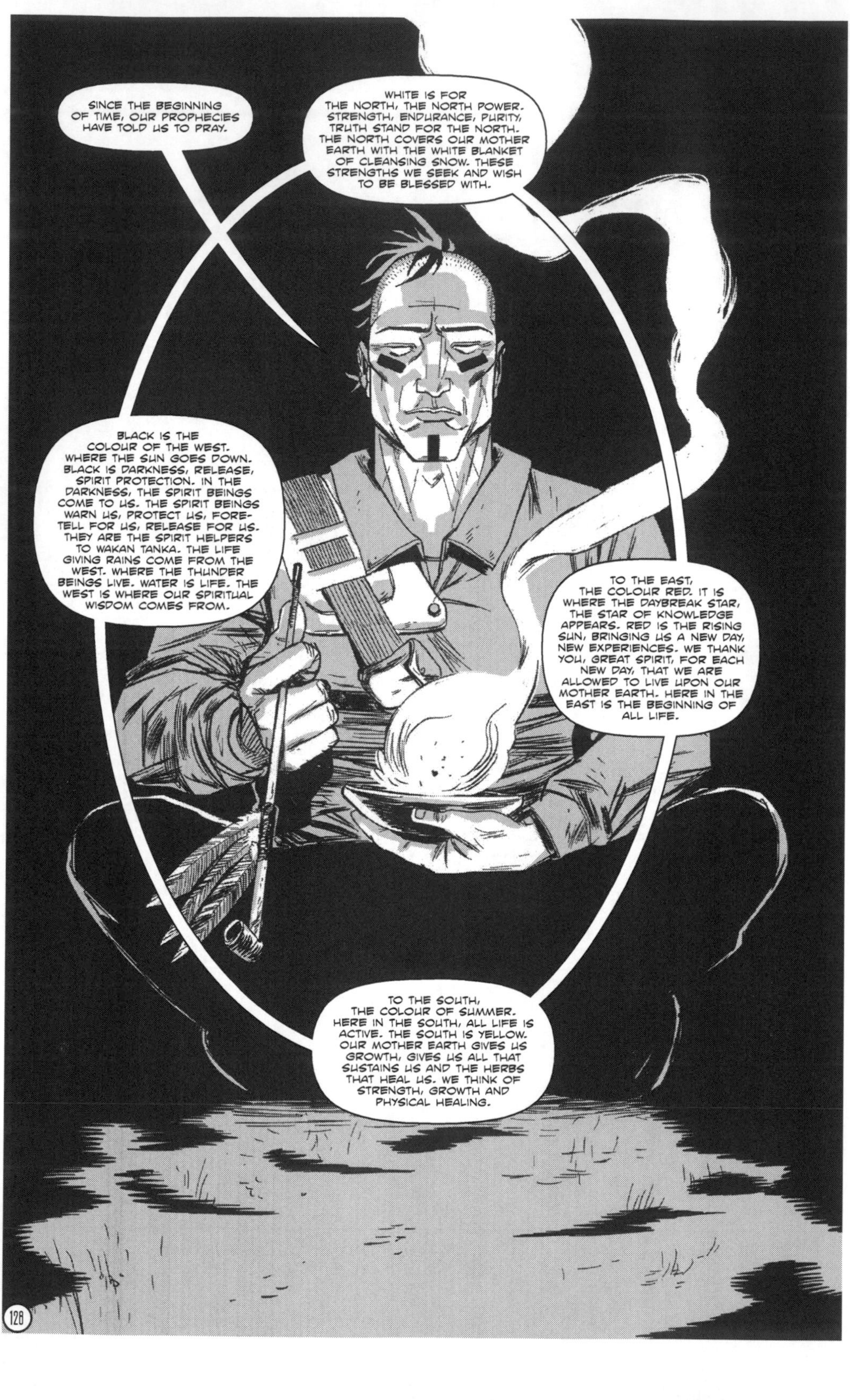
SINCE THE BEGINNING OF TIME, OUR PROPHECIES HAVE TOLD US TO PRAY.
WHITE IS FOR THE NORTH, THE NORTH POWER. STRENGTH, ENDURANCE, PURITY, TRUTH STAND FOR THE NORTH. THE NORTH COVERS OUR MOTHER EARTH WITH THE WHITE BLANKET OF CLEANSING SNOW. THESE STRENGTHS WE SEEK AND WISH TO BE BLESSED WITH.
BLACK IS THE COLOUR OF THE WEST. WHERE THE SUN GOES DOWN. BLACK IS DARKNESS, RELEASE, SPIRIT PROTECTION. IN THE DARKNESS, THE SPIRIT BEINGS COME TO US. THE SPIRIT BEINGS WARN US, PROTECT US, FORETELL FOR US, RELEASE FOR US. THEY ARE THE SPIRIT HELPERS TO WAKAN TANKA. THE LIFE GIVING RAINS COME FROM THE WEST. WHERE THE THUNDER BEINGS LIVE. WATER IS LIFE. THE WEST IS WHERE OUR SPIRITUAL WISDOM COMES FROM.
TO THE EAST, THE COLOUR RED. IT IS WHERE THE DAYBREAK STAR, THE STAR OF KNOWLEDGE APPEARS. RED IS THE RISING SUN, BRINGING US A NEW DAY, NEW EXPERIENCES. WE THANK YOU, GREAT SPIRIT, FOR EACH NEW DAY, THAT WE ARE ALLOWED TO LIVE UPON OUR MOTHER EARTH. HERE IN THE EAST IS THE BEGINNING OF ALL LIFE.
TO THE SOUTH, THE COLOUR OF SUMMER. HERE IN THE SOUTH, ALL LIFE IS ACTIVE. THE SOUTH IS YELLOW. OUR MOTHER EARTH GIVES US GROWTH, GIVES US ALL THAT SUSTAINS US AND THE HERBS THAT HEAL US. WE THINK OF STRENGTH, GROWTH AND PHYSICAL HEALING.

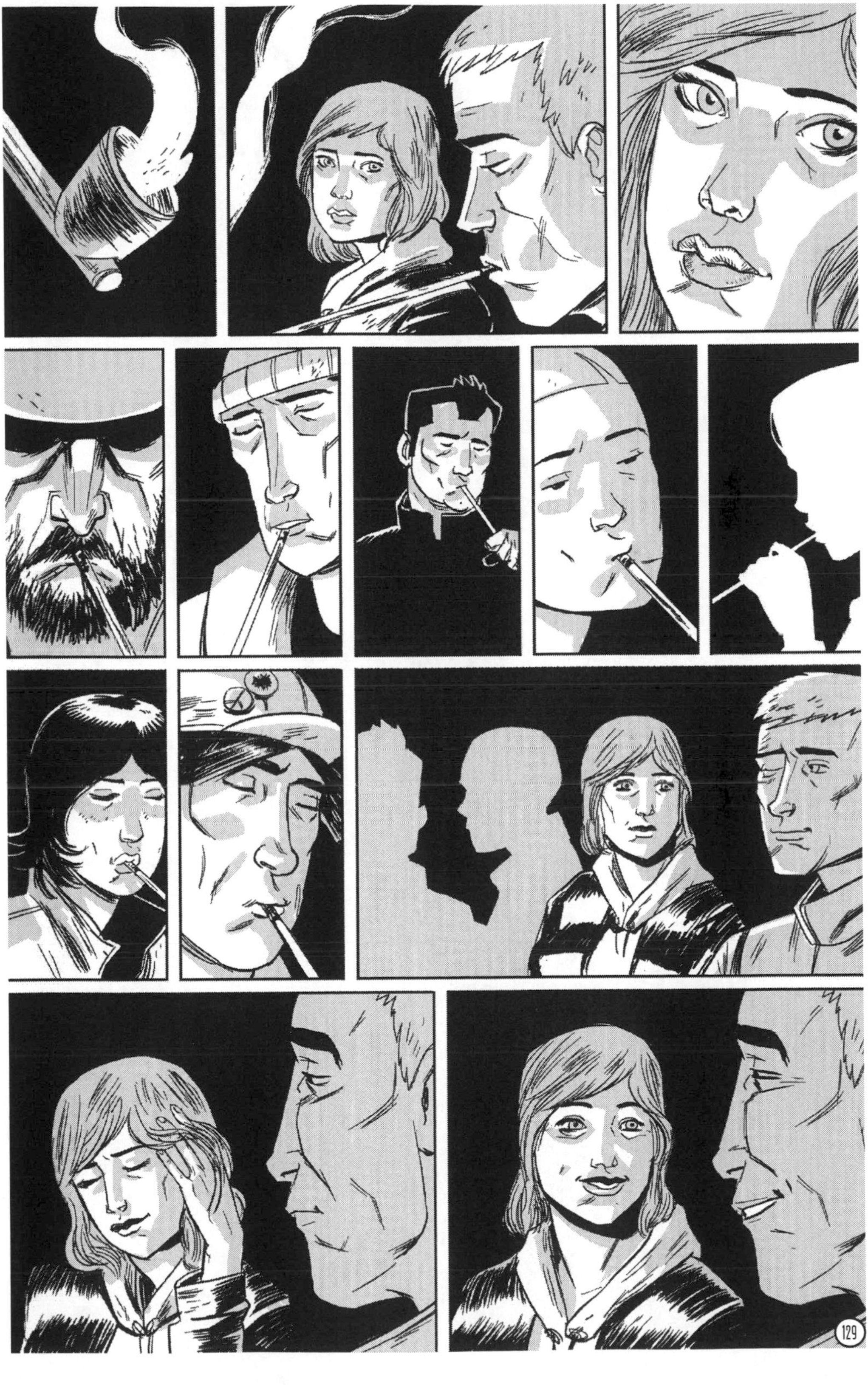

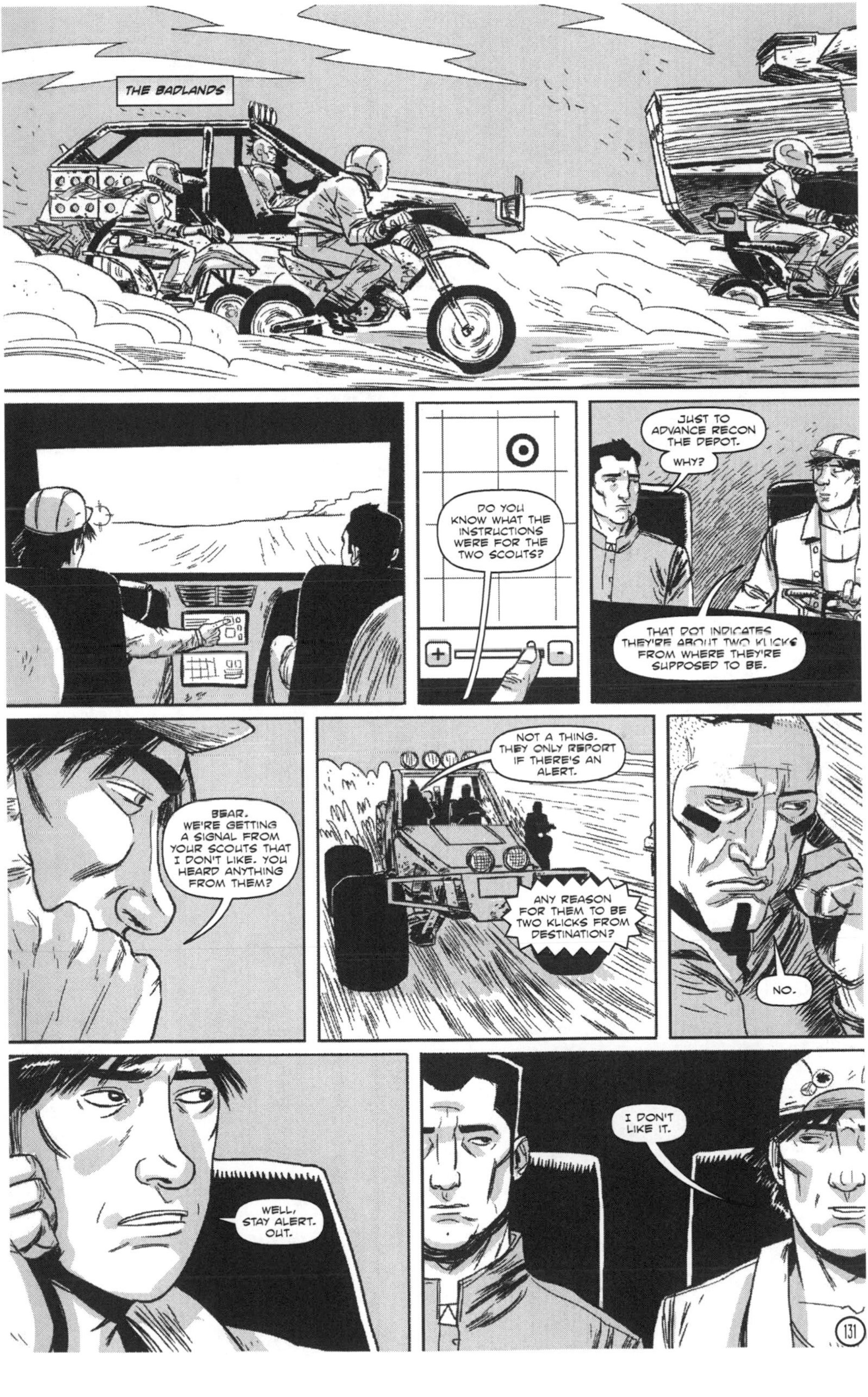
THE BADLANDS
DO YOU KNOW WHAT THE INSTRUCTIONS WERE FOR THE TWO SCOUTS?
JUST TO ADVANCE RECON THE DEPOT.
WHY?
THAT DOT INDICATES THEY'RE ABOUT TWO KLICKS FROM WHERE THEY'RE SUPPOSED TO BE.
BEAR. WE'RE GETTING A SIGNAL FROM YOUR SCOUTS THAT I DON'T LIKE. YOU HEARD ANYTHING FROM THEM?
NOT A THING. THEY ONLY REPORT IF THERE'S AN ALERT.
ANY REASON FOR THEM TO BE TWO KLICKS FROM DESTINATION?
NO.
WELL, STAY ALERT. OUT.
I DON'T LIKE IT.

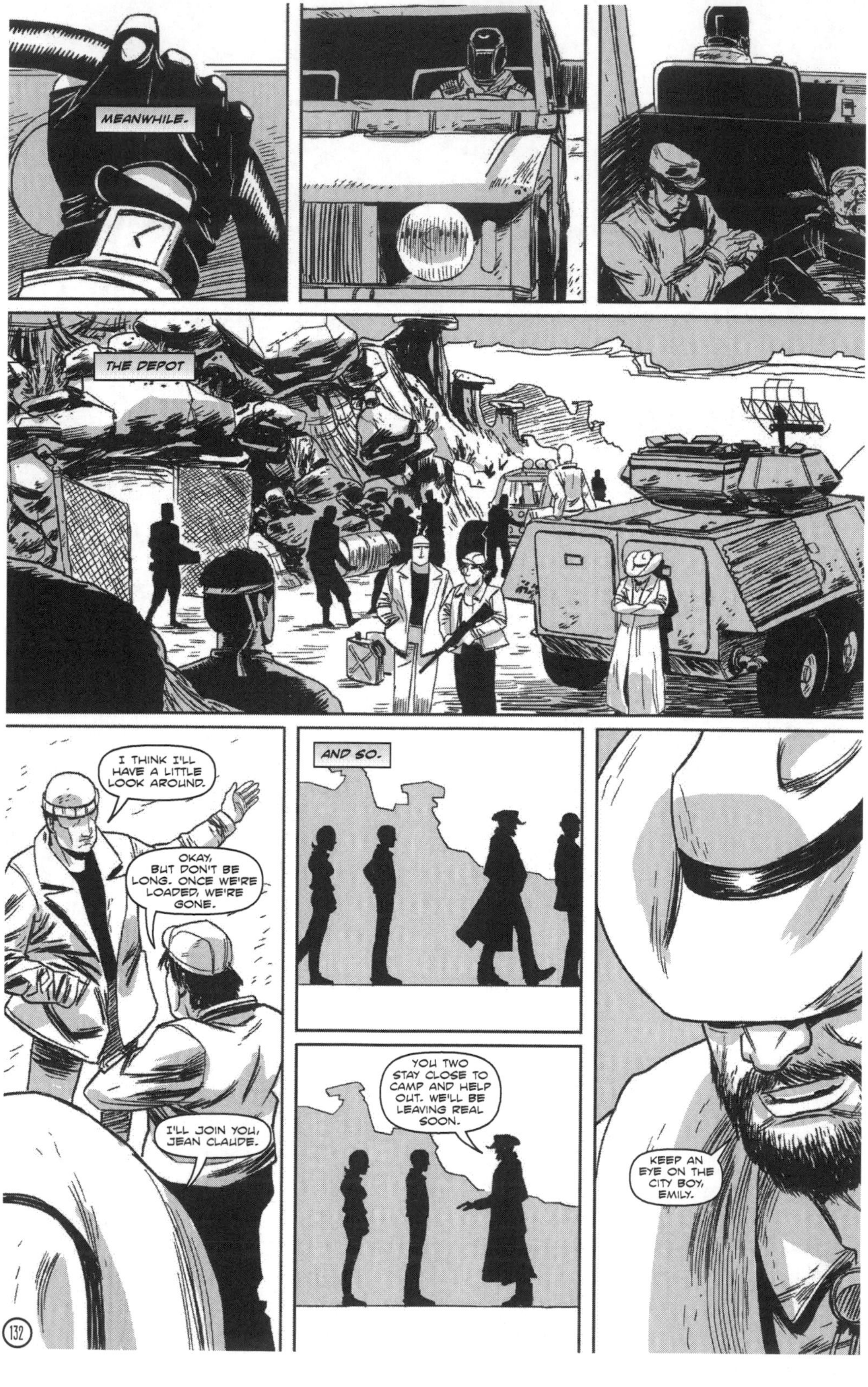
MEANWHILE.
THE DEPOT
I THINK I'LL HAVE A LITTLE LOOK AROUND.
OKAY, BUT DON'T BE LONG. ONCE WE'RE LOADED, WE'RE GONE.
I'LL JOIN YOU, JEAN CLAUDE.
AND SO.
YOU TWO STAY CLOSE TO CAMP AND HELP OUT. WE'LL BE LEAVING REAL SOON.
KEEP AN EYE ON THE CITY BOY, EMILY.

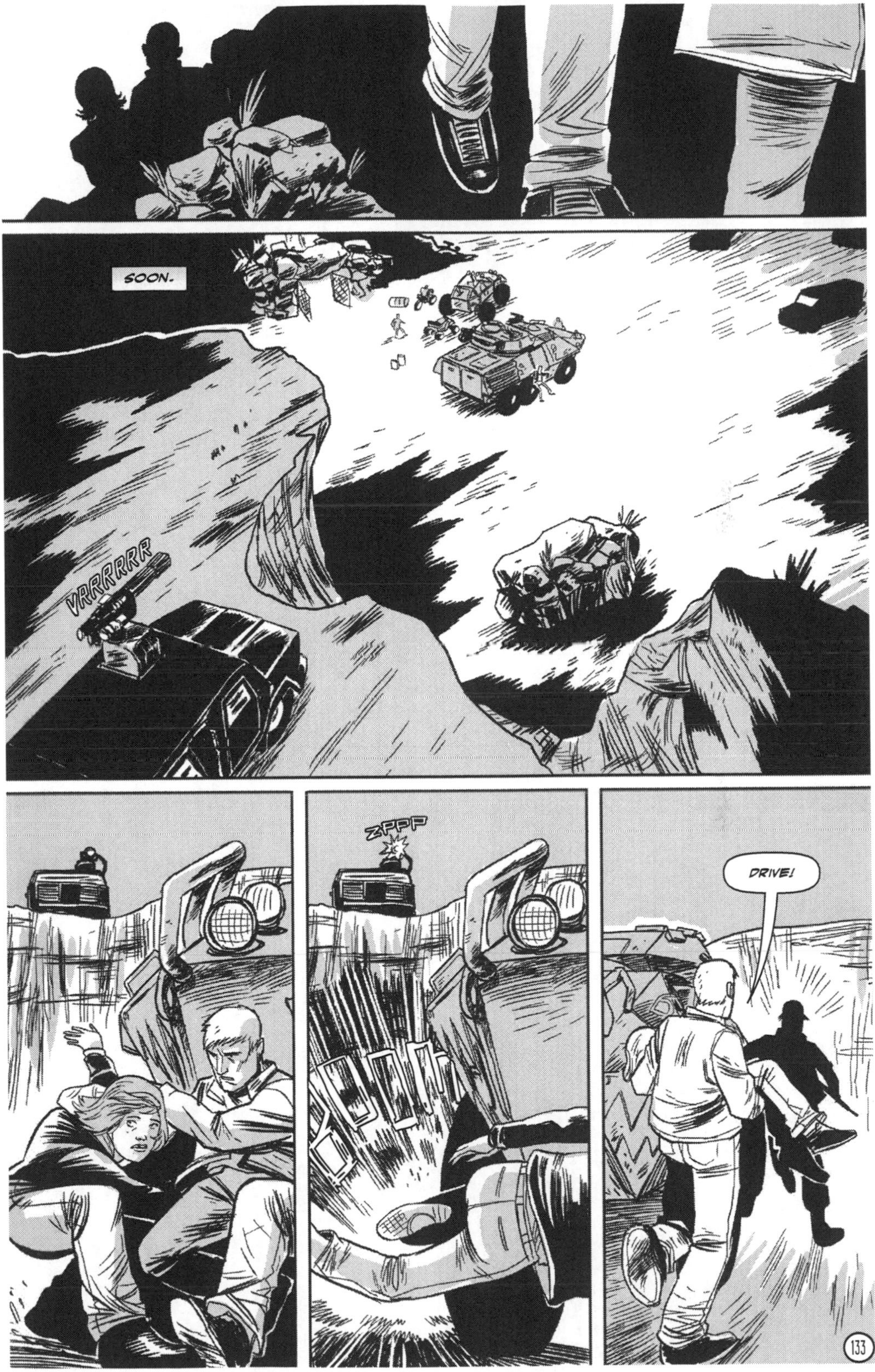
SOON.
VRRRRRRR
ZPPP
DRIVE!

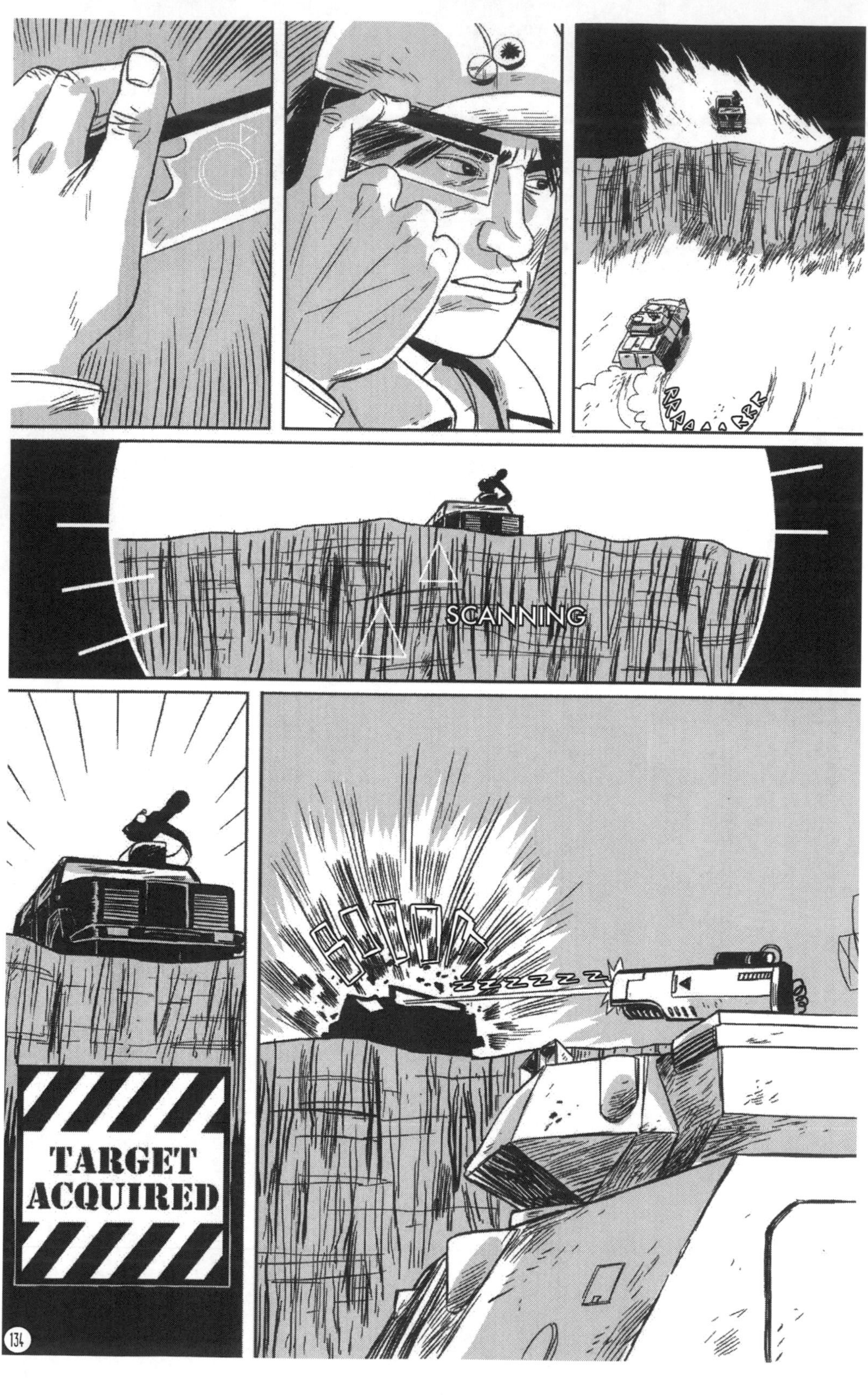
RRRAAAARRK
SCANNING
TARGET ACQUIRED
ZZZZZZZZ

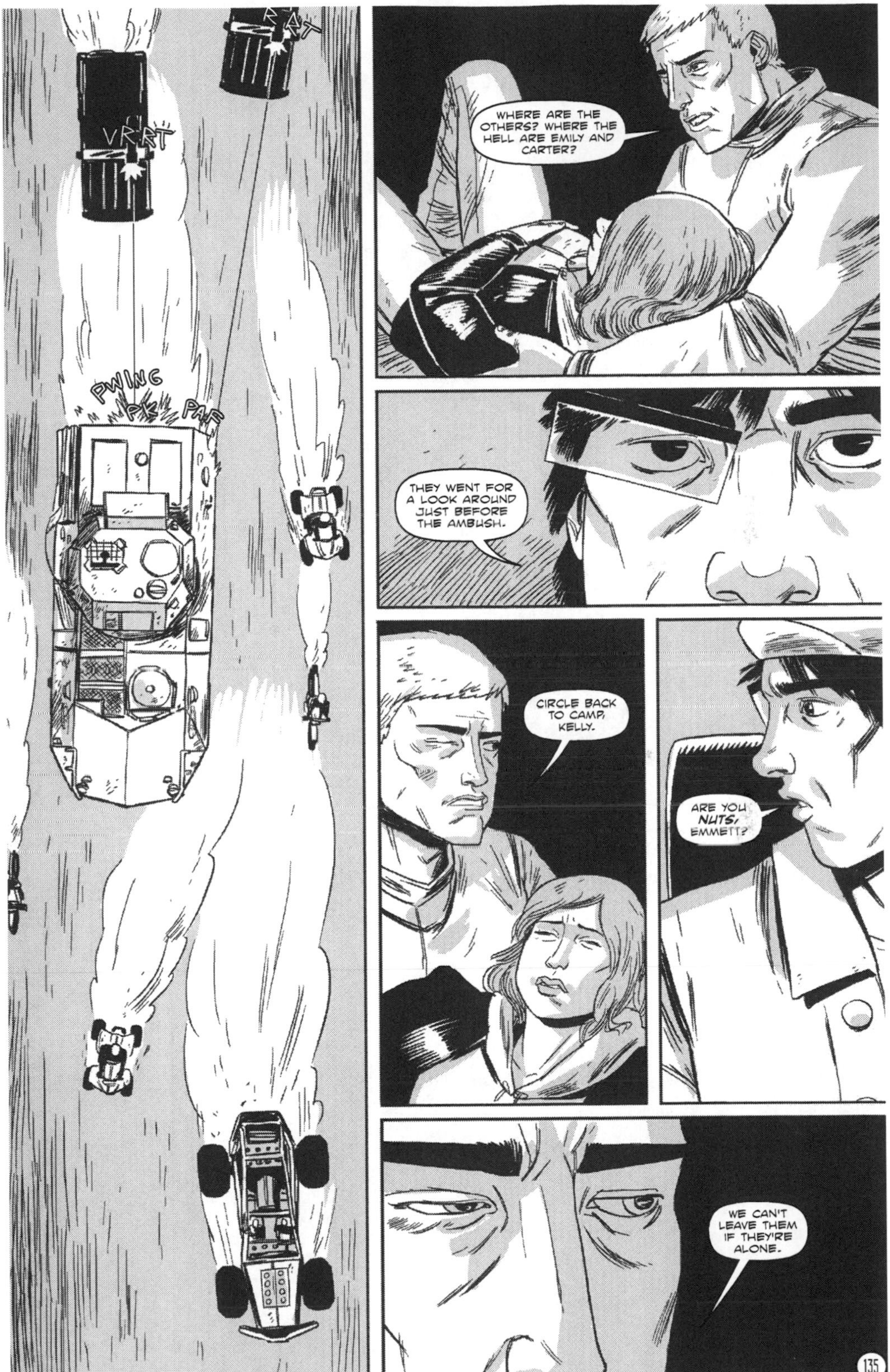
RAT
VRRT
PWING
PK
PAF
WHERE ARE THE OTHERS? WHERE THE HELL ARE EMILY AND CARTER?
THEY WENT FOR A LOOK AROUND JUST BEFORE THE AMBUSH.
CIRCLE BACK TO CAMP, KELLY.
ARE YOU NUTS, EMMETT?
WE CAN'T LEAVE THEM IF THEY'RE ALONE.

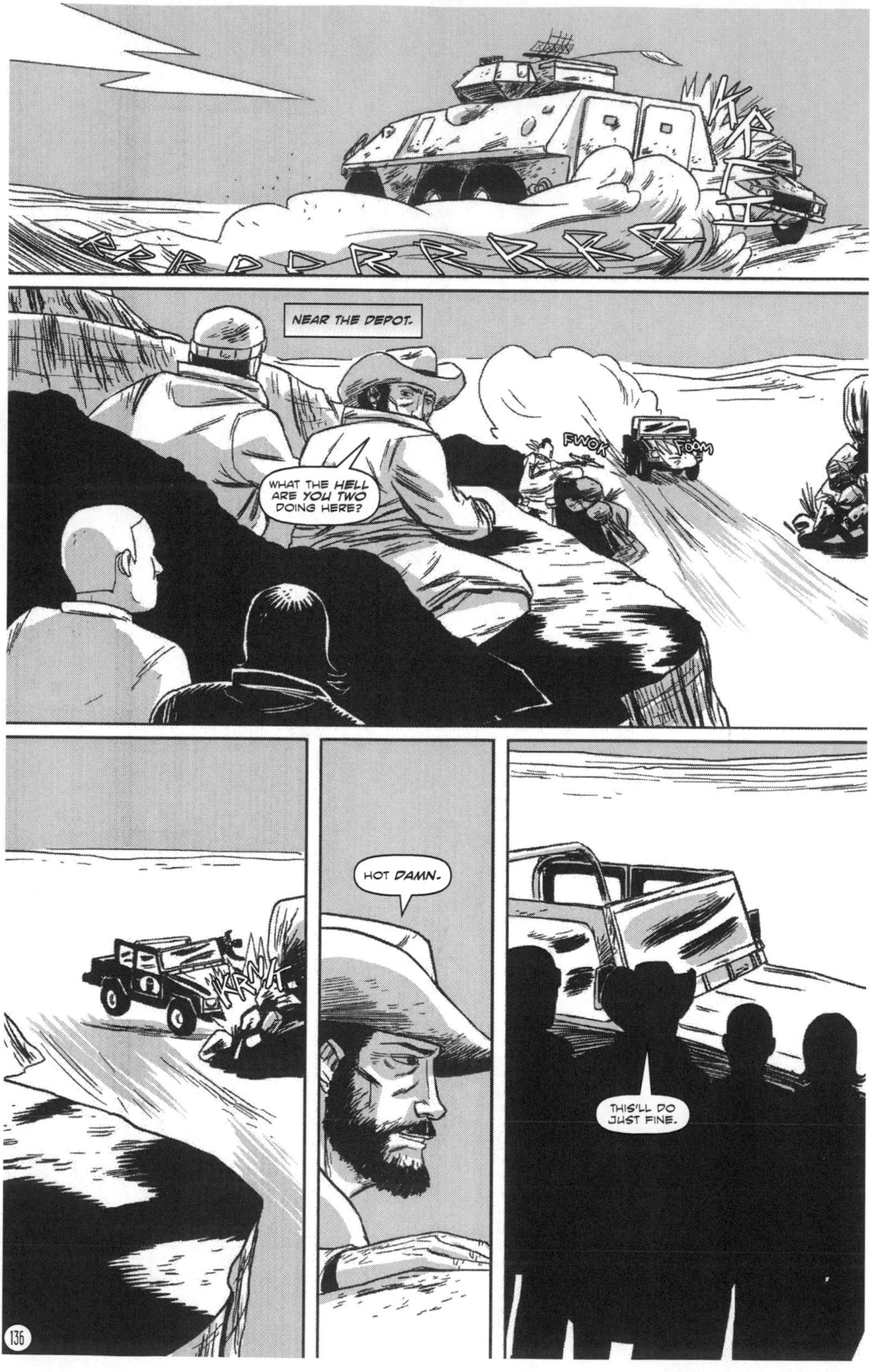
NEAR THE DEPOT.
WHAT THE HELL ARE YOU TWO DOING HERE?
FWOK
FOOM
KRNK
HOT DAMN.
THIS'LL DO JUST FINE.

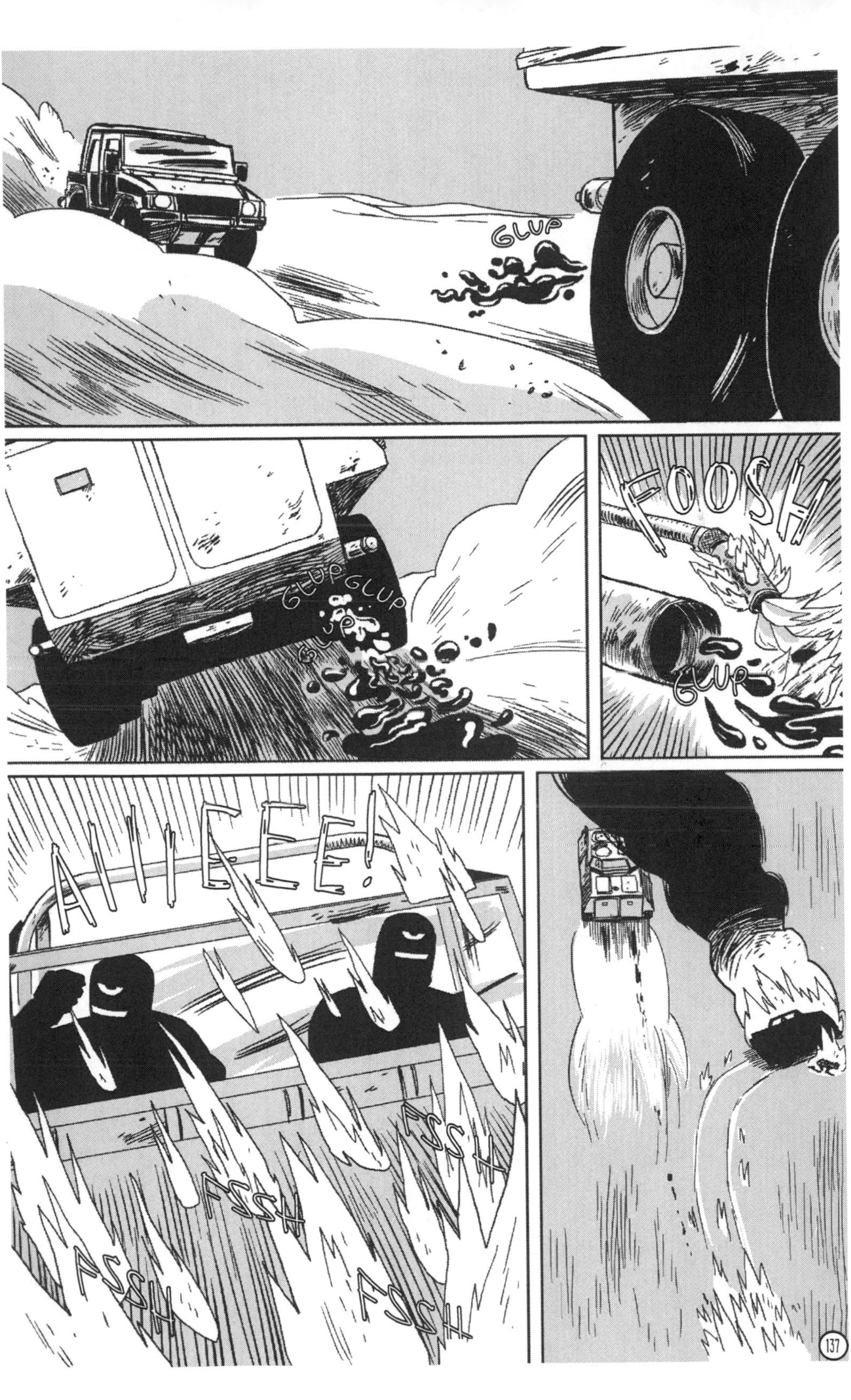
GLUP
GLUP GLUP
GLUP
GLUP
FOOSH
GLUP
AIIEEE!
FSSH
FSSH
FSSH
FSSH

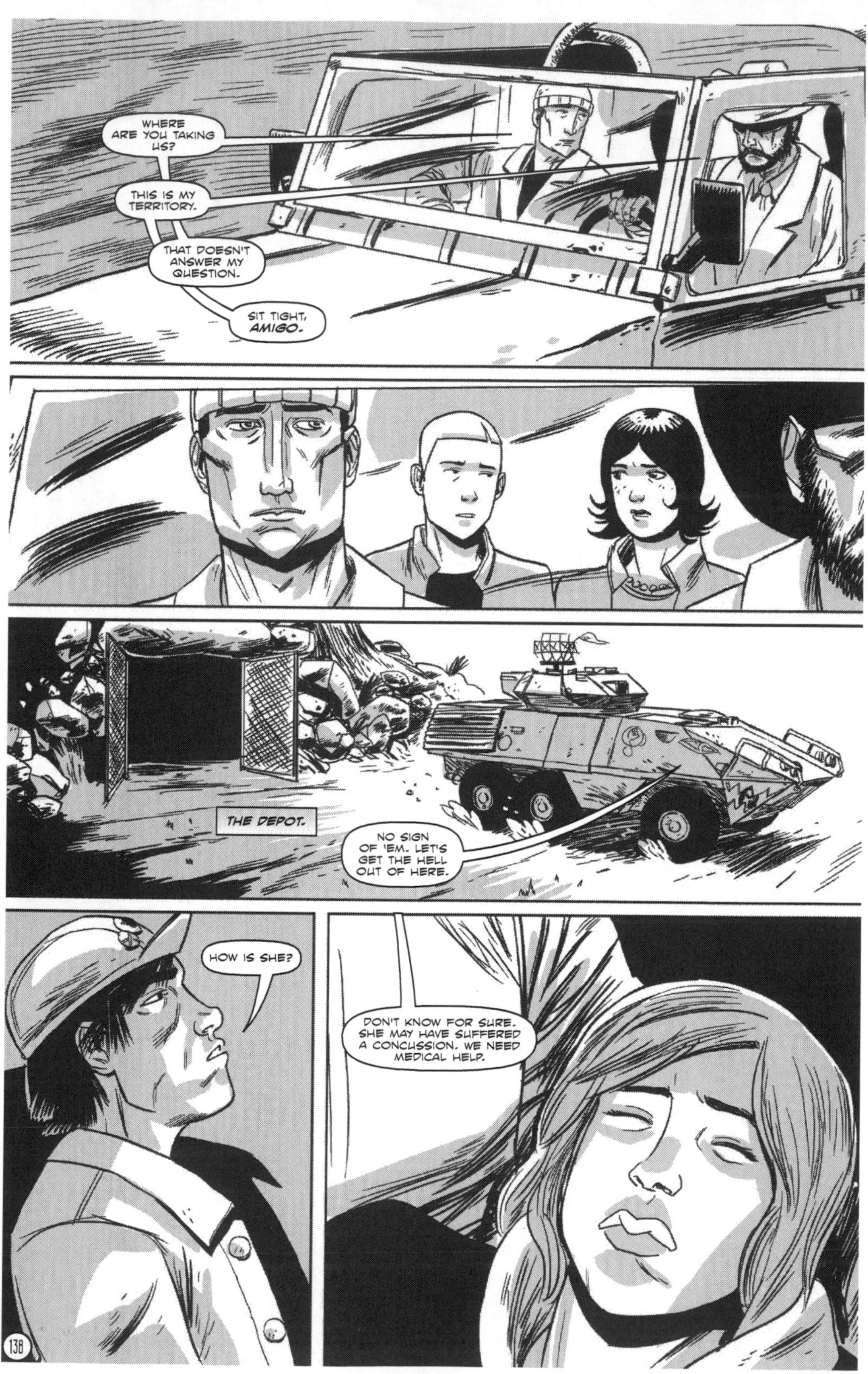

WHERE ARE YOU TAKING US?
THIS IS MY TERRITORY.
THAT DOESN'T ANSWER MY QUESTION.
SIT TIGHT, *AMIGO*.
THE DEPOT.
NO SIGN OF 'EM. LET'S GET THE HELL OUT OF HERE.
HOW IS SHE?
DON'T KNOW FOR SURE. SHE MAY HAVE SUFFERED A CONCUSSION. WE NEED MEDICAL HELP.

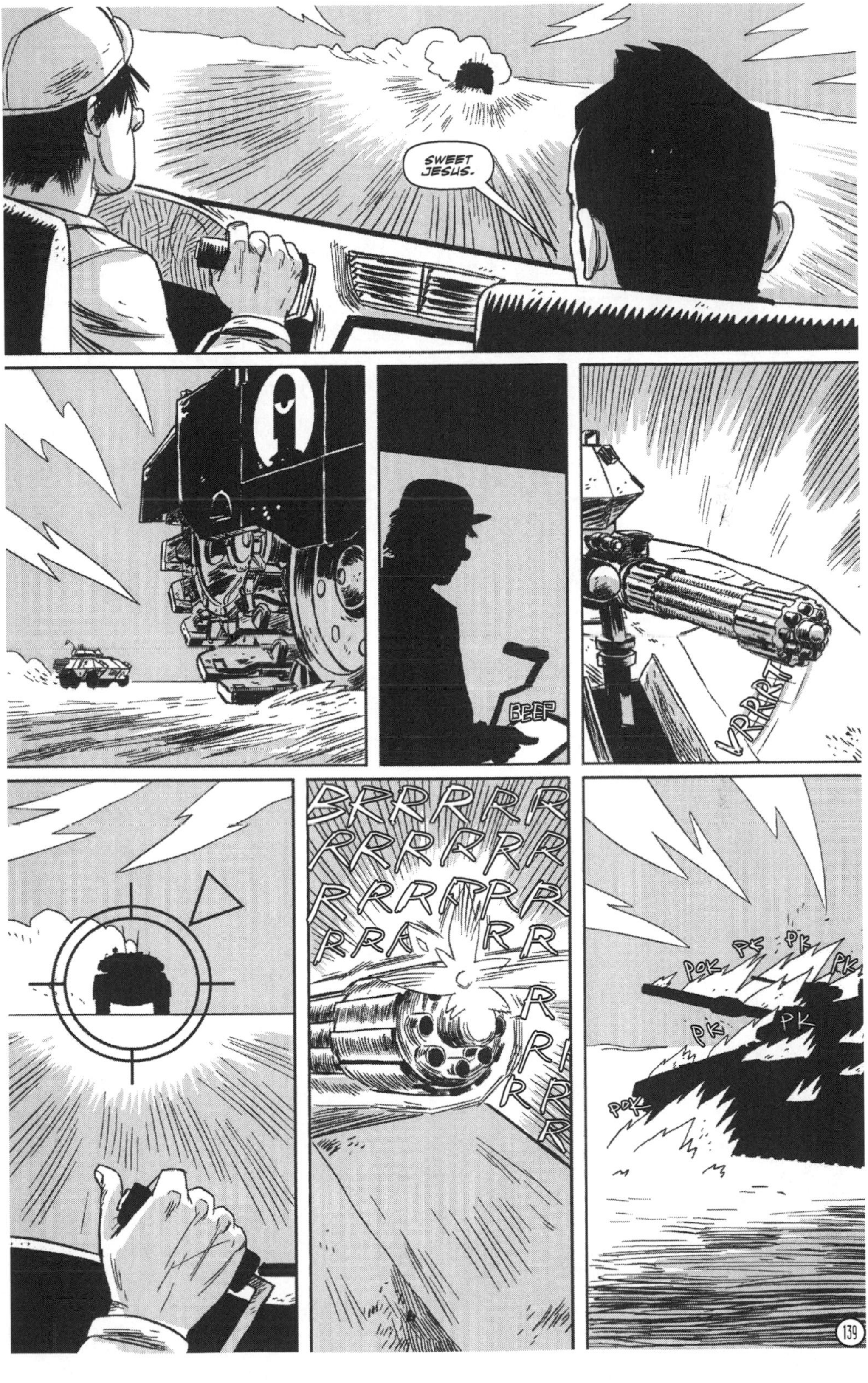
SWEET JESUS.
BEEP
VRRRRT
BRRRRRR RRRRRRR RRRRRRR RRA RR R RR RR R
POK PK PK PK PK PK POK

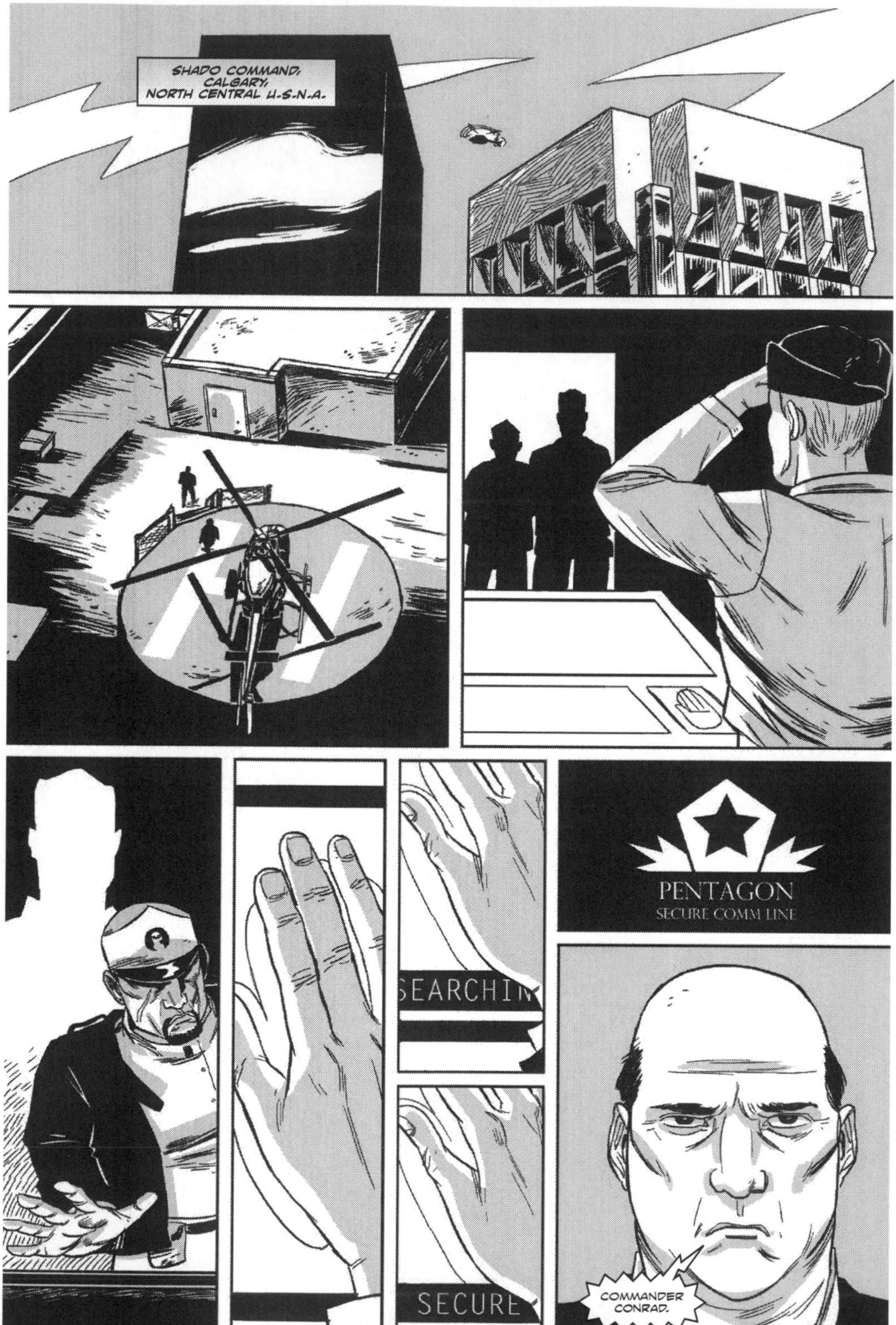
SHADO COMMAND,
CALGARY,
NORTH CENTRAL U.S.N.A.
SEARCHIN
SECURE
PENTAGON
SECURE COMM LINE
COMMANDER CONRAD.

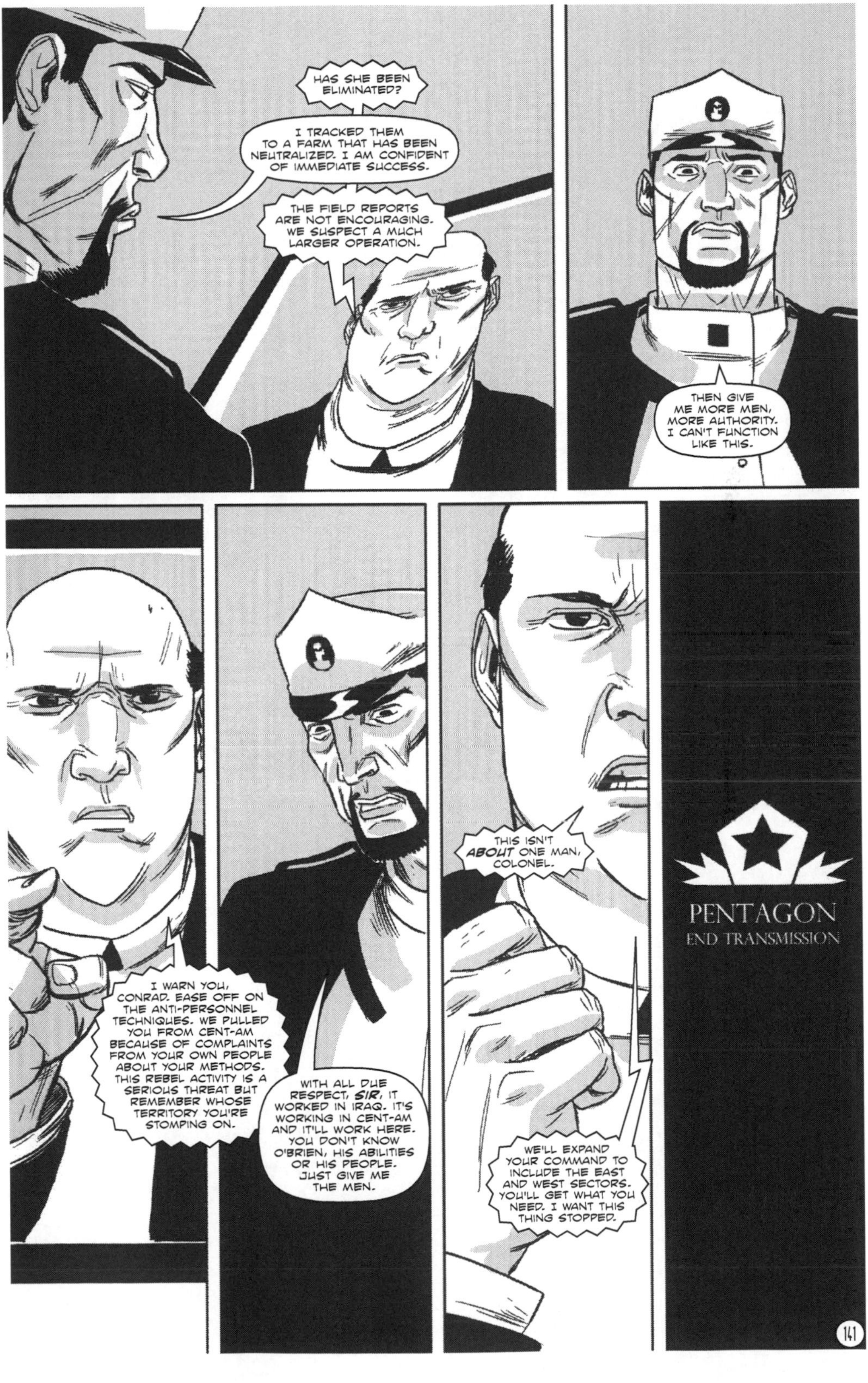
HAS SHE BEEN ELIMINATED?
I TRACKED THEM TO A FARM THAT HAS BEEN NEUTRALIZED. I AM CONFIDENT OF IMMEDIATE SUCCESS.
THE FIELD REPORTS ARE NOT ENCOURAGING. WE SUSPECT A MUCH LARGER OPERATION.
THEN GIVE ME MORE MEN, MORE AUTHORITY. I CAN'T FUNCTION LIKE THIS.
I WARN YOU, CONRAD. EASE OFF ON THE ANTI-PERSONNEL TECHNIQUES. WE PULLED YOU FROM CENT-AM BECAUSE OF COMPLAINTS FROM YOUR OWN PEOPLE ABOUT YOUR METHODS. THIS REBEL ACTIVITY IS A SERIOUS THREAT BUT REMEMBER WHOSE TERRITORY YOU'RE STOMPING ON.
WITH ALL DUE RESPECT, *SIR*, IT WORKED IN IRAQ. IT'S WORKING IN CENT-AM AND IT'LL WORK HERE. YOU DON'T KNOW O'BRIEN, HIS ABILITIES OR HIS PEOPLE. JUST GIVE ME THE MEN.
THIS ISN'T *ABOUT* ONE MAN, COLONEL.
WE'LL EXPAND YOUR COMMAND TO INCLUDE THE EAST AND WEST SECTORS. YOU'LL GET WHAT YOU NEED. I WANT THIS THING STOPPED.
PENTAGON
END TRANSMISSION

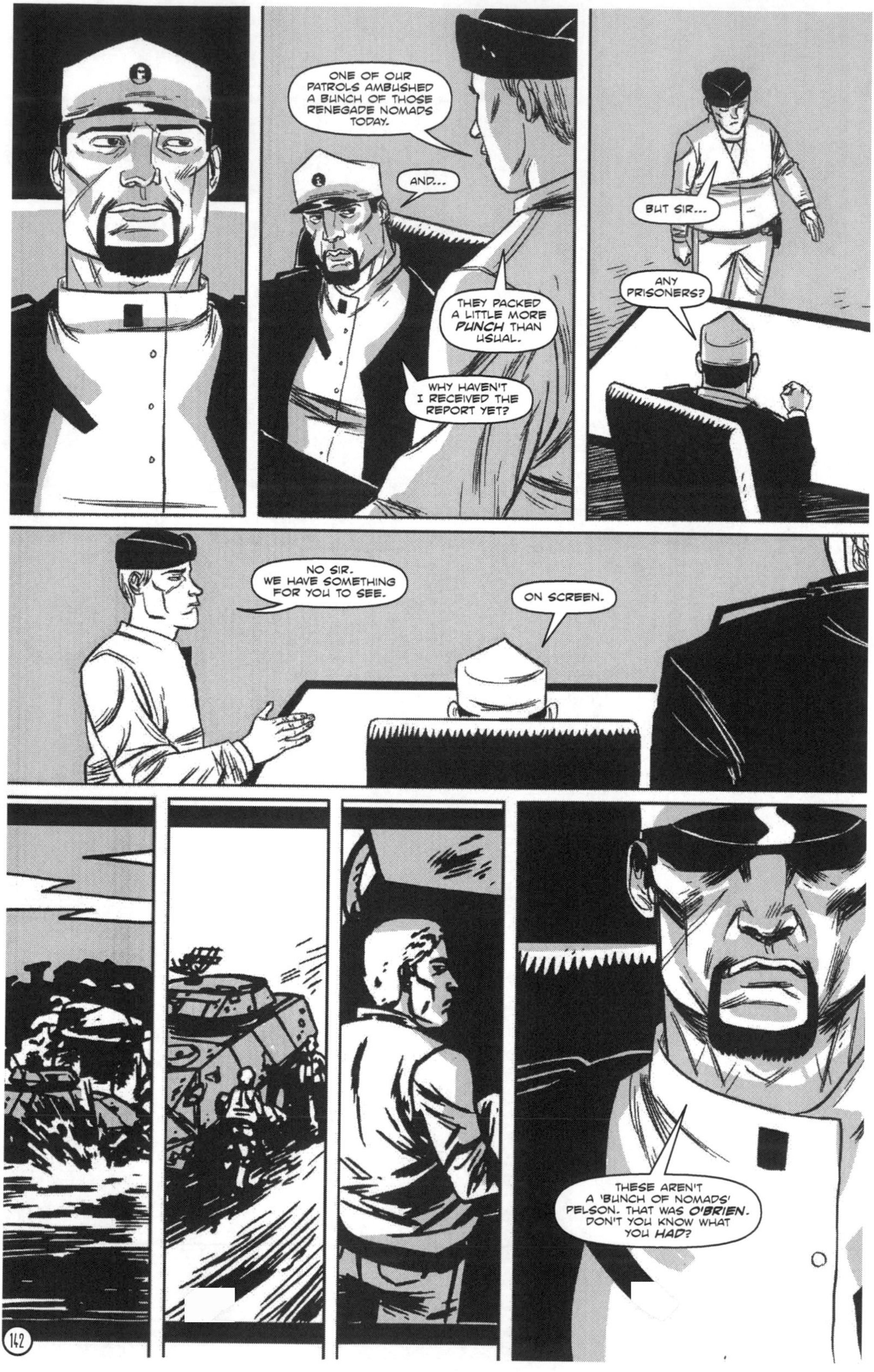

ONE OF OUR PATROLS AMBUSHED A BUNCH OF THOSE RENEGADE NOMADS TODAY.
AND...
THEY PACKED A LITTLE MORE PUNCH THAN USUAL.
WHY HAVEN'T I RECEIVED THE REPORT YET?
BUT SIR...
ANY PRISONERS?
NO SIR. WE HAVE SOMETHING FOR YOU TO SEE.
ON SCREEN.
THESE AREN'T A 'BUNCH OF NOMADS' PELSON. THAT WAS O'BRIEN. DON'T YOU KNOW WHAT YOU HAD?

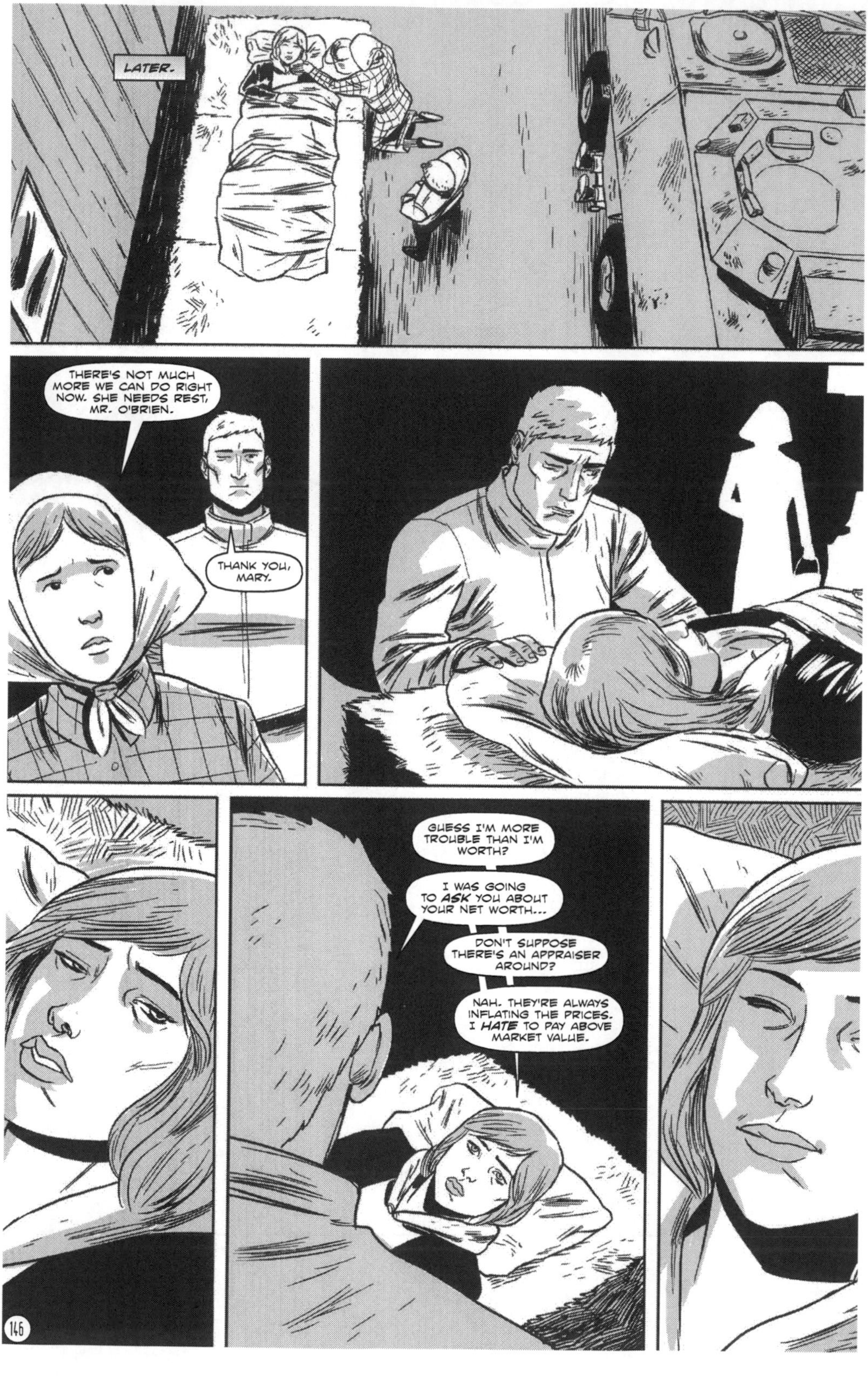
LATER.
THERE'S NOT MUCH MORE WE CAN DO RIGHT NOW. SHE NEEDS REST, MR. O'BRIEN.
THANK YOU, MARY.
GUESS I'M MORE TROUBLE THAN I'M WORTH?
I WAS GOING TO ASK YOU ABOUT YOUR NET WORTH...
DON'T SUPPOSE THERE'S AN APPRAISER AROUND?
NAH. THEY'RE ALWAYS INFLATING THE PRICES. I HATE TO PAY ABOVE MARKET VALUE.

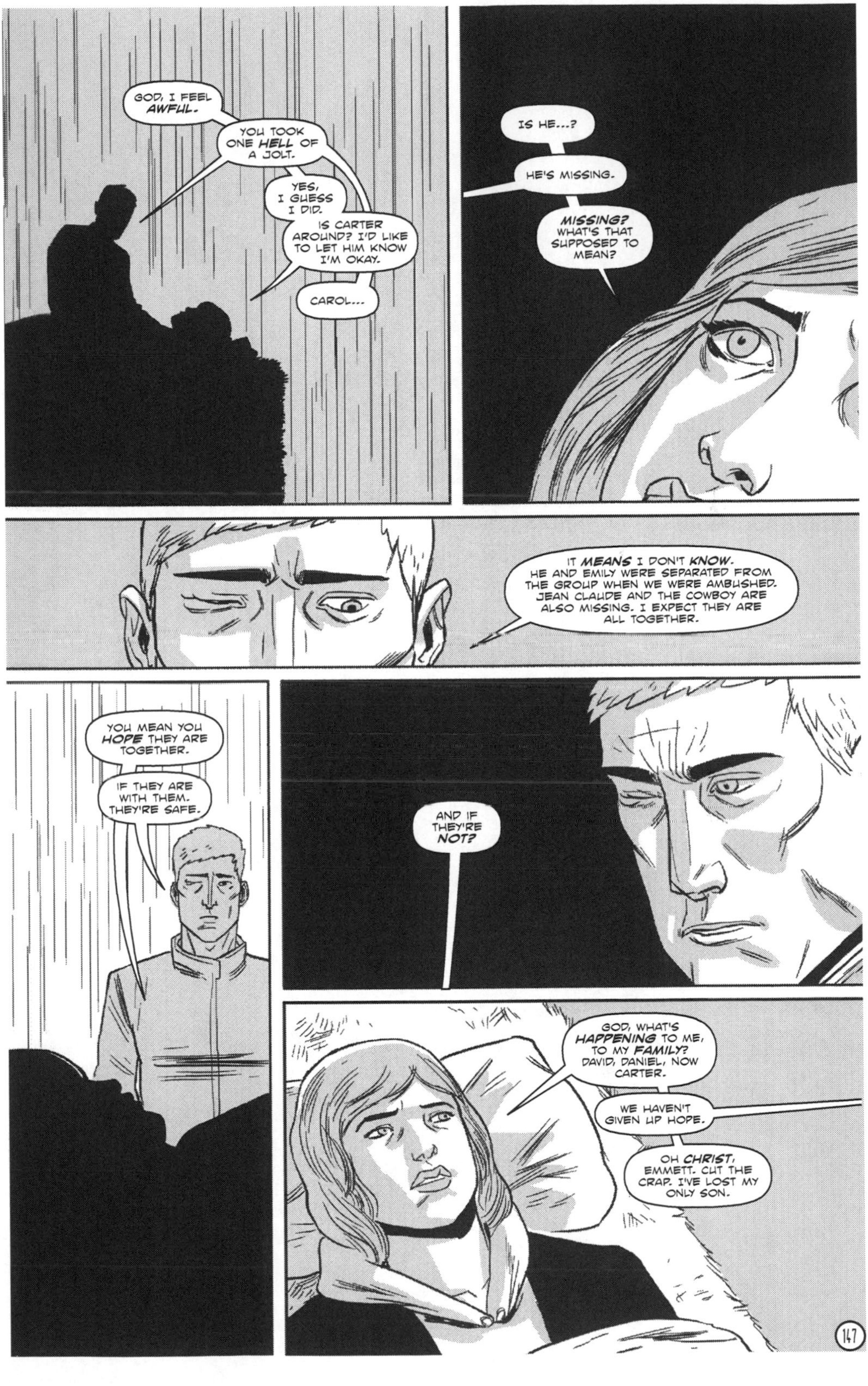
GOD, I FEEL *AWFUL.*
YOU TOOK ONE *HELL* OF A JOLT.
YES, I GUESS I DID.
IS CARTER AROUND? I'D LIKE TO LET HIM KNOW I'M OKAY.
CAROL...
IS HE...?
HE'S MISSING.
MISSING? WHAT'S THAT SUPPOSED TO MEAN?
IT *MEANS* I DON'T *KNOW.* HE AND EMILY WERE SEPARATED FROM THE GROUP WHEN WE WERE AMBUSHED. JEAN CLAUDE AND THE COWBOY ARE ALSO MISSING. I EXPECT THEY ARE ALL TOGETHER.
YOU MEAN YOU *HOPE* THEY ARE TOGETHER.
IF THEY ARE WITH THEM. THEY'RE SAFE.
AND IF THEY'RE *NOT?*
GOD, WHAT'S *HAPPENING* TO ME, TO MY *FAMILY?* DAVID, DANIEL, NOW CARTER.
WE HAVEN'T GIVEN UP HOPE.
OH *CHRIST,* EMMETT. CUT THE CRAP. I'VE LOST MY ONLY SON.
147

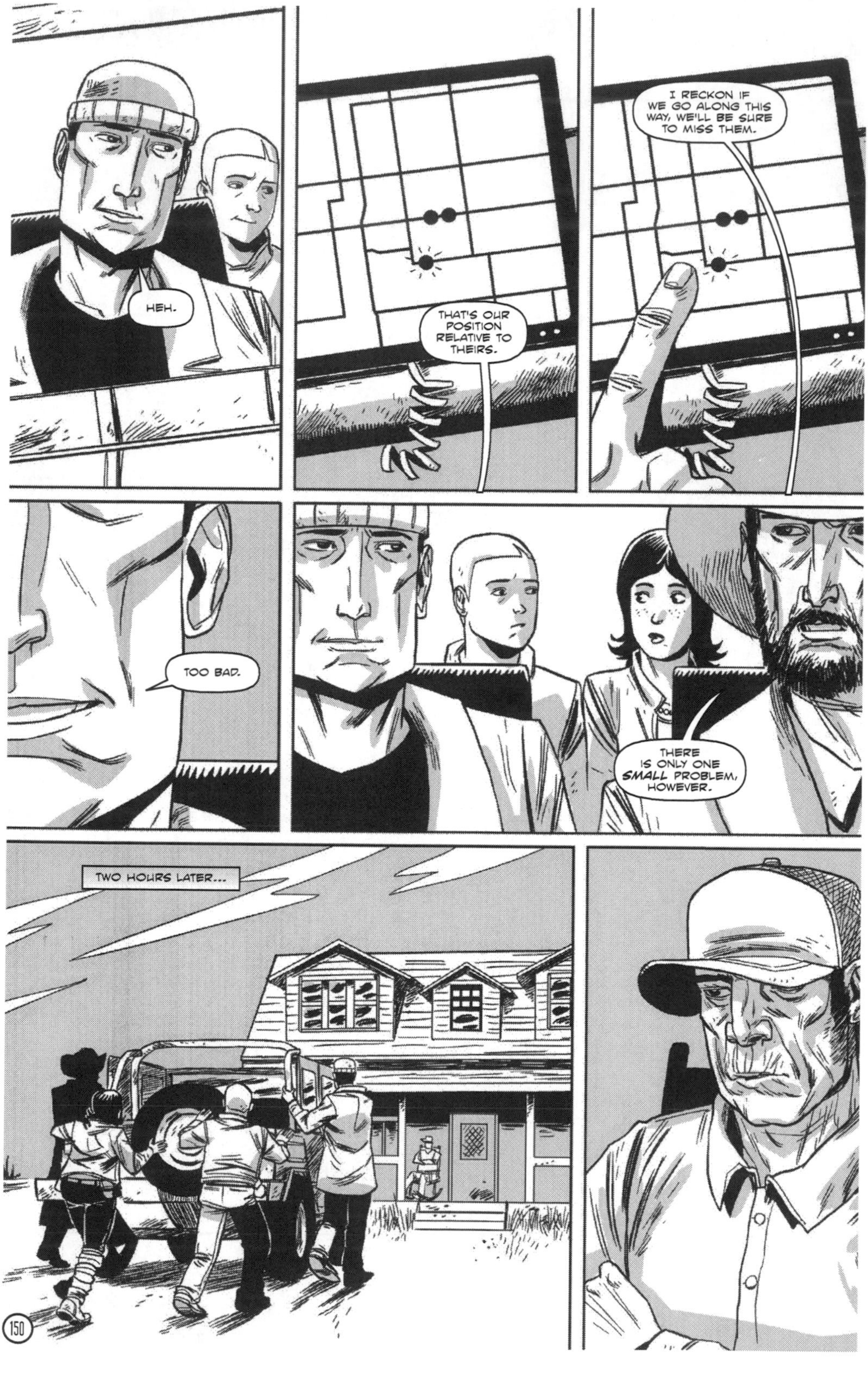
HEH.
THAT'S OUR POSITION RELATIVE TO THEIRS.
I RECKON IF WE GO ALONG THIS WAY, WE'LL BE SURE TO MISS THEM.
TOO BAD.
THERE IS ONLY ONE SMALL PROBLEM, HOWEVER.
TWO HOURS LATER...

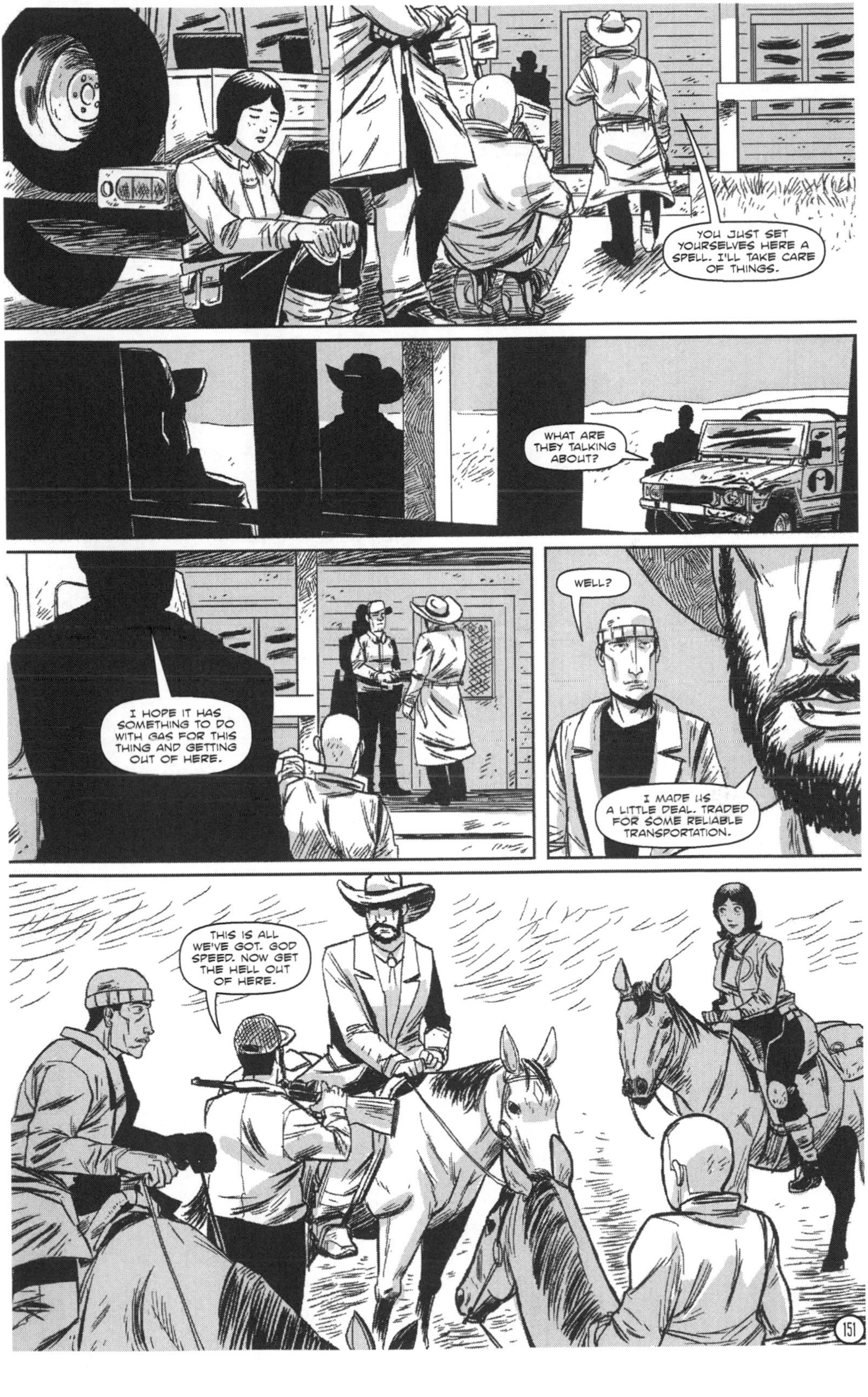
YOU JUST SET YOURSELVES HERE A SPELL. I'LL TAKE CARE OF THINGS.
WHAT ARE THEY TALKING ABOUT?
I HOPE IT HAS SOMETHING TO DO WITH GAS FOR THIS THING AND GETTING OUT OF HERE.
WELL?
I MADE US A LITTLE DEAL. TRADED FOR SOME RELIABLE TRANSPORTATION.
THIS IS ALL WE'VE GOT. GOD SPEED. NOW GET THE HELL OUT OF HERE.

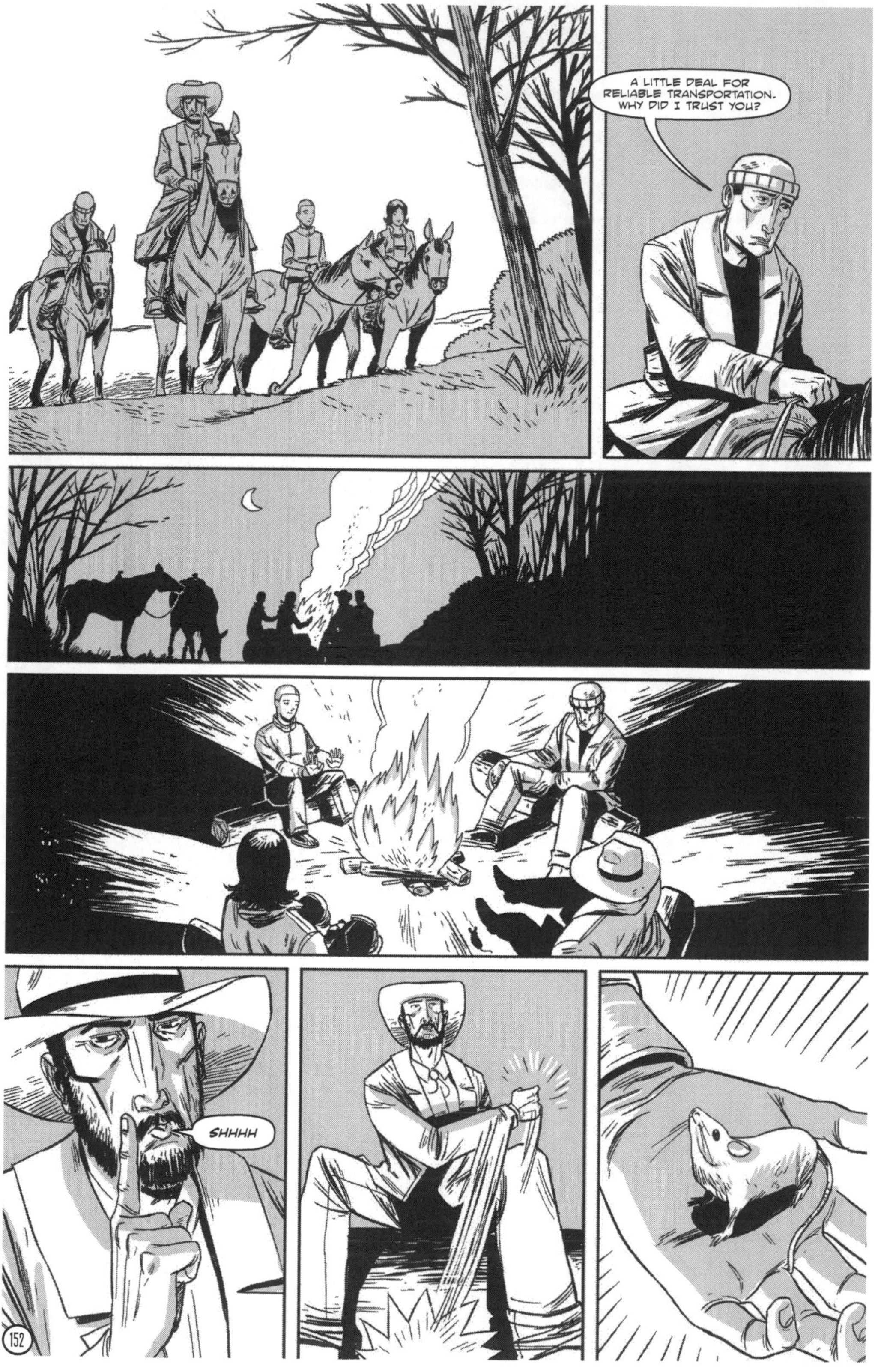
A LITTLE DEAL FOR RELIABLE TRANSPORTATION. WHY DID I TRUST YOU?
SHHHH

NEVER AGAIN. WHY DIDN'T YOU TRADE FOR *FUEL*?

'CAUSE THIS IS HORSE COUNTRY.

THIS MAY BE HORSE COUNTRY TO YOU, BUT IT'S *MISERY* TO ME.

"SAY YOU DON'T LIKE HORSEBACK RIDING? LET ME TELL YOU FRIEND. THAT ONCE YOU'VE REALLY TRIED IT, IT'LL GET YOU IN THE END." S. OMAR BARKER.

EVERYONE'S A BLOODY POET.

MAYBE...

HE SAYS NO ONE COULD HAVE BROUGHT HIM TO CANADA OVERLAND BUT YOU. DID YOU RIDE ALL THE WAY FROM THE FOUR CORNERS?

YEAH, THAT'S WHERE WE FIRST MET. IRON BEAR WAS WITH US.

WHEN IT WAS DECIDED THAT EMMETT SHOULD RETURN, HE CAME TO ME AND ASKED ME TO LEAD HIM. HE SAID I WAS THE ONLY MAN HE'D MET WHO HAD SPENT HIS LIFE LEARNING THE COWBOY SKILLS; LIVING THE LAND.

SOMETIMES A MAN GETS TO WONDERING IF HE'S WASTED HIS LIFE LEARNING WHAT HE'S LEARNED. THAT EMMETT, HE KNOWS HOW TO MAKE A MAN FEEL PROUD OF HIS HERITAGE AND HIS LIFE. AND HE KNOWS HOW TO LET A MAN ALONE AND BE AT PEACE.

I THINK MAYBE *I* OWE HIM A LOT.

EMMETT SAYS HE OWES A LOT TO YOU.

153

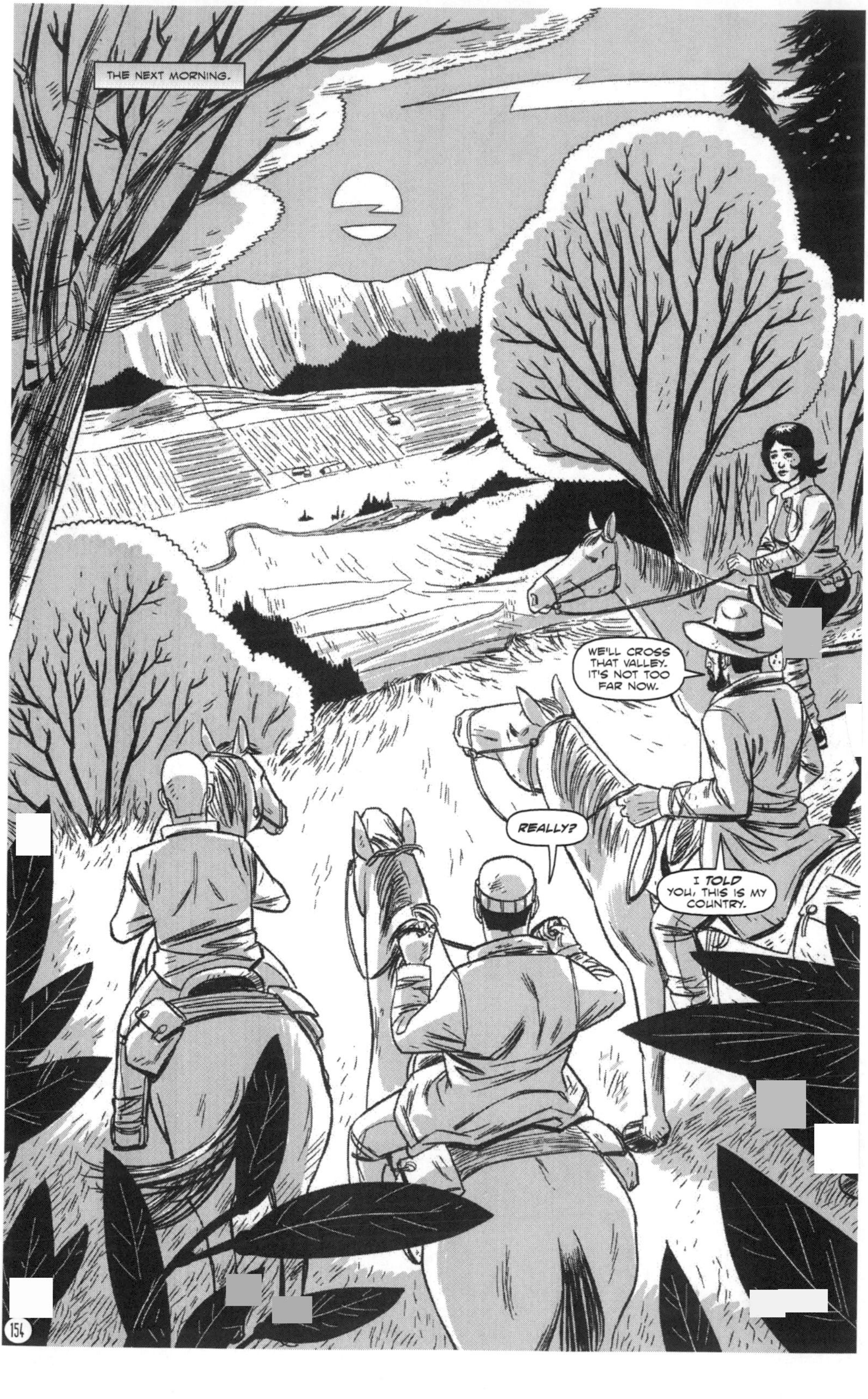
THE NEXT MORNING.
WE'LL CROSS THAT VALLEY. IT'S NOT TOO FAR NOW.
REALLY?
I *TOLD* YOU, THIS IS MY COUNTRY.

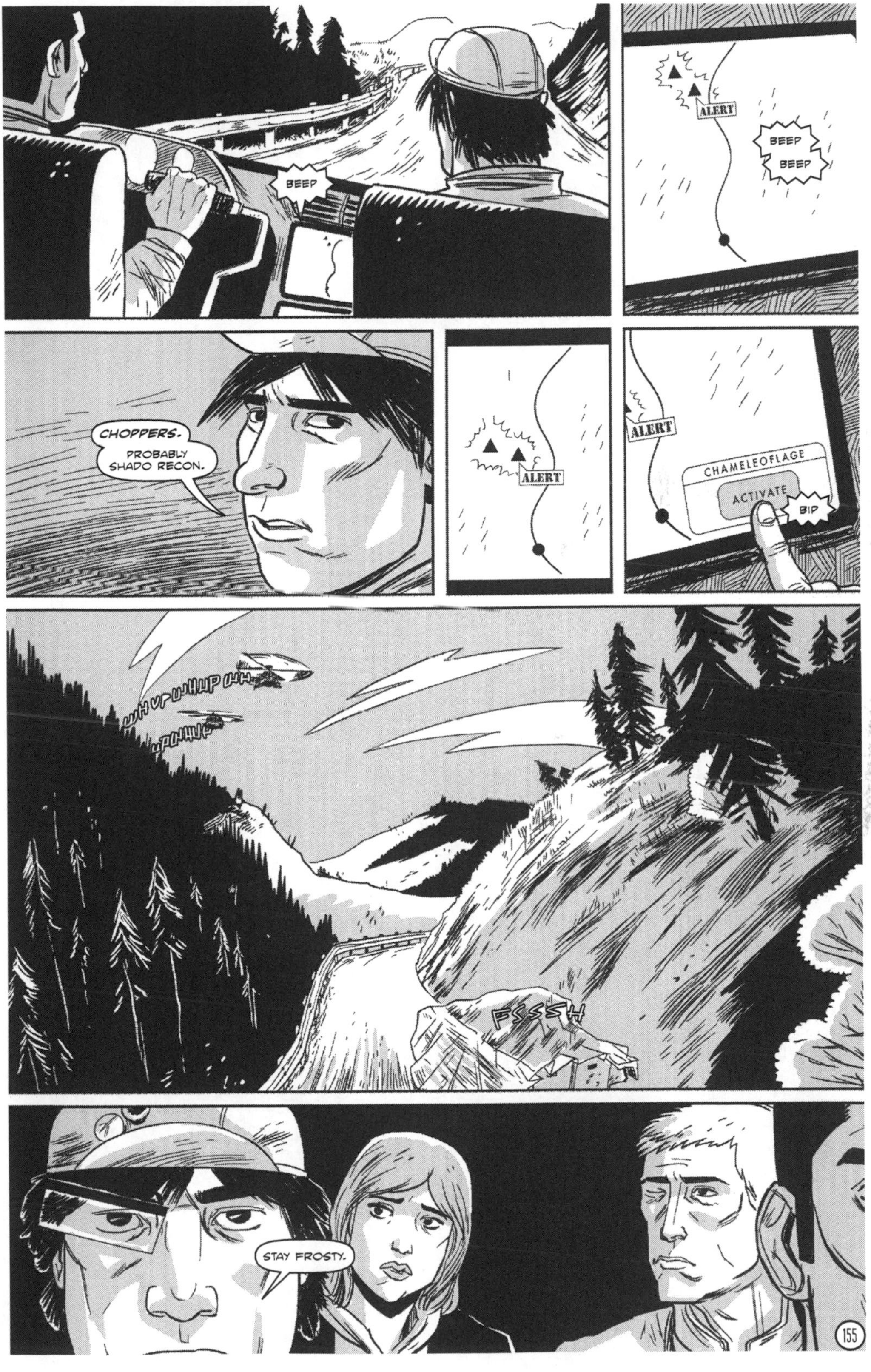
BEEP
ALERT
BEEP
BEEP
CHOPPERS.
PROBABLY SHADO RECON.
ALERT
ALERT
CHAMELEOFLAGE
ACTIVATE
BIP
FSSSH
STAY FROSTY.

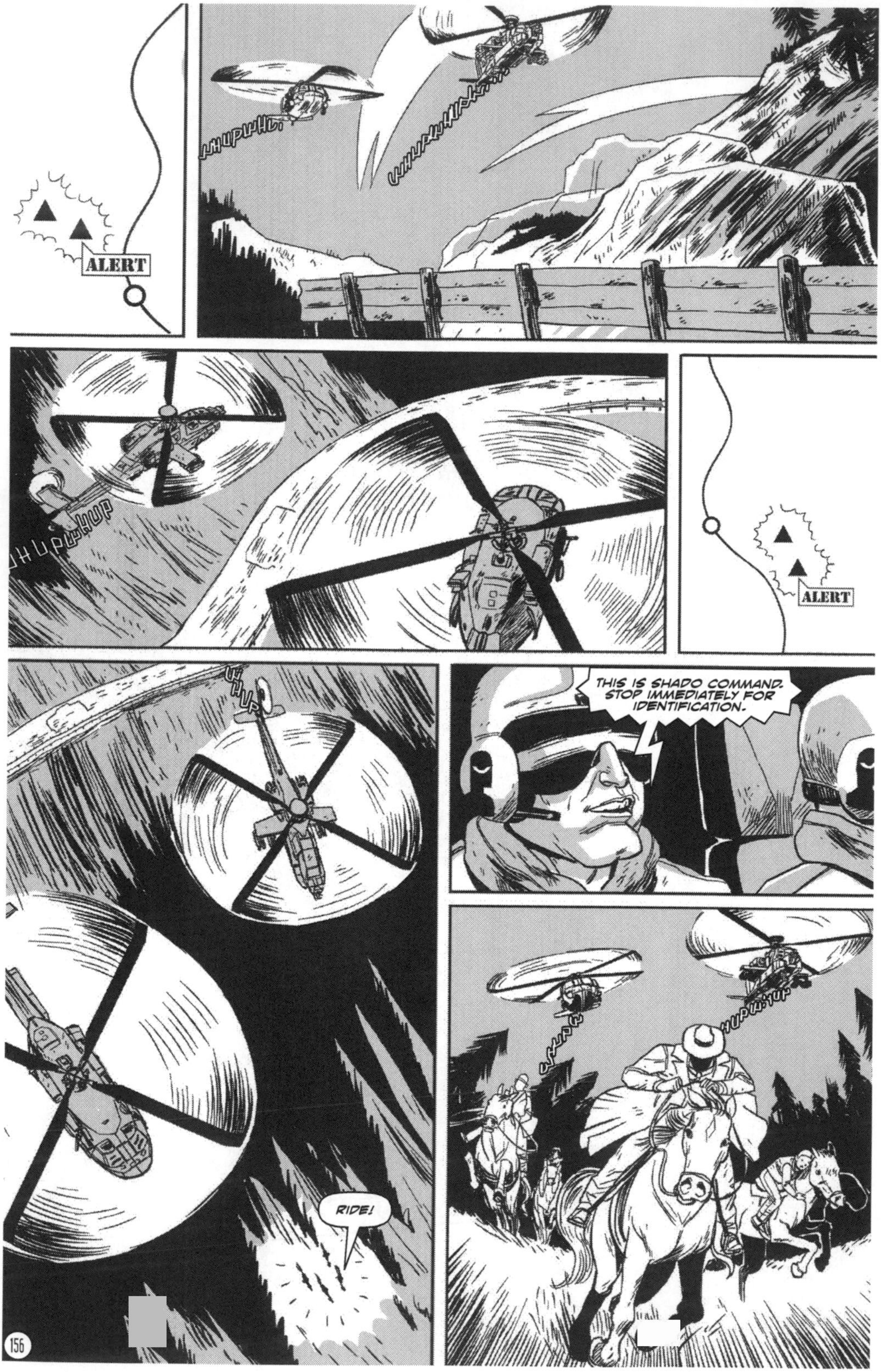
ALERT
ALERT
THIS IS SHADO COMMAND. STOP IMMEDIATELY FOR IDENTIFICATION.
RIDE!

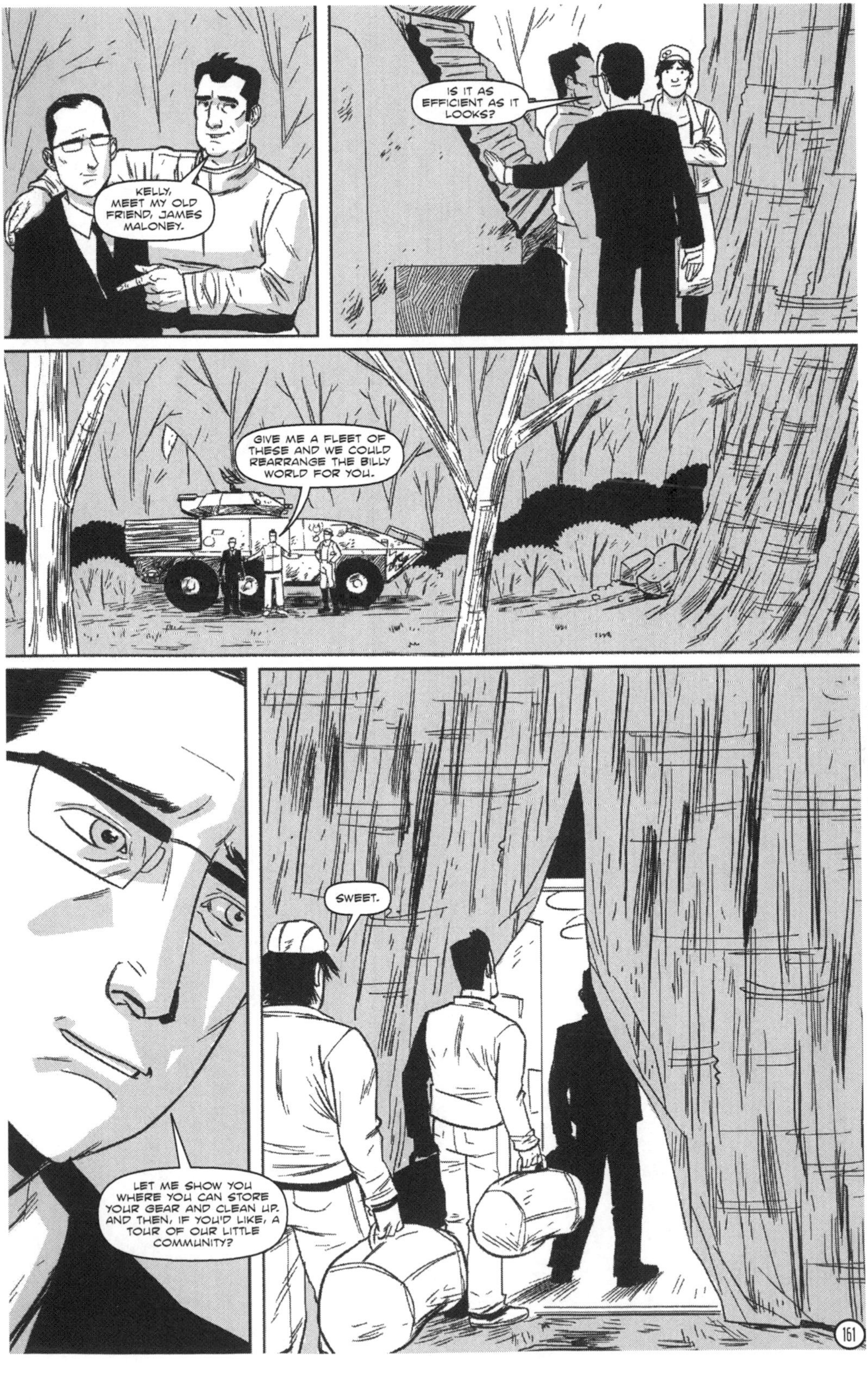
KELLY, MEET MY OLD FRIEND, JAMES MALONEY.
IS IT AS EFFICIENT AS IT LOOKS?
GIVE ME A FLEET OF THESE AND WE COULD REARRANGE THE BILLY WORLD FOR YOU.
LET ME SHOW YOU WHERE YOU CAN STORE YOUR GEAR AND CLEAN UP. AND THEN, IF YOU'D LIKE, A TOUR OF OUR LITTLE COMMUNITY?
SWEET.

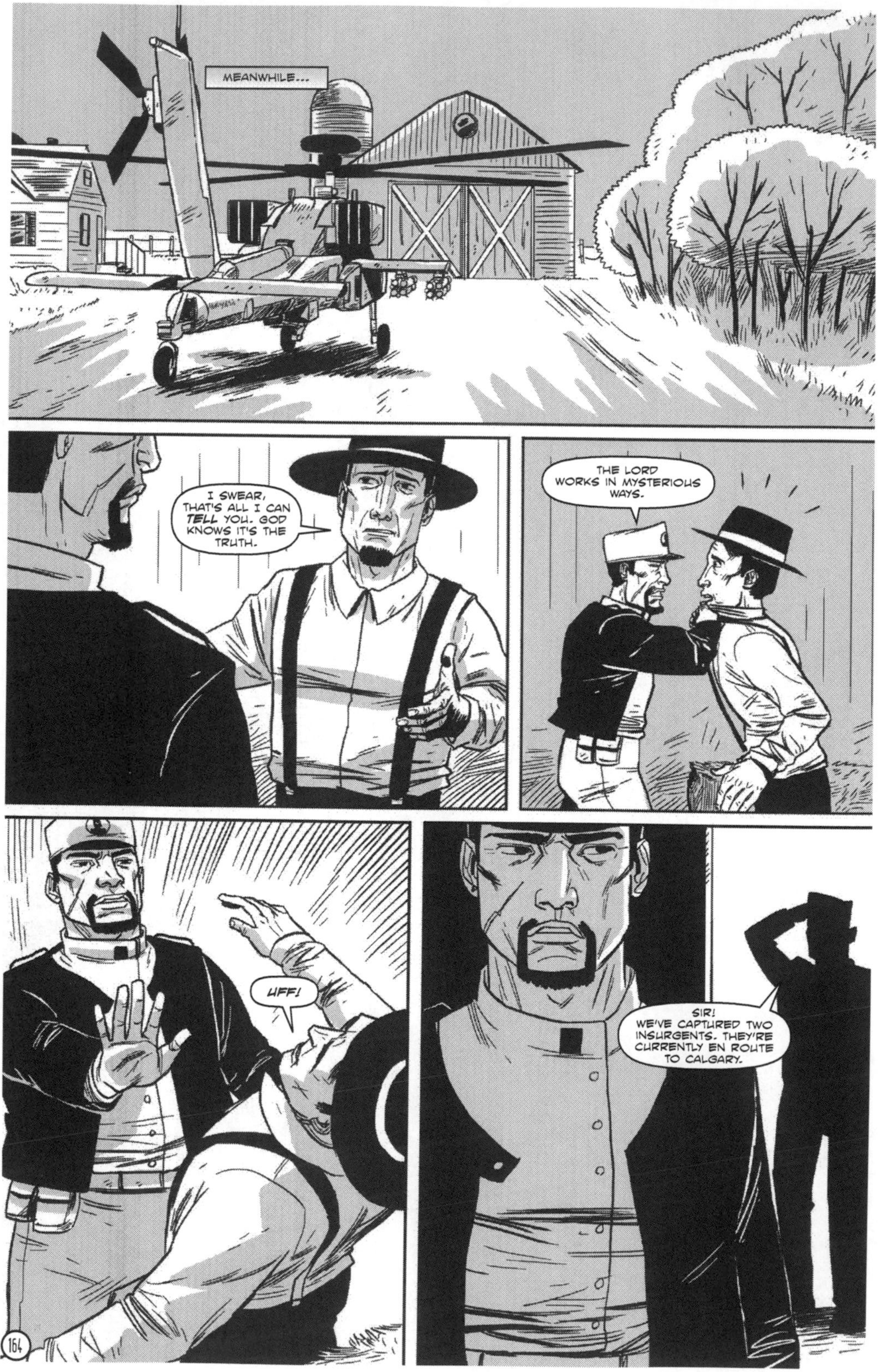
MEANWHILE...
I SWEAR, THAT'S ALL I CAN TELL YOU. GOD KNOWS IT'S THE TRUTH.
THE LORD WORKS IN MYSTERIOUS WAYS.
UFF!
SIR! WE'VE CAPTURED TWO INSURGENTS. THEY'RE CURRENTLY EN ROUTE TO CALGARY.

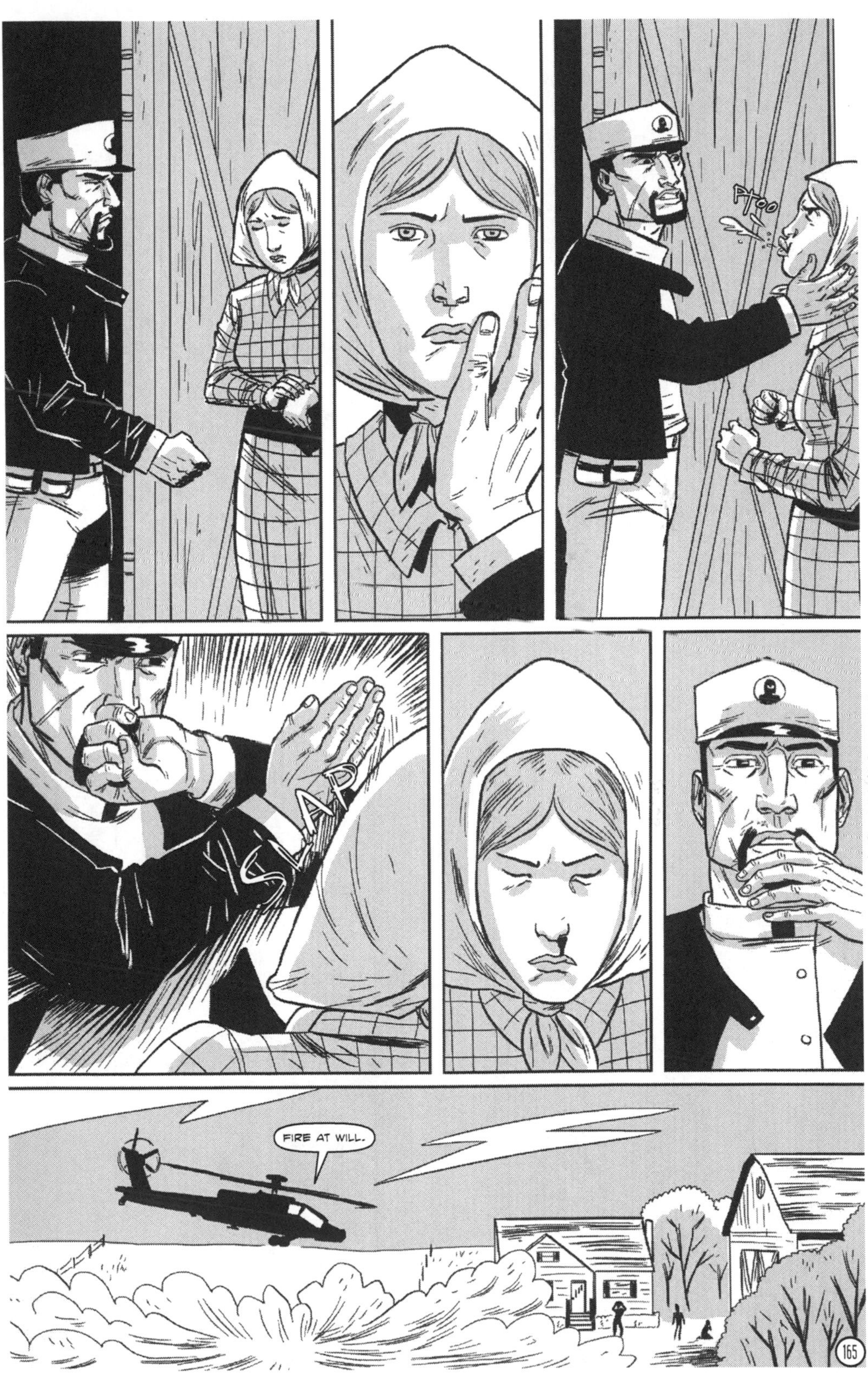
PTOO
SLAP
FIRE AT WILL.

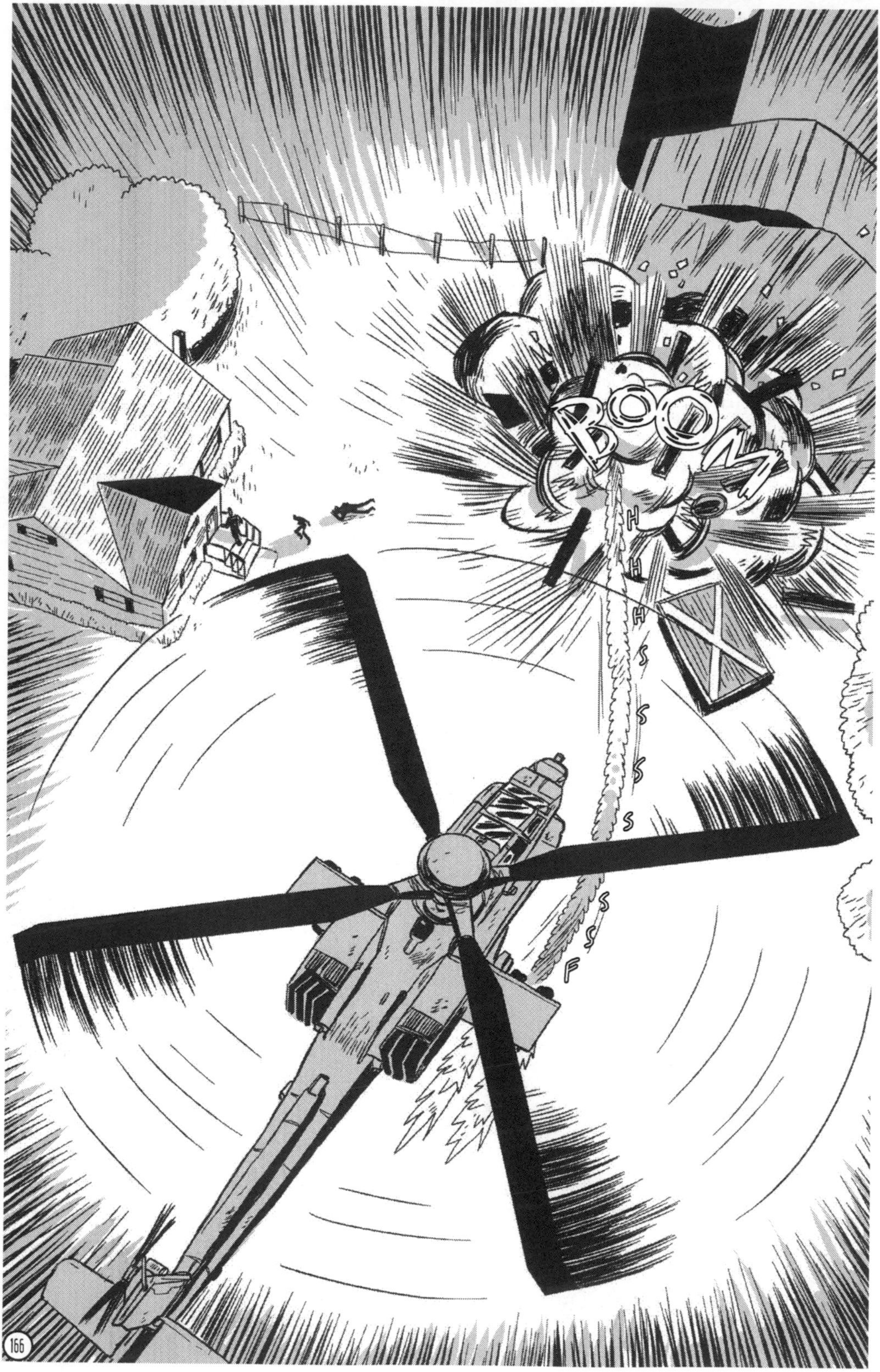
BOOM
FSSSSSSHHH

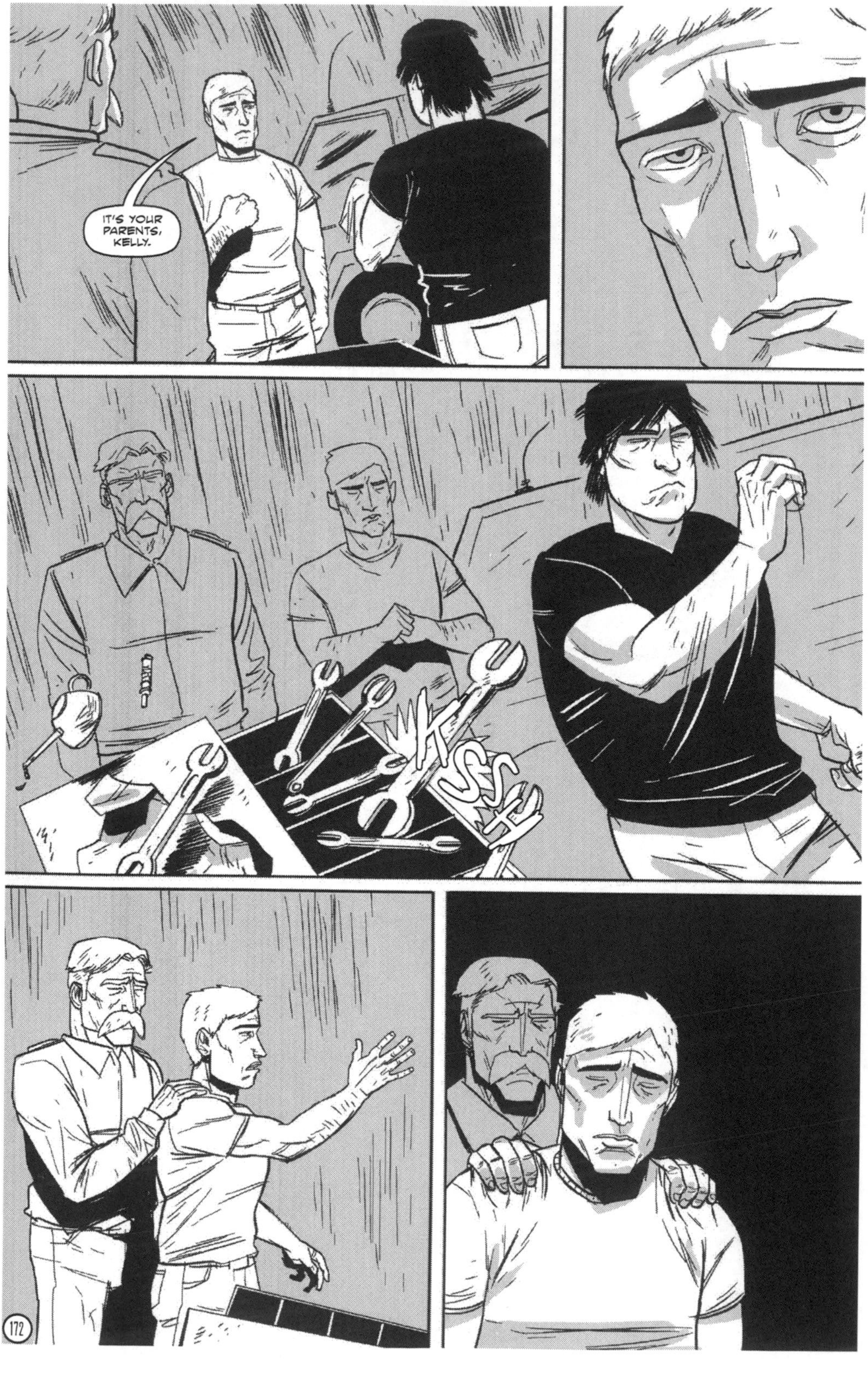
IT'S YOUR PARENTS, KELLY.
KSSH

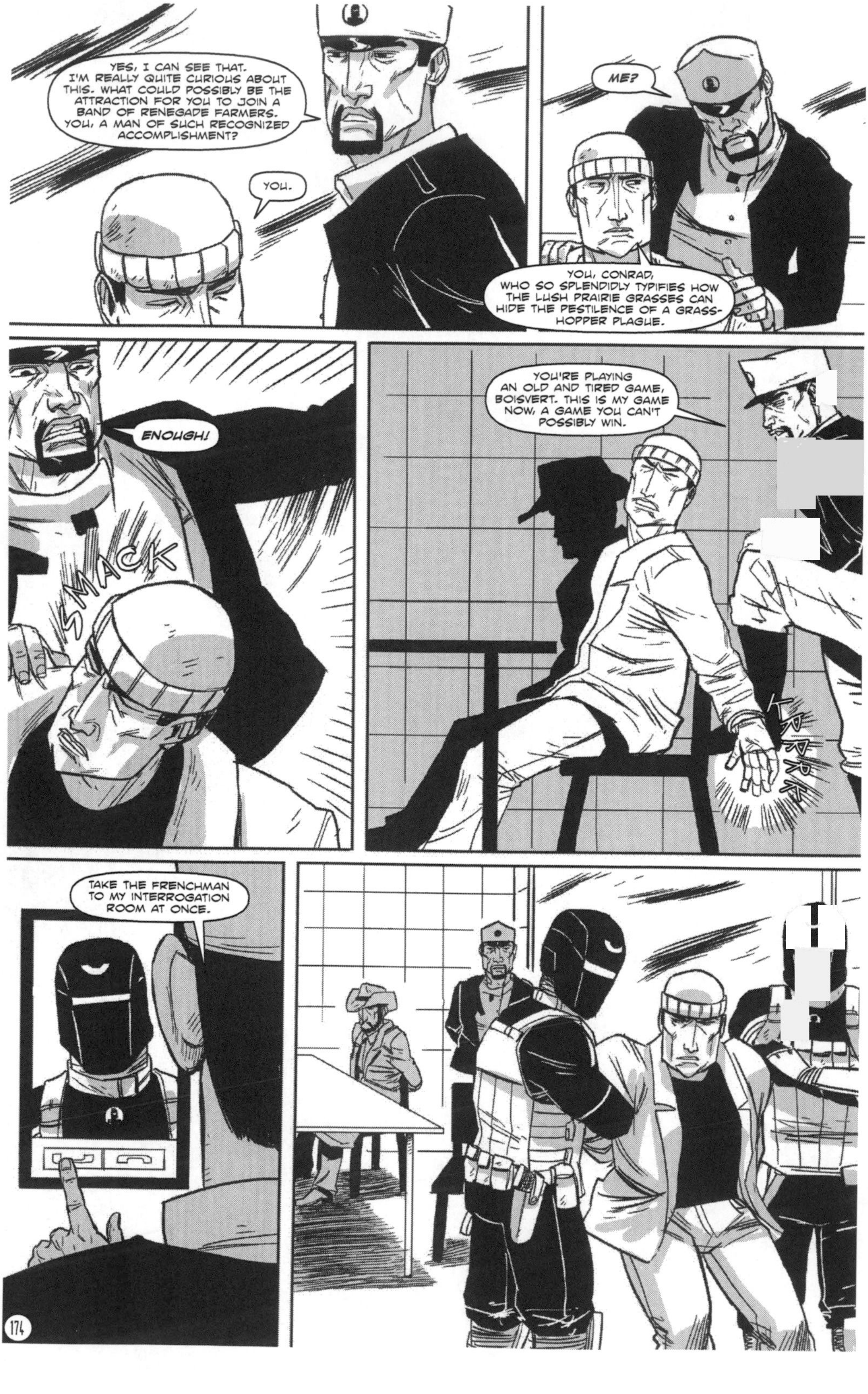
YES, I CAN SEE THAT. I'M REALLY QUITE CURIOUS ABOUT THIS. WHAT COULD POSSIBLY BE THE ATTRACTION FOR YOU TO JOIN A BAND OF RENEGADE FARMERS. YOU, A MAN OF SUCH RECOGNIZED ACCOMPLISHMENT?
YOU.
ME?
YOU, CONRAD, WHO SO SPLENDIDLY TYPIFIES HOW THE LUSH PRAIRIE GRASSES CAN HIDE THE PESTILENCE OF A GRASS-HOPPER PLAGUE.
ENOUGH!
SMACK
YOU'RE PLAYING AN OLD AND TIRED GAME, BOISVERT. THIS IS MY GAME NOW, A GAME YOU CAN'T POSSIBLY WIN.
KRRRK
TAKE THE FRENCHMAN TO MY INTERROGATION ROOM AT ONCE.

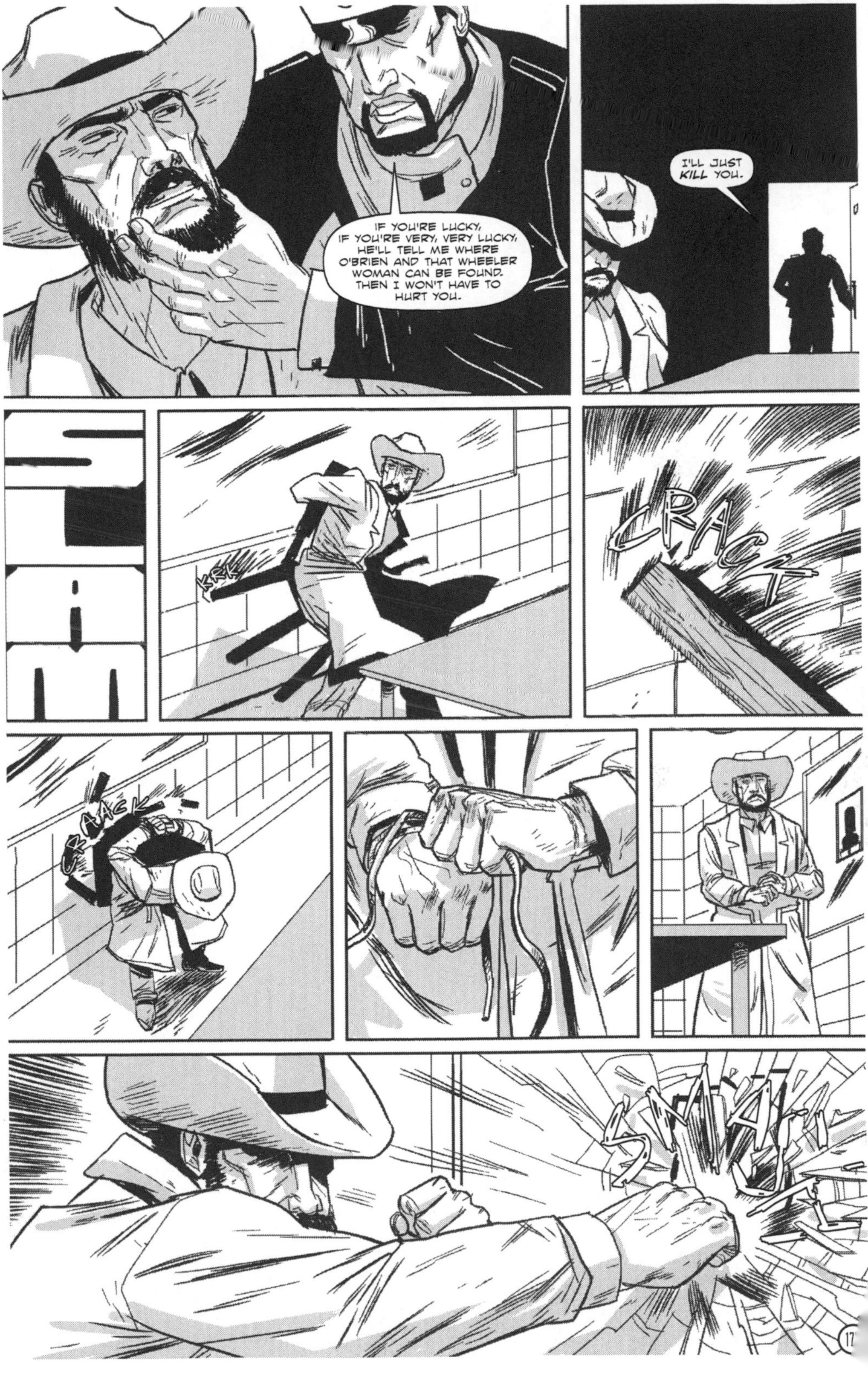
IF YOU'RE LUCKY, IF YOU'RE VERY, VERY LUCKY, HE'LL TELL ME WHERE O'BRIEN AND THAT WHEELER WOMAN CAN BE FOUND. THEN I WON'T HAVE TO HURT YOU.
I'LL JUST KILL YOU.
SLAM
KRK
CRACK
KRAACK
SMASH

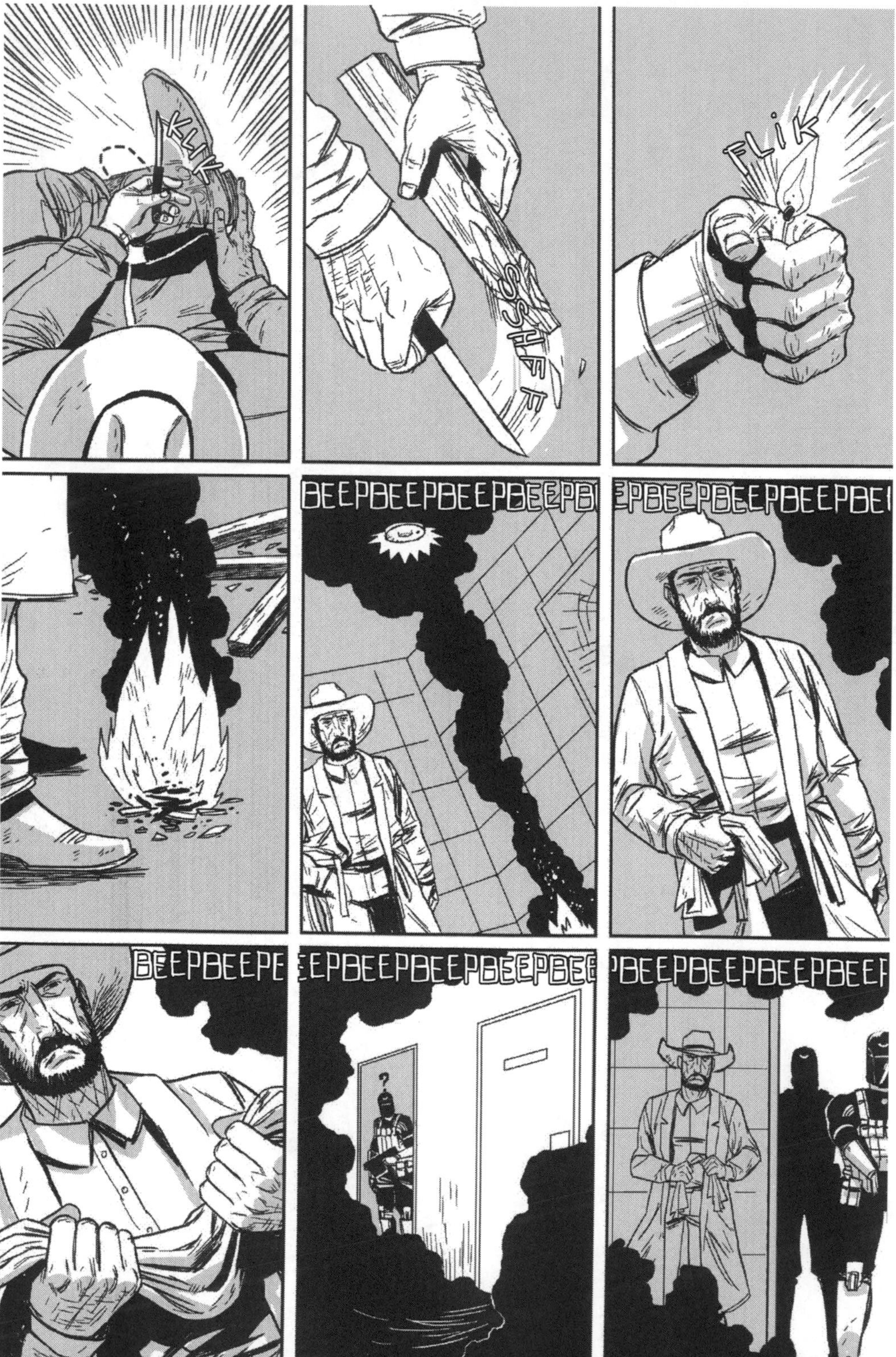
KLIK
SSHFF
FLIK
BEEPBEEPBEEPBEEP
BEEPBEEPBEEP
BEEPBEEP
BEEPBEEPBEEPBEEP
BEEPBEEPBEEP

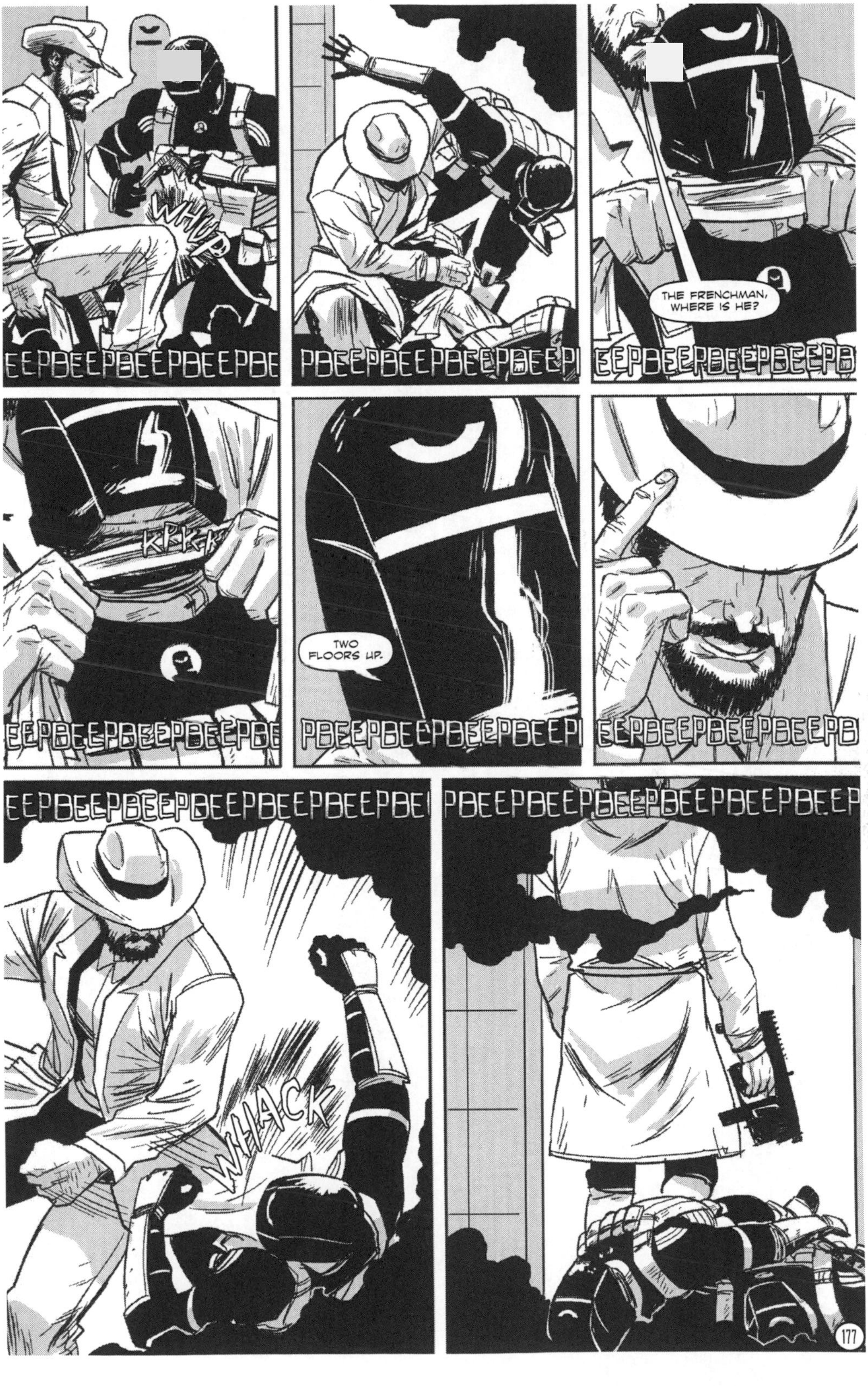
WHUP
EEPBEEPBEEPBEEPBE
PBEEPBEEPBEEPBEEP
THE FRENCHMAN, WHERE IS HE?
EEPBEEPBEEPBEEPB
EEPBEEPBEEPBEEPBE
TWO FLOORS UP.
PBEEPBEEPBEEPBEEP
EEPBEEPBEEPBEEPB
EEPBEEPBEEPBEEPBEEPBE
WHACK
PBEEPBEEPBEEPBEEPBEEPBEEP

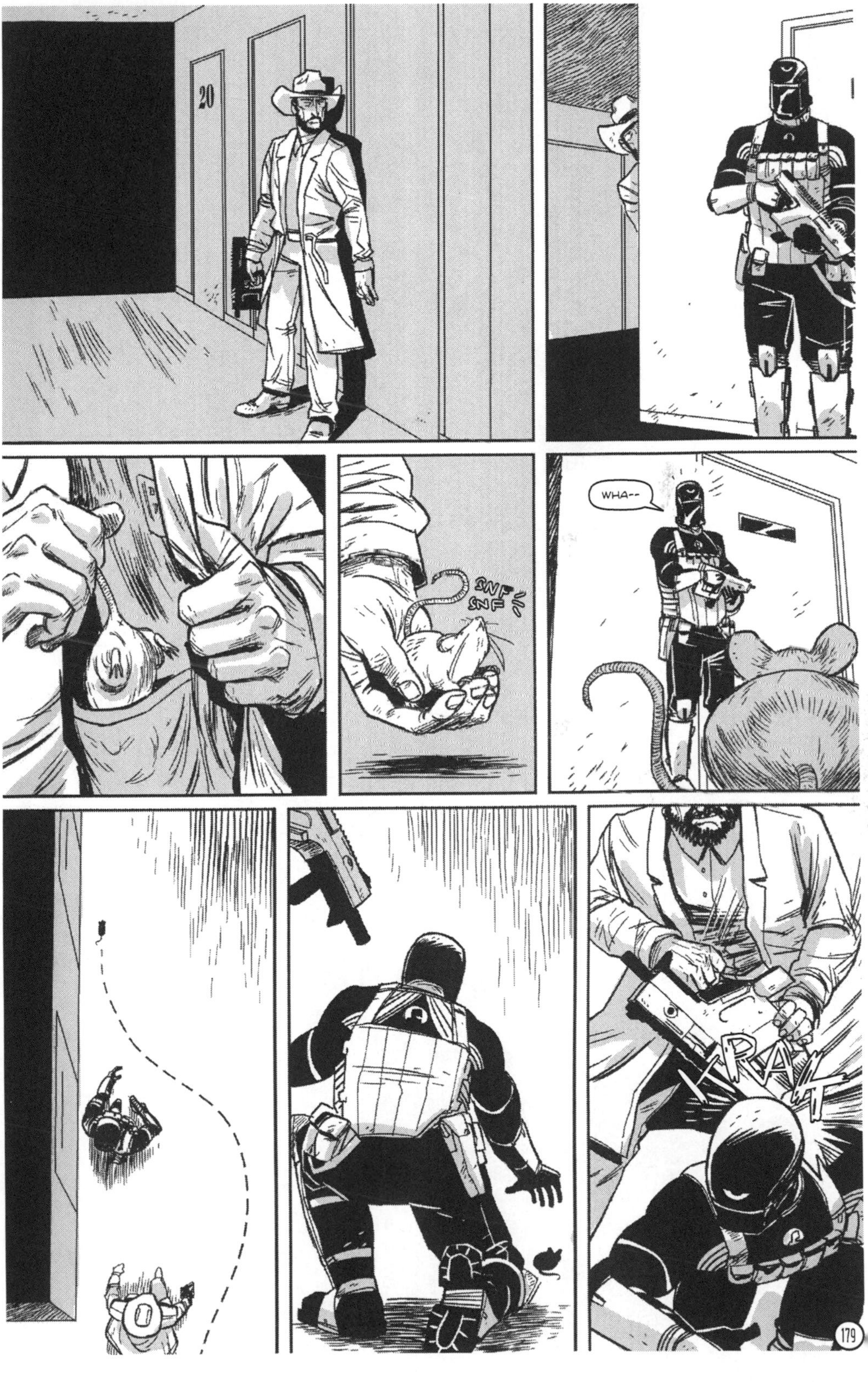
SNF SNF
WHA--
KRAK

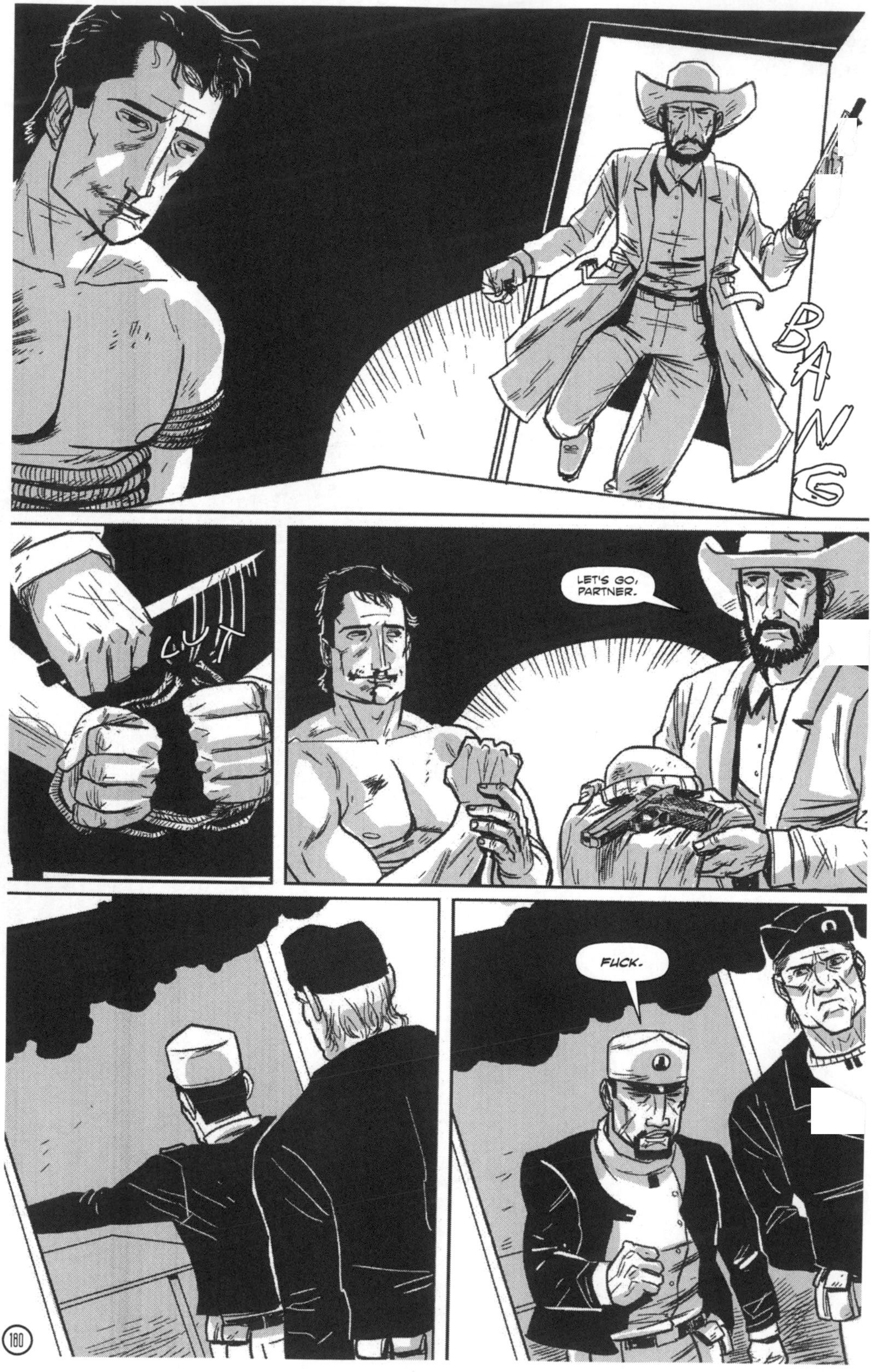
BANG
CUT
LET'S GO, PARTNER.
FUCK.

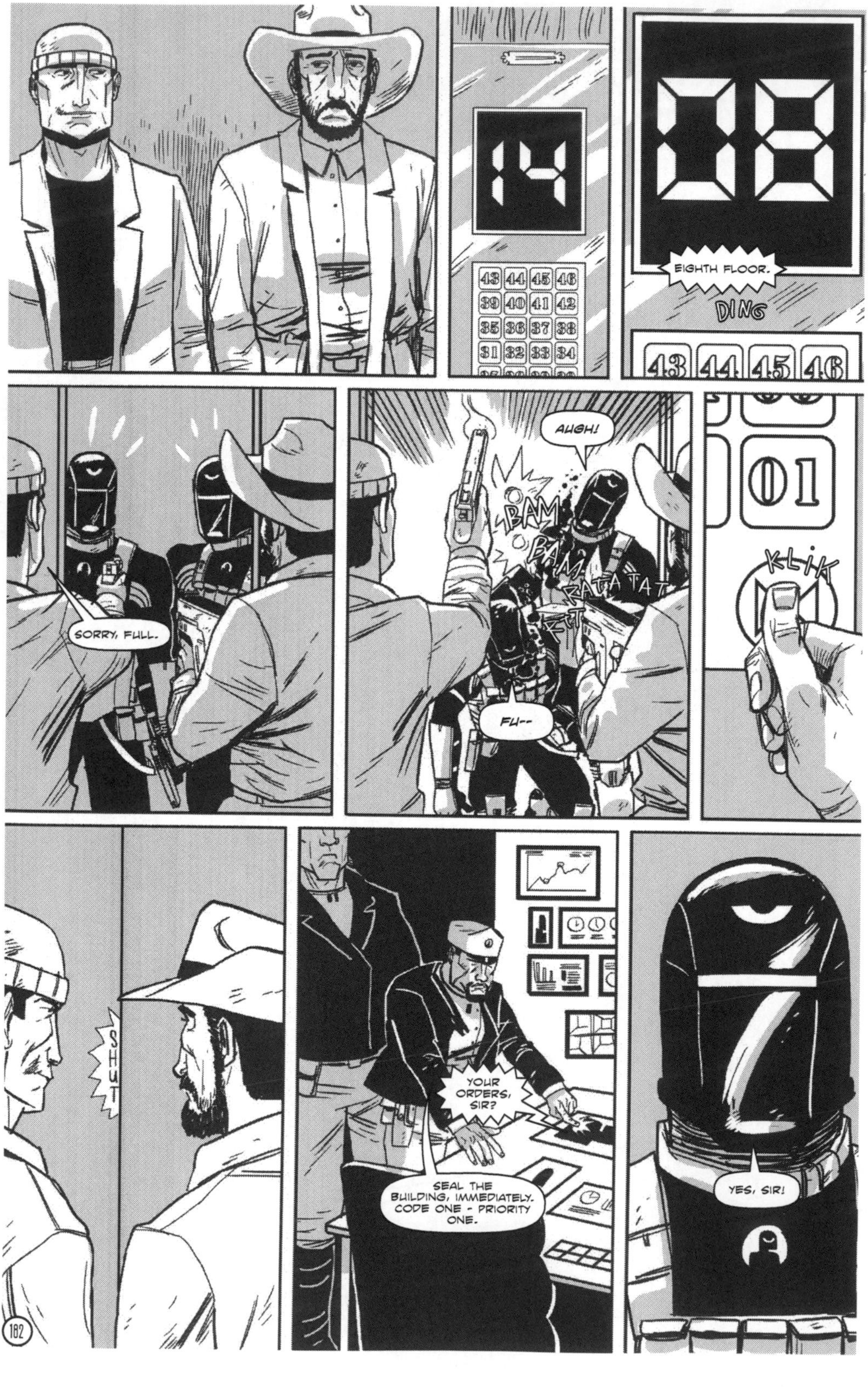

14
43 44 45 46
39 40 41 42
35 36 37 38
31 32 33 34
08
EIGHTH FLOOR.
DING
43 44 45 46
SORRY, FULL.
AUGH!
BAM
BAM
RATATAT
FU--
01
KLIK
SHUT
YOUR ORDERS, SIR?
SEAL THE BUILDING, IMMEDIATELY. CODE ONE - PRIORITY ONE.
YES, SIR!

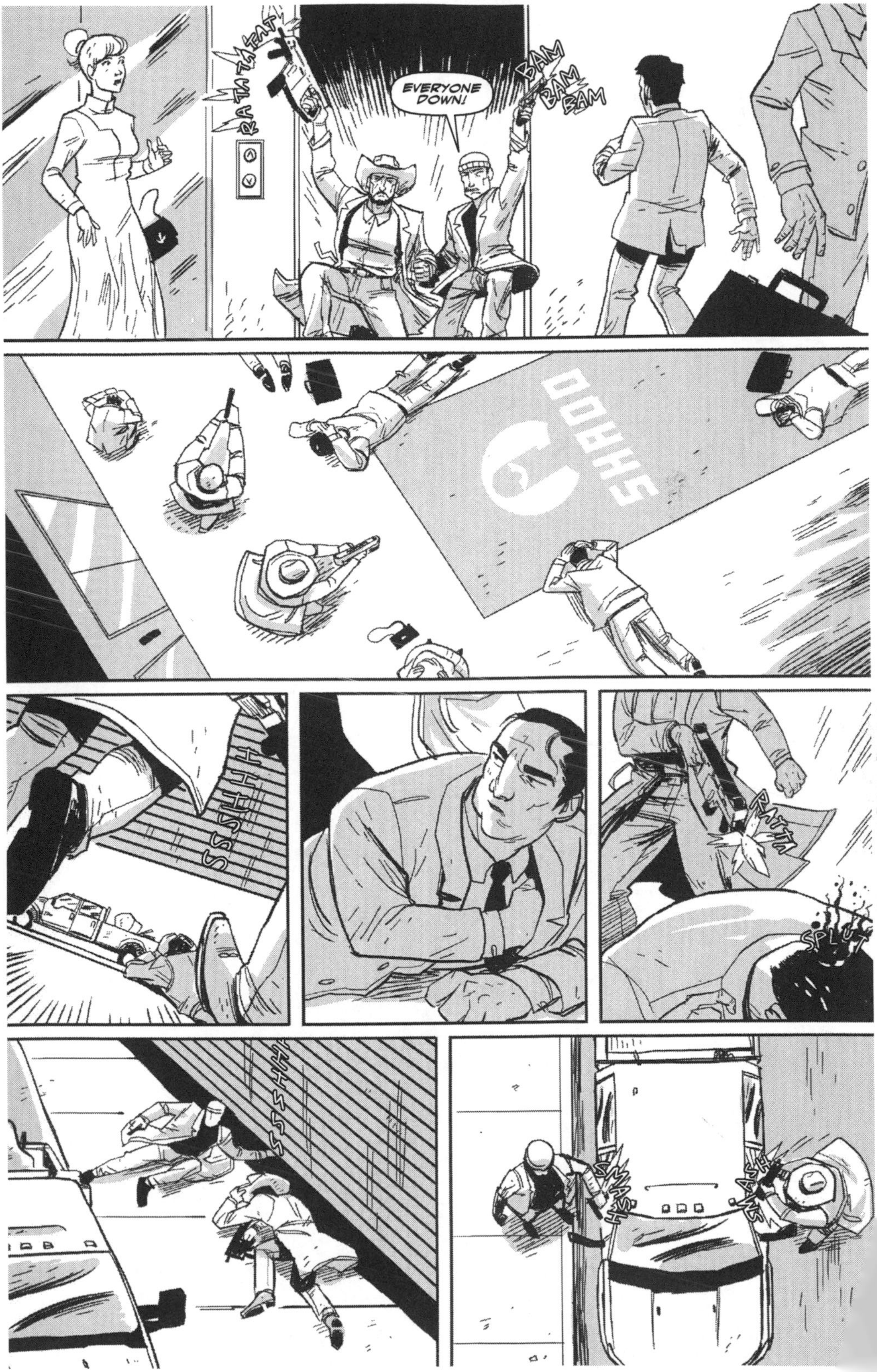
RA TA TA TAT
EVERYONE DOWN!
BAM BAM BAM
SHADOO
SSSHHH
RATTA
SPLUT
SSSHH
SMASH
SMASH

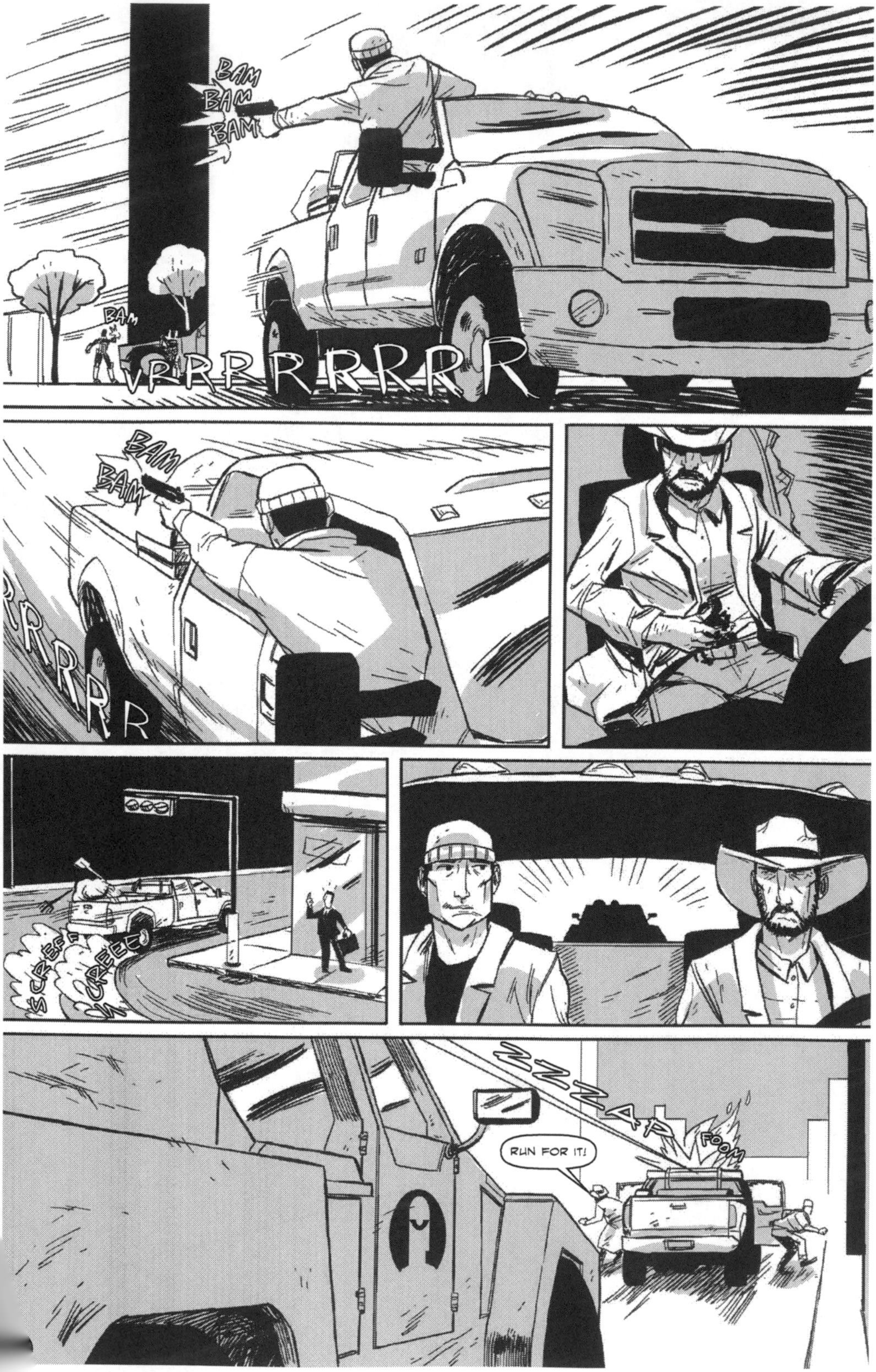
BAM
BAM
BAM
BAM
VRRRRRRRRR
BAM
BAM
RRRRRR
SCREEE
SCREEE
ZZZZAP
FOOM
RUN FOR IT!

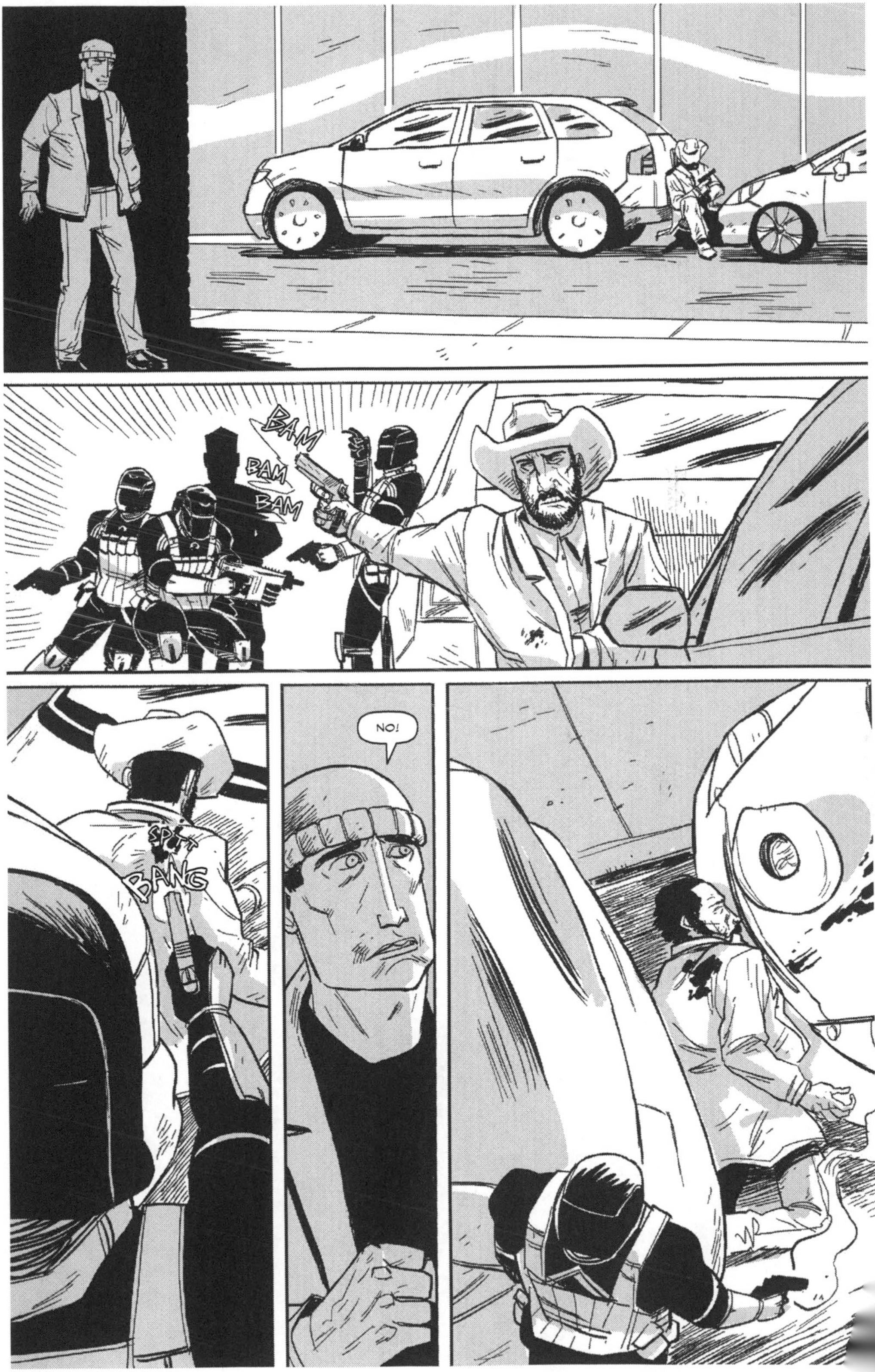
BAM
BAM
BAM
SPTT
BANG
NO!

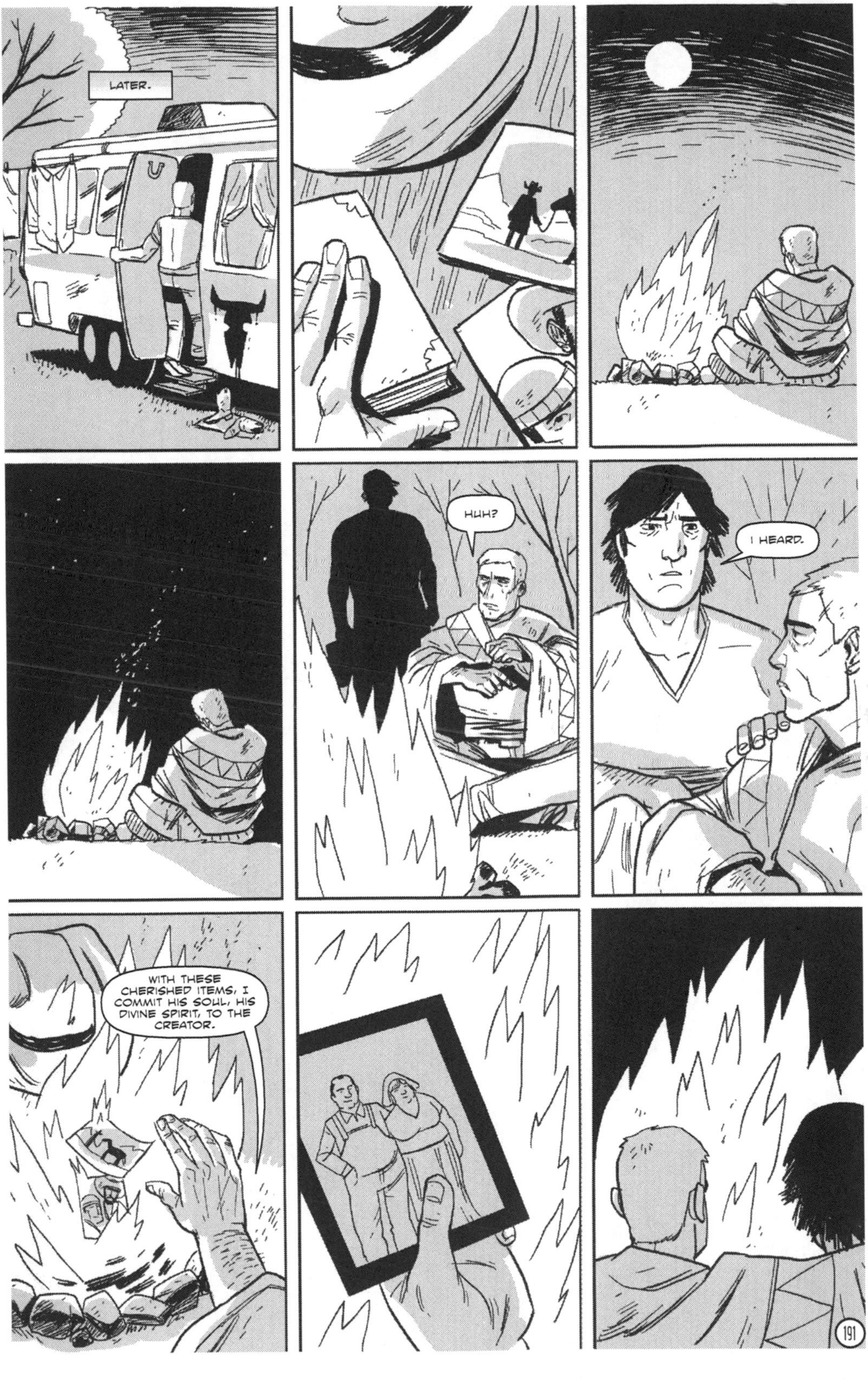

LATER.
HUH?
I HEARD.
WITH THESE CHERISHED ITEMS, I COMMIT HIS SOUL, HIS DIVINE SPIRIT, TO THE CREATOR.

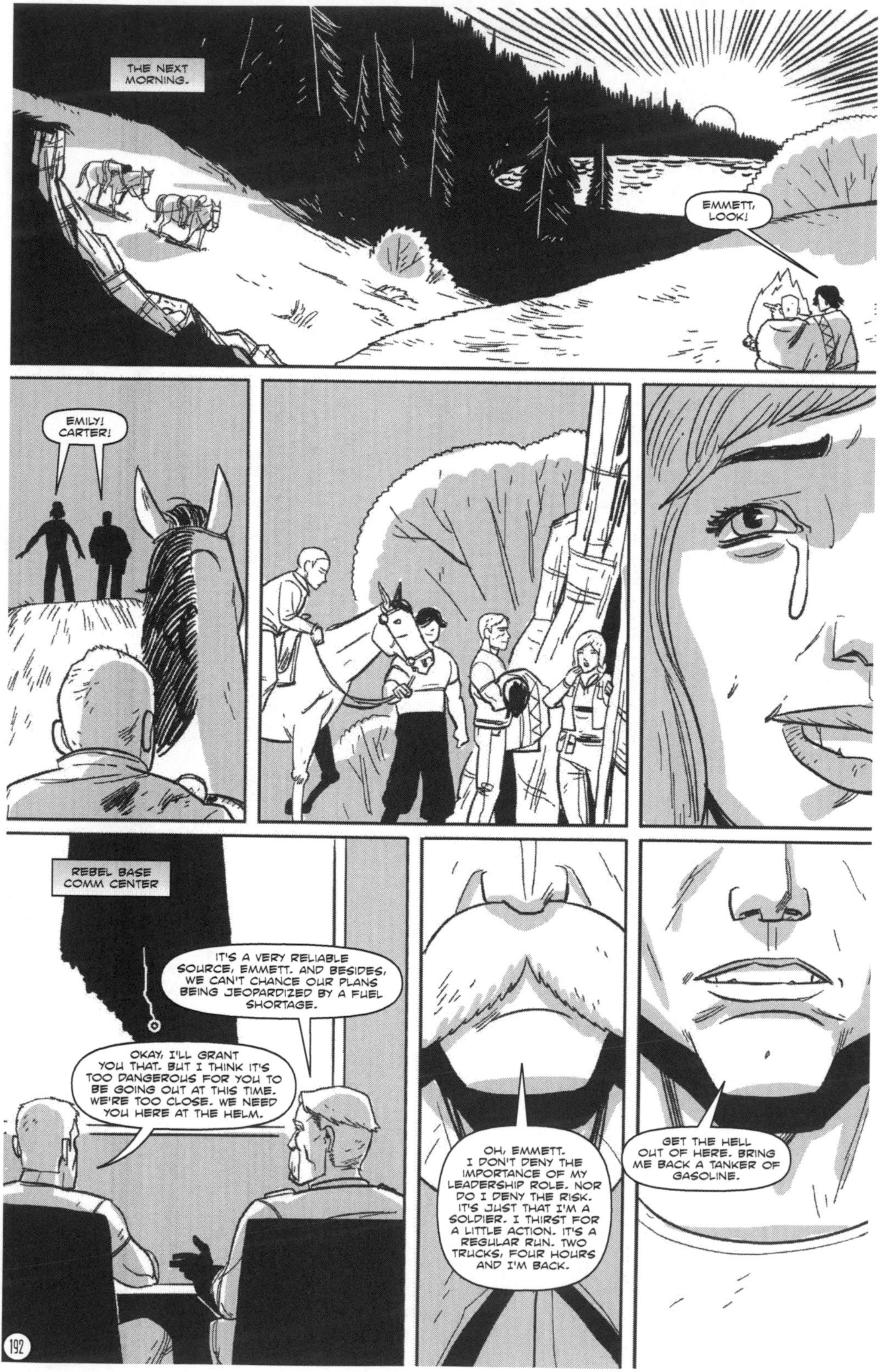
THE NEXT MORNING.
EMMETT, LOOK!
EMILY! CARTER!
REBEL BASE COMM CENTER
IT'S A VERY RELIABLE SOURCE, EMMETT. AND BESIDES, WE CAN'T CHANCE OUR PLANS BEING JEOPARDIZED BY A FUEL SHORTAGE.
OKAY, I'LL GRANT YOU THAT. BUT I THINK IT'S TOO DANGEROUS FOR YOU TO BE GOING OUT AT THIS TIME. WE'RE TOO CLOSE. WE NEED YOU HERE AT THE HELM.
OH, EMMETT. I DON'T DENY THE IMPORTANCE OF MY LEADERSHIP ROLE. NOR DO I DENY THE RISK. IT'S JUST THAT I'M A SOLDIER. I THIRST FOR A LITTLE ACTION. IT'S A REGULAR RUN. TWO TRUCKS, FOUR HOURS AND I'M BACK.
GET THE HELL OUT OF HERE. BRING ME BACK A TANKER OF GASOLINE.

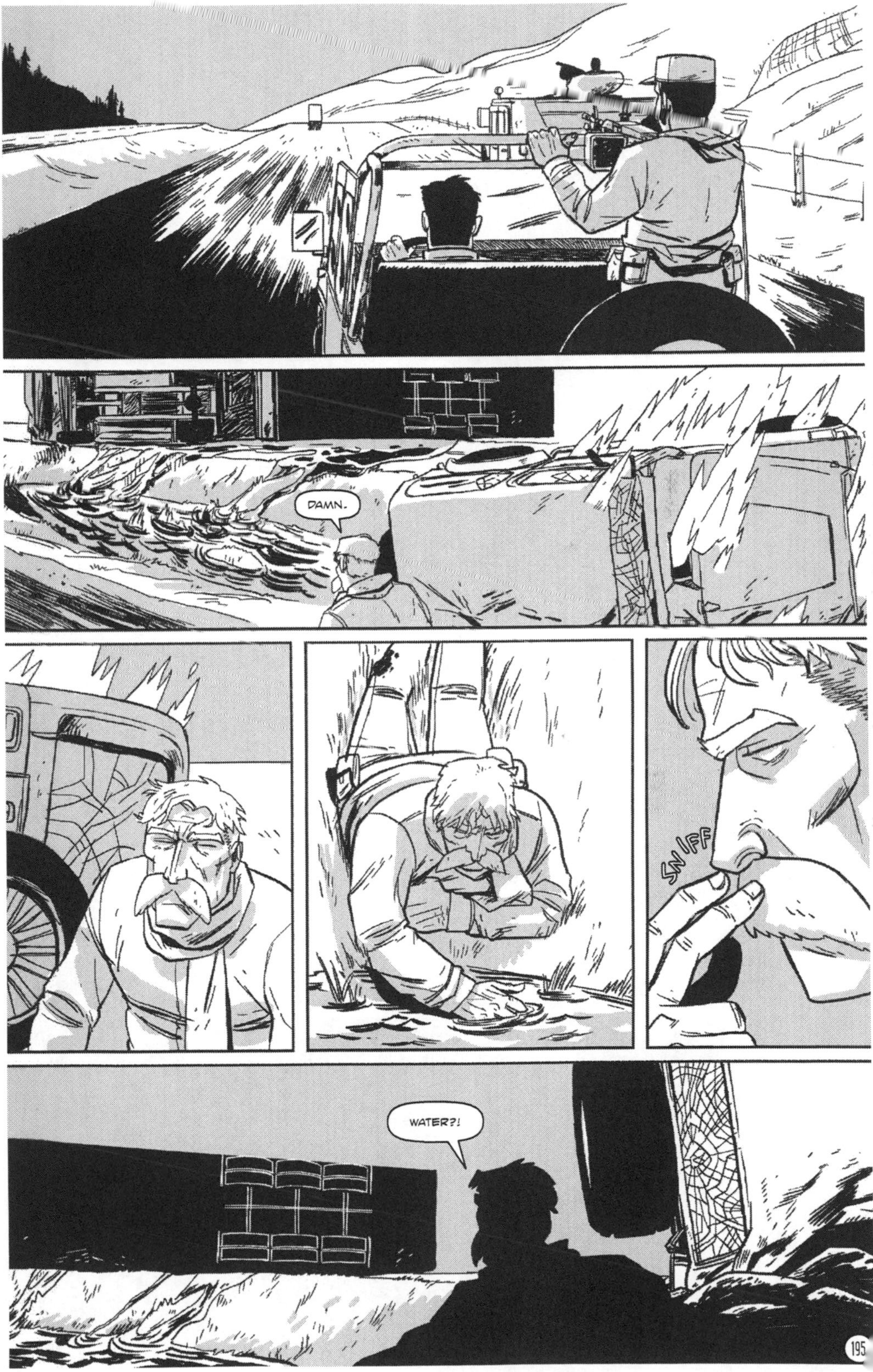
DAMN.
SNIFF
WATER?!

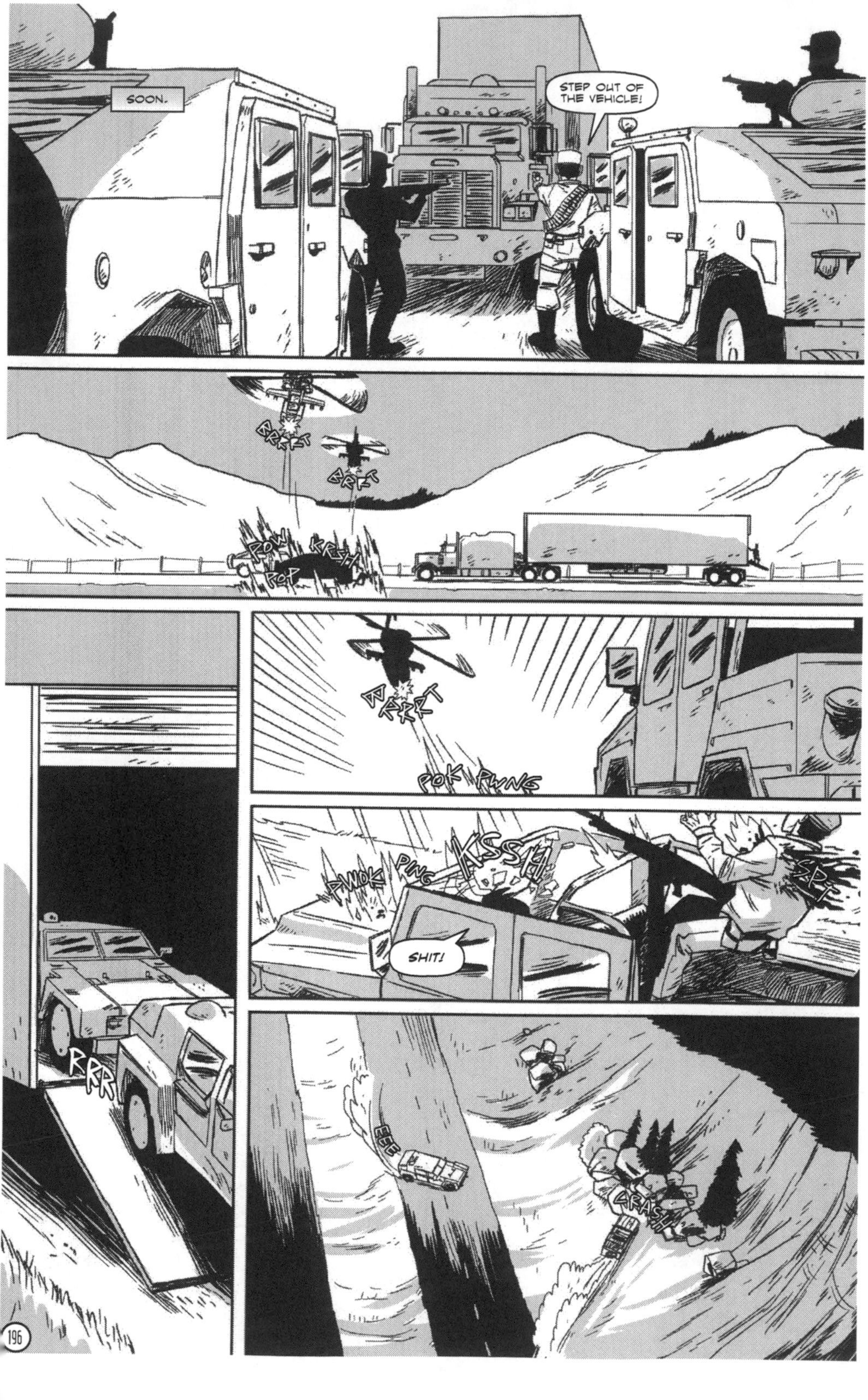
SOON.
STEP OUT OF THE VEHICLE!
BRRRT
BRRT
POW
KRSH
POP
RRR
BRRRT
POK
PWNG
PWOK
PING
KSSH
SPT
SHIT!
EEE
CRASH

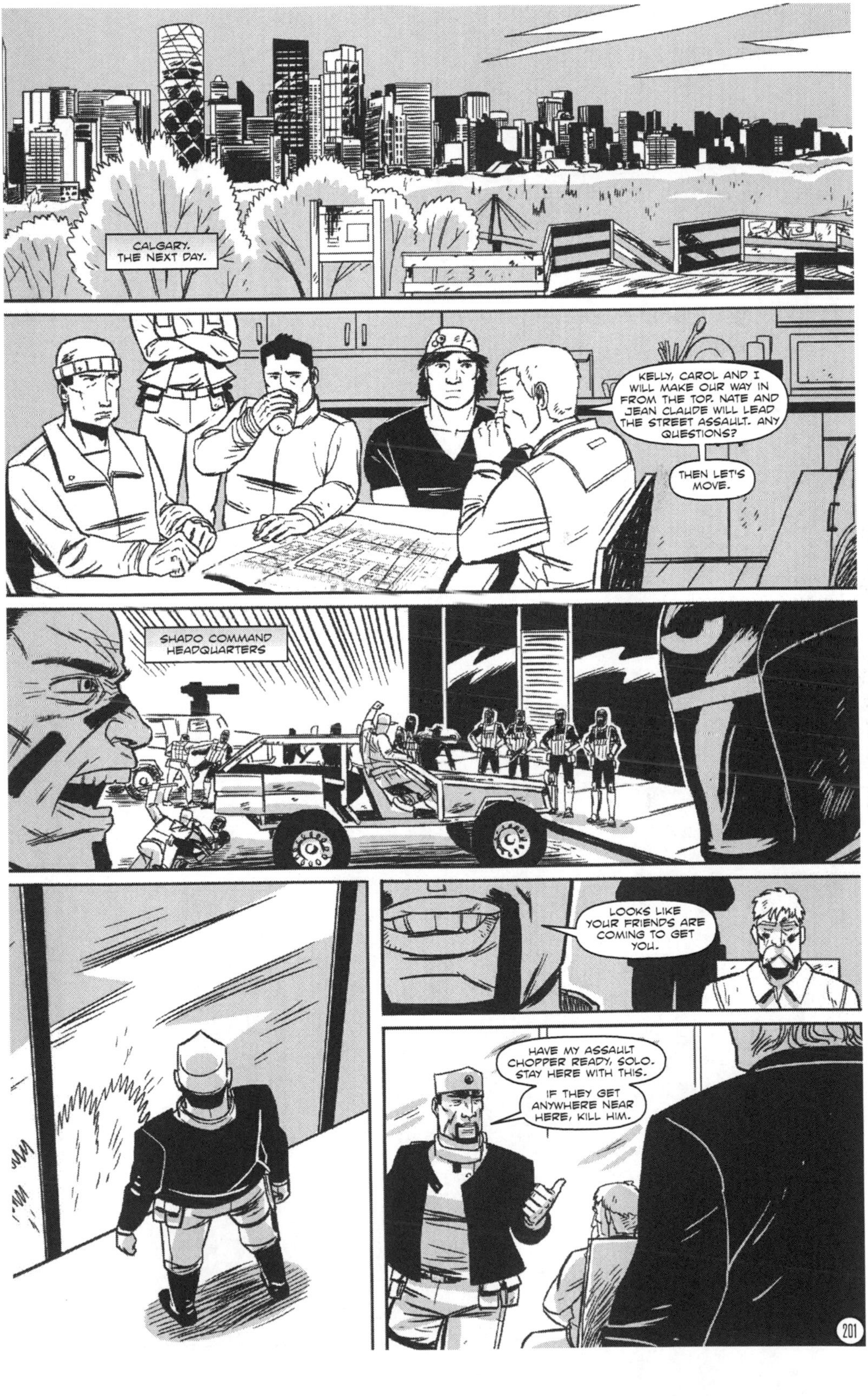
CALGARY. THE NEXT DAY.
KELLY, CAROL AND I WILL MAKE OUR WAY IN FROM THE TOP. NATE AND JEAN CLAUDE WILL LEAD THE STREET ASSAULT. ANY QUESTIONS?
THEN LET'S MOVE.
SHADO COMMAND HEADQUARTERS
LOOKS LIKE YOUR FRIENDS ARE COMING TO GET YOU.
HAVE MY ASSAULT CHOPPER READY, SOLO. STAY HERE WITH THIS.
IF THEY GET ANYWHERE NEAR HERE, KILL HIM.

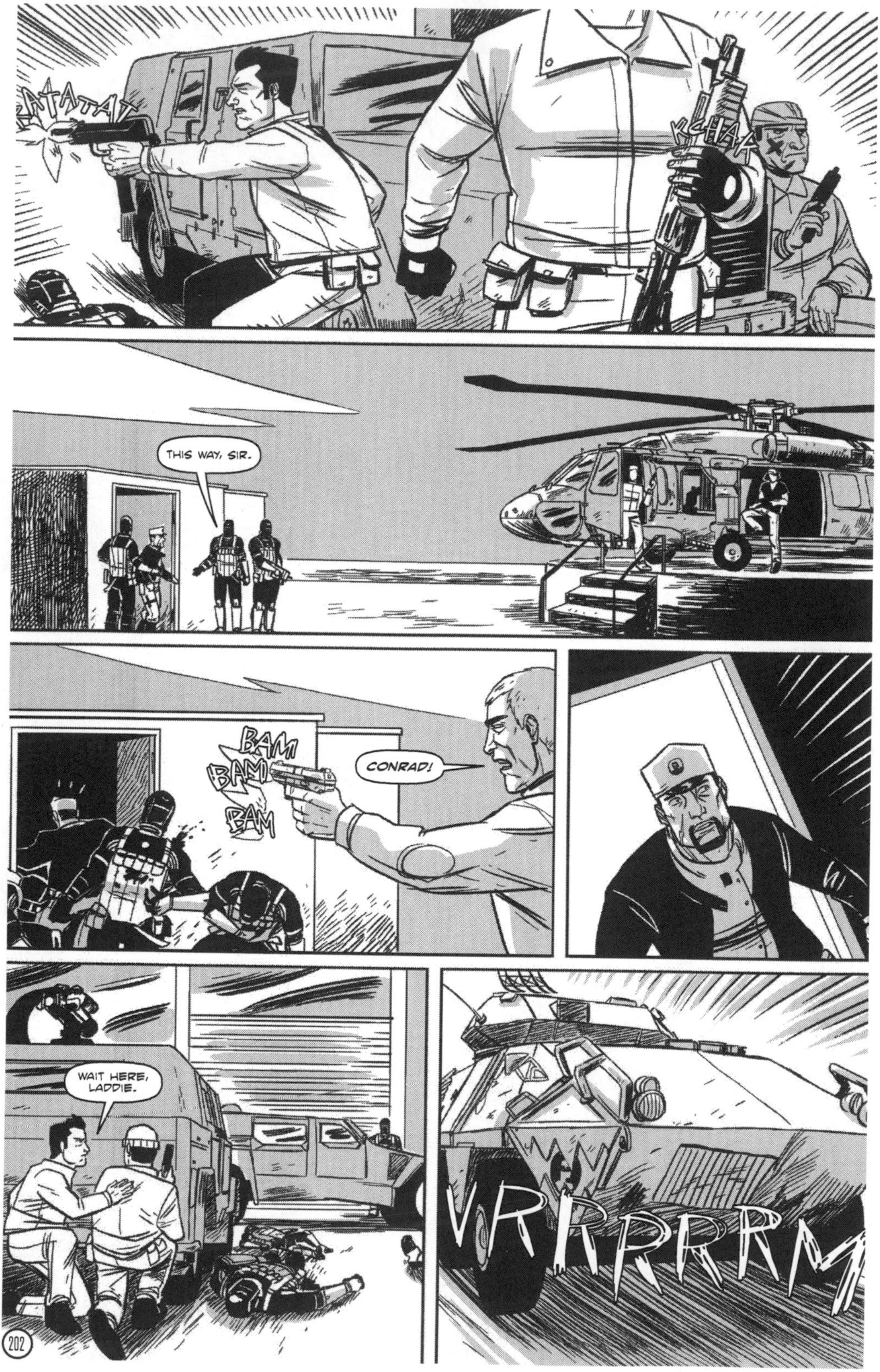
RATATAT
KCHAK
THIS WAY, SIR.
BAM
BAM
BAM
CONRAD!
WAIT HERE, LADDIE.
VRRRRRM

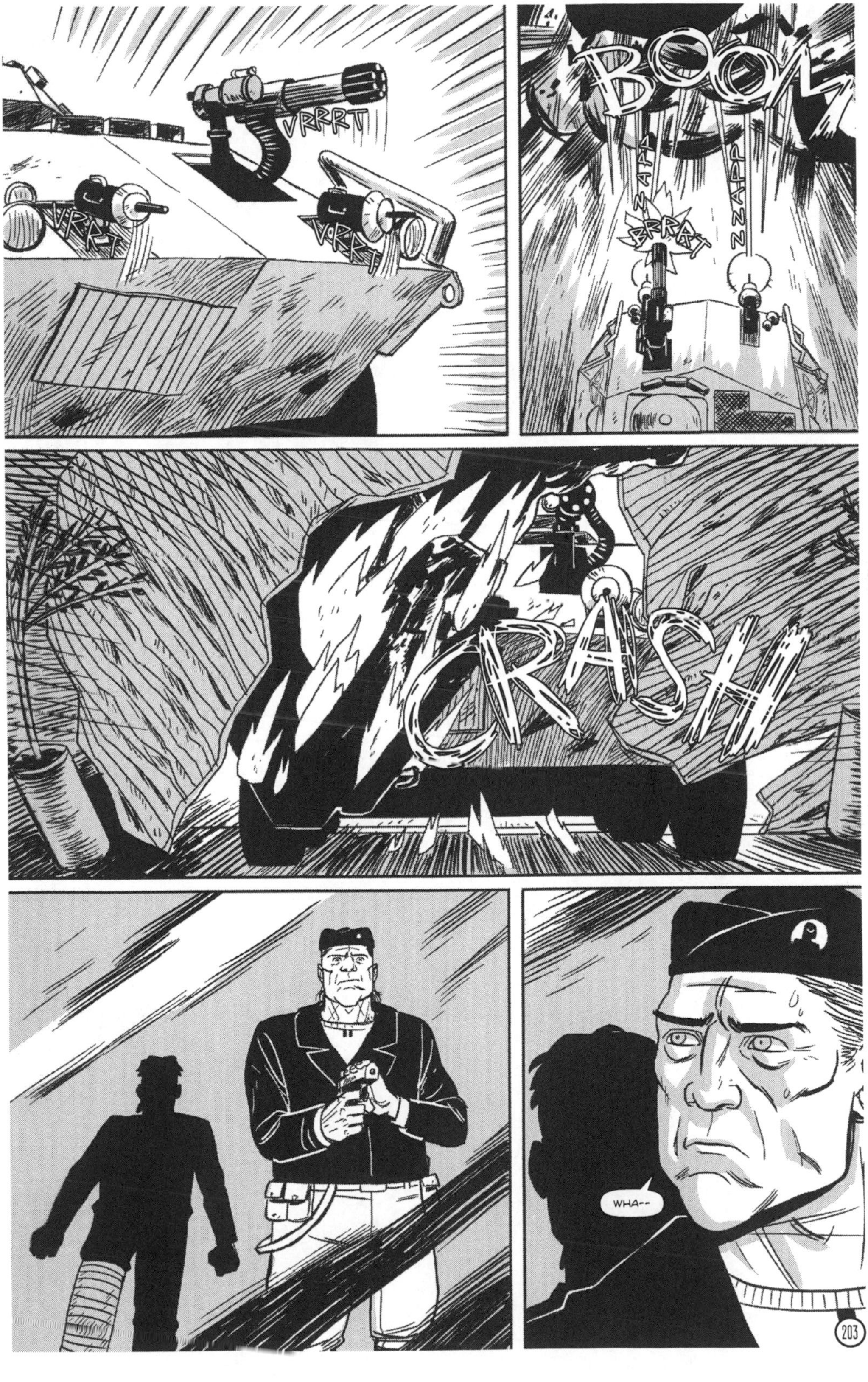
VRRRT
VRRRT
VRRRT
BOOM
ZAPP
BRRRAT
ZZAPP
CRASH
WHA--

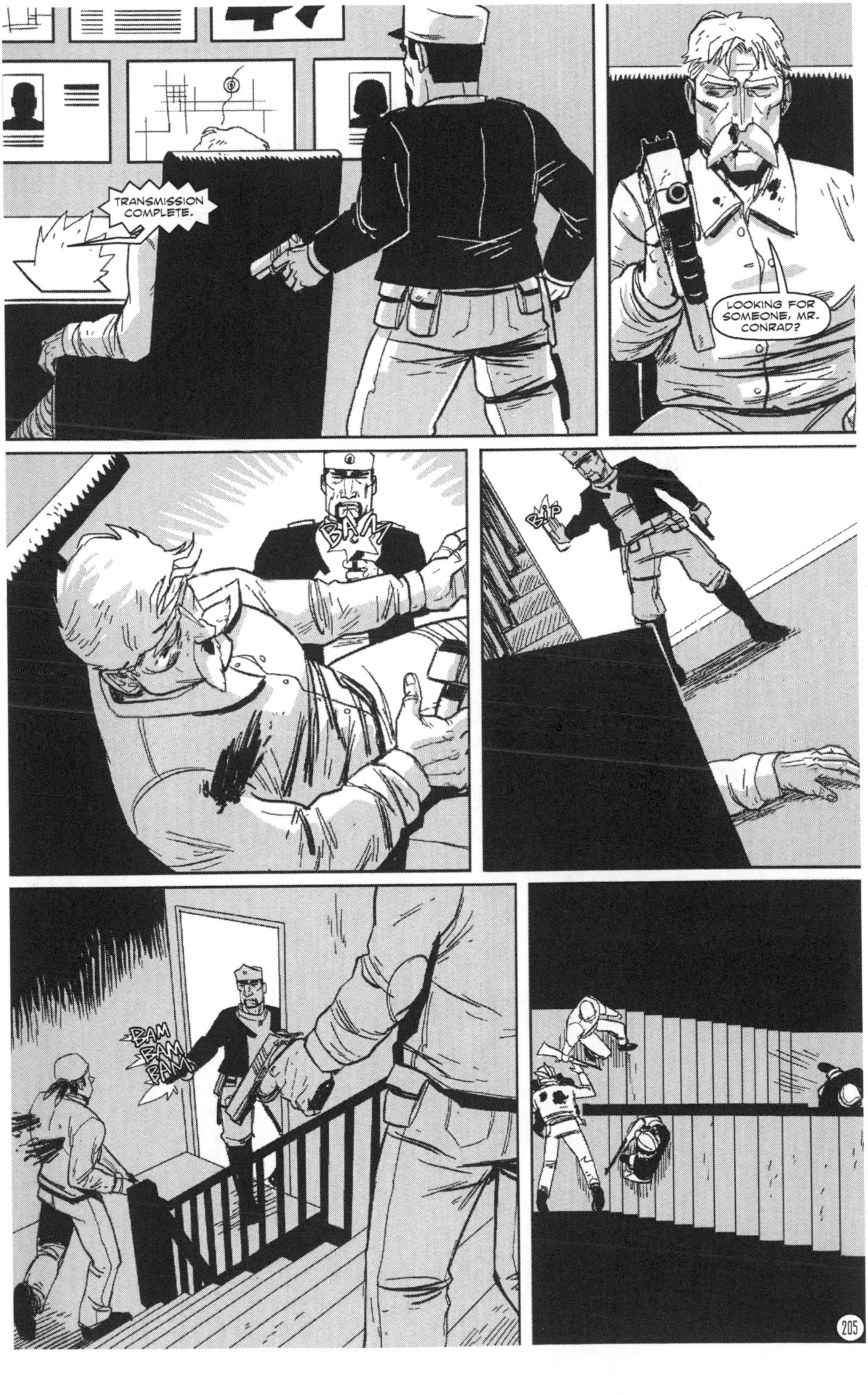
TRANSMISSION COMPLETE.
LOOKING FOR SOMEONE, MR. CONRAD?
BAM
BIP
BAM BAM BAM

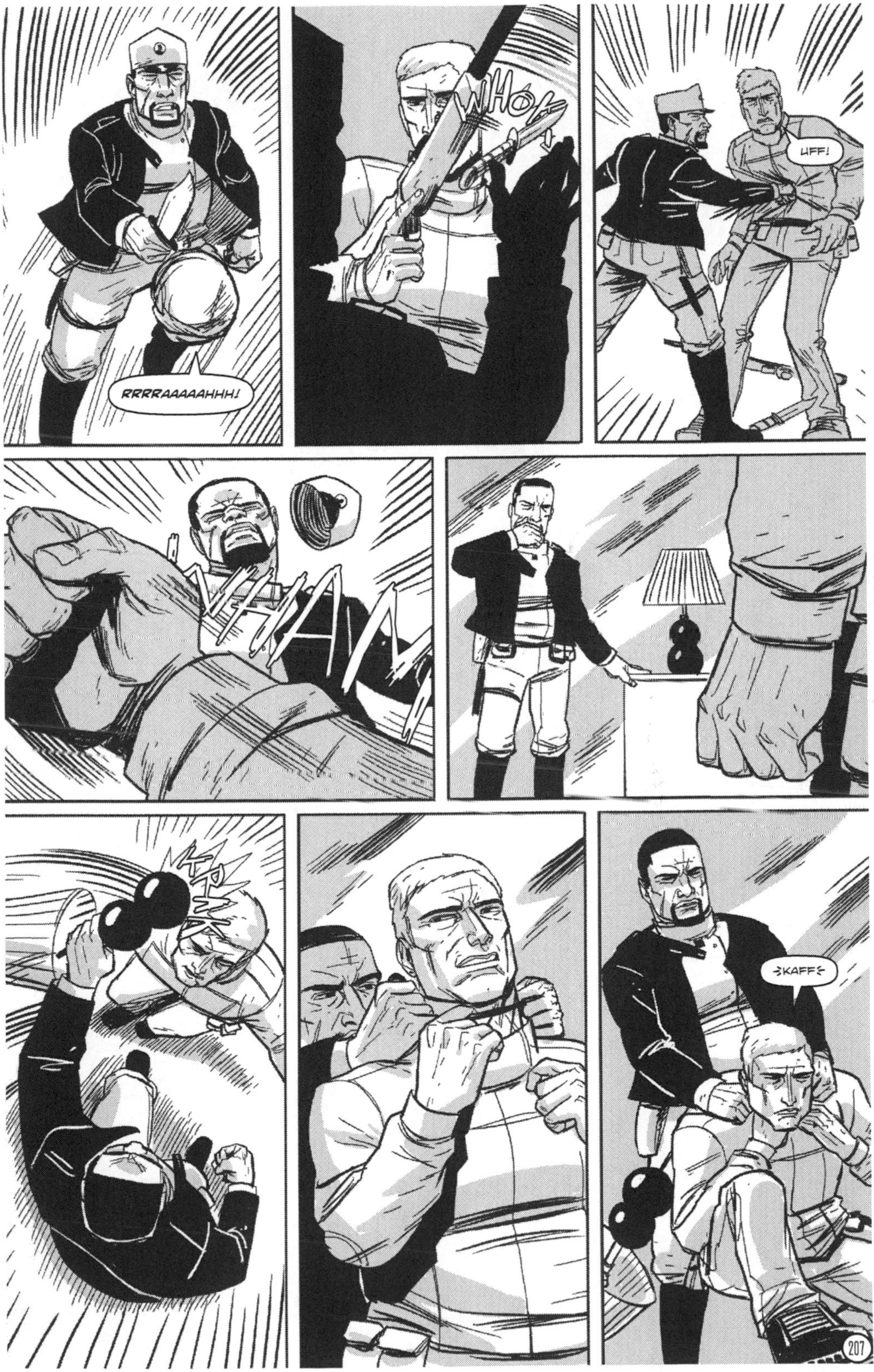
RRRRAAAAAHHH!
WHOK
UFF!
WHAM
KRAK
-KAFF-

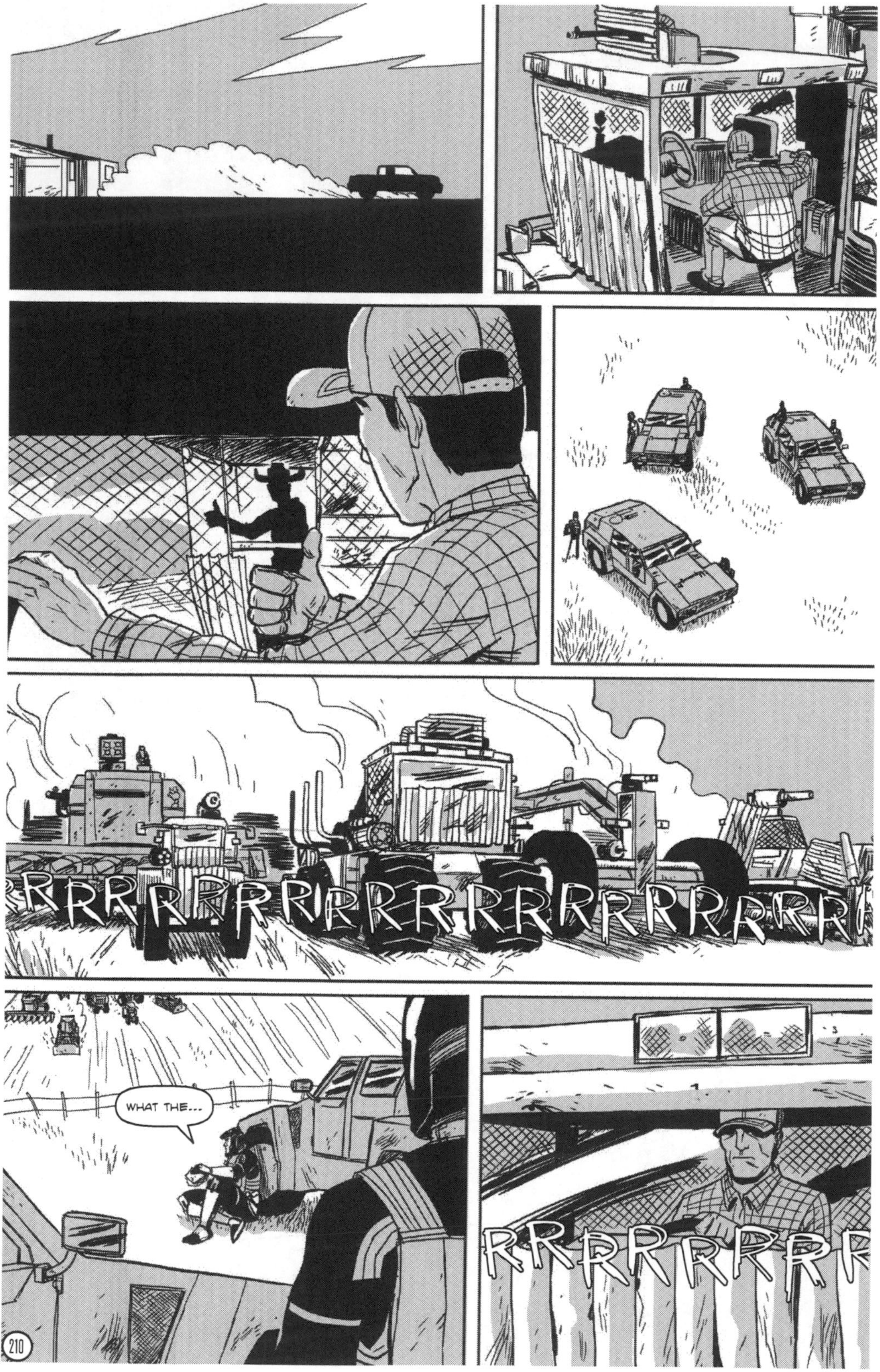
RRRRRRRRRRRRRRRRRRRRRR
WHAT THE...
RRRRRRRRR

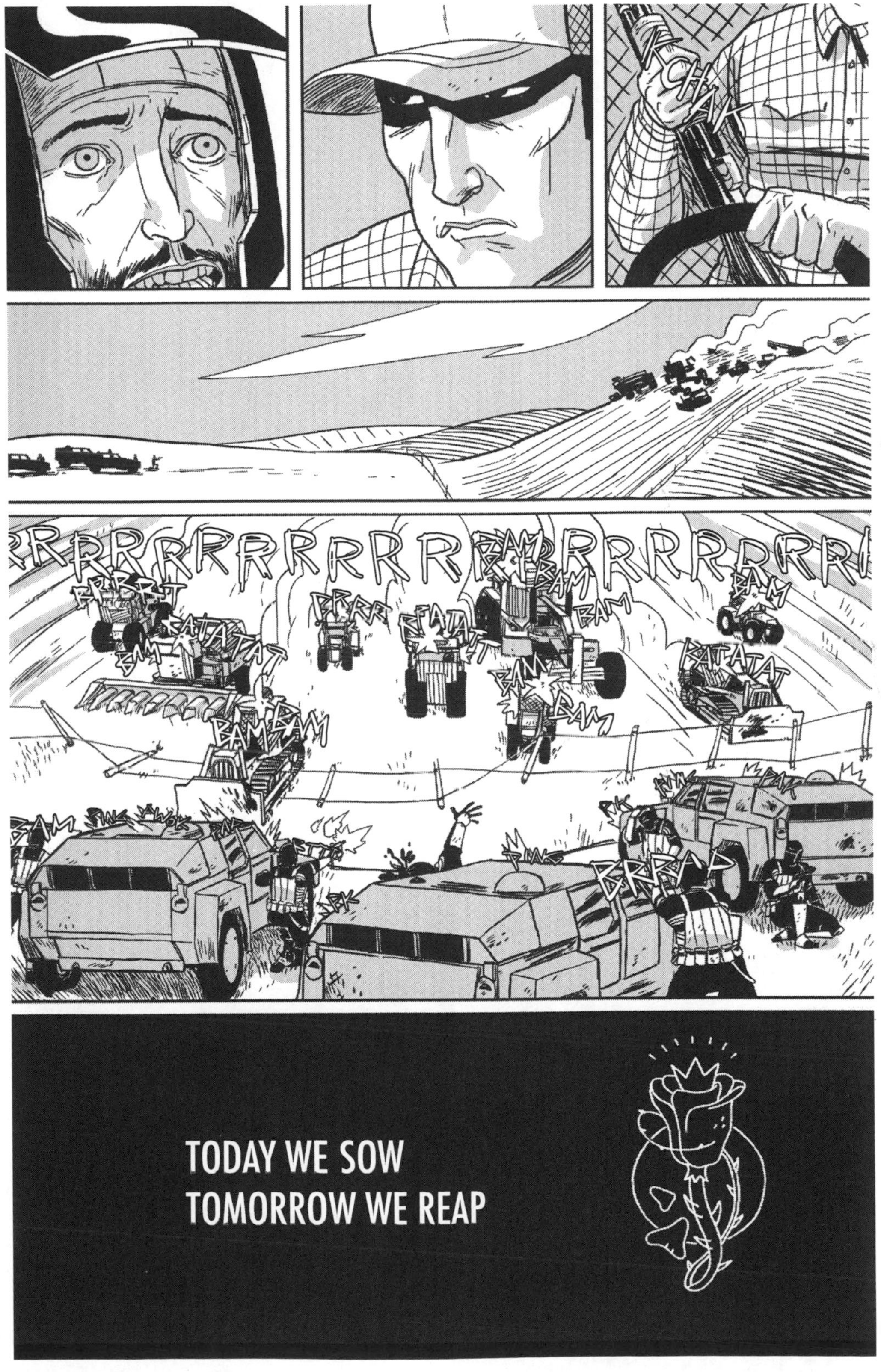
K-CHAK
RRRRRRRRRRRRRRRRR
BAM
RATATAT
BAM BAM
BRRRAP

TODAY WE SOW
TOMORROW WE REAP

Made in the USA
Charleston, SC
13 December 2012